Past or Future Crimes

A Volume in the
Crime, Law, and Deviance
Series

Past or Future Crimes

Crimes

Deservedness and Dangerousness in the Sentencing of Criminals

Andrew von Hirsch

RUTGERS UNIVERSITY PRESS
New Brunswick and London

First paperback printing, 1987
Second cloth printing, 1987

Library of Congress Cataloging in Publication
Data

von Hirsch, Andrew.
  Past or future crimes.

  (Crime, law, and deviance series)
  Bibliography: p.
  Includes index.
  1. Prison sentences—United States. 2.
Punishment—United   States.   3.   Recidivism—
United States. I. Title. II. Series.

HV9471.V66 1985   364.6'5'0973   84-29834
ISBN 0-8135-1262-X

British cataloguing information available.

To Kaethe and Ruth Bachert
Donald von Hirsch

Contents

List of Figures   ix
Preface   xi
Acknowledgments   xiii

PART I
The Issues in Perspective   1

1 *Evolution of the Debate   3*
2 *Sentencing Guidelines   19*

PART II
The Conception of Desert   29

3 *Why Punish Proportionately?   31*
4 *Proportionality: Determining or Limiting?   38*
5 *Why Punish at All?   47*

PART III
How Much Punishment Is Deserved?   61

6 *Gauging the Seriousness of Crimes   63*
7 *Previous Convictions   77*
8 *Anchoring the Penalty Scale   92*

PART IV
Selective Incapacitation   103

9   *Predictive Efficacy   105*
10 *Impact on Crime Rates and Prison Populations*   115
11 *Ethical Problems: The "No Conflict" Thesis   128*
12 *Prediction within Broad Desert Limits?   139*

PART V
Synthesizing Past and Future   147

13 *Categorial Incapacitation   149*
14 *Strategies for Synthesis   160*
15 *Concluding Observations   167*

APPENDIXES
1 *The Question of False Positives   175*
2 *A Note on Minnesota's Sentencing Guidelines   179*

Notes   183
Bibliography   201
Index   213

List of Figures

2.1   *The Sentencing Grid*   *23*

2.2   *Cells in the Sentencing Grid*   *24*

2.3   *Sample In-Out Line*   *25*

7.1   *In-Out Line in Desert Model, Disregarding Prior Criminality*   *86*

7.2   *In-Out Line in Desert Model, Utilizing Prior Criminality*   *87*

7.3   *The First-Offender Discount*   *89*

7.4   *Overlap between Desert Lines*   *90*

8.1   *Limitations of Cardinal Proportionality*   *94*

8.2   *Example of Excessively Lenient In-Out Line: More Prison Capacity Needed*   *97*

8.3   *Example of Excessively Severe In-Out Line: Prison Capacity Should Be Reduced*   *98*

8.4   *Example of Acceptable In-Out Line: Retain Current Prison Capacity*   *99*

11.1   *In-Out Line in Selective Incapacitation Rationale*   *134*

12.1   *Commissioner A's Proposed In-Out Line*   *142*

12.2   *Commissioner B's Proposed In-Out Line*   *143*

13.1   *Categorial Incapacitation and Fixing the In-Out Line*   *158*

Preface

This book grew more or less of its own accord. My first sketch of a theory of criminal sentencing was published in 1976—*Doing Justice,* the report of the Committee for the Study of Incarceration. Having spent more than four years on that project, I thought I had exhausted what I might have to say.

My intention was to focus next on the implementation of sentencing reform. I obtained a grant to study parole, which evolved into Kathleen Hanrahan's and my 1979 book, *The Question of Parole.* I then became involved in a study of determinate sentencing as it had been carried out in several jurisdictions.

During these projects, however, questions of sentencing theory kept intruding. The desert model for sentencing advocated in *Doing Justice* was generating more interest than I had anticipated—and I found myself confronted with questions about various aspects of the model. Studying determinate sentencing also raised theoretical questions about the role of previous convictions, about gauging the seriousness of crimes, and about finding the anchoring points for a penalty scale. The resurgence of interest in predictive sentencing in the early 1980s forced me to take a second look at prediction, and its empirical and ethical problems. I wrote articles on these various topics, as they claimed my attention.

Recently, I had some leisure to look those efforts over and found they had become a patchwork of writings in separate journals, with some overlap and with major gaps. The time had come to do a more systematic work on desert and prediction in sentencing—one that would incorporate the usable parts of those articles and address the issues I had not dealt with previously. The result is this book.

I have tried to make my ideas specific enough to provide guidance to rulemakers. Having served as consultant to several sentencing commissions, I have seen how seriously the members and staff were willing to take ideas, provided they are made relevant to the writing of guidelines. I learned to share commission members' impatience with broad theories whose application is left unspecified.

Punishment has always been a nasty business. No theory can improve it, without the necessary political will and an understanding of the actual workings of the penal system. A coherent theory, however, is needed so we can comprehend better what our aims should be. One can reform sentencing only by knowing what reform means.

Acknowledgments

My principal debt in writing this book is to Julia M. Mueller. As my graduate assistant for two years, she helped me with the research on this book and several of the articles that preceded it. She also reviewed the drafts as I wrote them, and I have benefited from her sound judgment.

I am grateful also to Marianne Frierson, who was my graduate assistant during the final months of preparing the book for publication. She was of great help to me in revising the draft and preparing the notes and bibliography.

I would like to thank the dean of the School of Criminal Justice at Rutgers, Don M. Gottfredson, for permitting me to make use of portions of a recent article we wrote together on the subject of selective incapacitation.

I owe my gratitude to several colleagues who devoted their valuable time to reviewing the first draft of the book and whose comments have helped me improve it: Jacqueline Cohen, Don Gottfredson, David Greenberg, Sten Heckscher, Peter Hoffman, Nils Jareborg, John Kleinig, Sheldon Messinger, John Monahan, Don Scheid, Kip Schlegel, and Richard Singer.

I would like to thank Joan Schroeder, who typed the manuscript, for her patient and painstaking work.

I also much appreciate the enthusiasm and support of Rutgers University Press, and of its editor-in-chief, Marlie Wasserman.

Finally, I should acknowledge my debt to Norval Morris. I continue our running theoretical debate in this book, but he has in his writings compelled me to rethink my ideas. He also deserves much of the credit for stimulating and maintaining our profession's interest in the conceptual underpinnings of sentencing policy.

In a number of chapters, I have used (with considerable alterations and additions) portions of articles of mine that have been published elsewhere. I am grateful to the following publishers, who have kindly allowed me to utilize those articles.

In chapter 1: "Recent Trends in American Criminal Sentencing Theory," *Maryland Law Review* 42 (1983): 6–36. Originally published in German as "Gegenwärtige Tendenzen in der Amerikanischen Strafzumessungslehre," *Zeitschrift für die Gesamte Strafrechtswissenschaft* 94 (1982): 1047–1079. Also, a book review of *The Decline of the Rehabilitative Ideal,* by Francis Allen, and *Imprisonment in America,* by Michael Sherman and Gordon Hawkins, *University of Pennsylvania Law Review* 131 (1983): 819–834.

In chapters 3 and 5: "'Neoclassicism,' Proportionality and the Rationale for Punishment: Thoughts on the Scandinavian Debate," *Crime and Delinquency* 29 (1983): 52–70, originally published in Swedish as "Nyklassicism, proportionalitet och straffets grunder." *Nordisk Tidsskrift for Kriminalvidenskab* 69 (1982): 97–117.

In chapter 4: "Equality, 'Anisonomy' and Justice: A Review of *Madness and the Criminal Law,*" *Michigan Law Review* 82 (1984): 1093–1112.

In chapter 7: "Desert and Previous Convictions in Sentencing," *Minnesota Law Review* 65 (1981): 591–634.

In chapters 6 and 8: "Commensurability and Crime Prevention: Evaluating Formal Sentencing Structures and Their Rationale," *Journal of Criminal Law and Criminology* 74 (1983): 209–248.

In chapters 9 and 10: "Selective Incapacitation: Some Queries about Research Design and Equity," *New York University Review of Law and Social Change* 12 (1983–1984): 11–51 (with Don M. Gottfredson).

Past or Future Crimes

PART I

The Issues in Perspective

PAST CRIMES OR FUTURE? When a convicted criminal faces sentence, should the blameworthiness of his criminal acts decide his punishment? Or should the sentence be based on how dangerous he is?

This question of past or future crimes prompts much of today's criminal sentencing debate. One influential school of thought emphasizes the past crime—the conduct for which the defendant stands convicted. It holds that punishment is a condemnatory institution, and its severity should comport with the degree of blameworthiness of the offender's criminal acts. Another school emphasizes risk of future criminality. Once the defendant has been convicted, his sentence should be determined chiefly by how likely he is to commit further offenses. The first theory, concerned with desert and proportionality, was not taken seriously in earlier decades, but during the last ten years it has acquired—and retains—a great deal of influence. The second, concerned with prediction, was historically influential, waned for some years, and has had a recent renaissance.

The debate is no abstract one, for it vitally affects the substance of sentencing policy. According to the first theory, punishments should be scaled to reflect the comparative gravity of offenses, and crimes of similar gravity should receive similar punishments. According to the second, offenders convicted of similar crimes should receive unequal sentences, when their probabilities of returning to crime are unequal. Sentencing guidelines will have different emphasis and content, depending on which of the two theories is the guide. This book examines the merits of the two conceptions, and the conflict between them.

Before proceeding with the analysis, however, it may be useful to put the question of past or future crimes in perspective. In chapter 1, I sketch the development of today's debate: the origins of the competing views, and the earlier conceptions they have replaced. In chapter 2, I describe the sentencing grid and explain how this device can be used to illustrate the issues.■

CHAPTER 1

Evolution of the Debate

Before about 1970, there was for several decades a recognizable consensus among penologists about the aims of sentencing. That consensus no longer exists today.

The Positivist Penal Ethic and Its Decline

The old consensus has often been described as one preoccupied with rehabilitation.[1] The belief supposedly once was, but no longer is, that sanctions should be chosen to serve the treatment needs of offenders.

A decline in the penal treatment ethic would scarcely be surprising, for it lived on watered intellectual capital. Despite years of rhetoric about rehabilitation, the ends of treatment were never carefully specified. Was it to protect the community by reducing recidivism? Or was it to enhance offenders' own lives, by offering them needed skills, guidance, and opportunities? Treatment advocates claimed it was both, without admitting the potential conflict between these aims.[2] Or worse, they oscillated between crime-prevention and social service conceptions in unprincipled fashion. Treatment programs were presented as a way of protecting the community against crime. When their effectiveness was questioned, it was said (on slender evidence) that they *probably* prevented crime, but that even if not, they enabled offenders to live more fulfilled lives. When offenders resisted the profferred help, it was then said that their consent was not needed, because the treatment helped reduce recidivism, and so on.

Equally vague was the specification of the means for treatment. Virtually any intervention, even the daily routine of the prison itself ("milieu therapy"), was said to be rehabilitative—with little serious inquiry into how (or why) that intervention could be expected to work.[3] It was only a matter of time before the inadequacies of rehabilitative techniques became a matter of public knowledge. After decades of talk of treatment, American criminologists began in the 1950s and 1960s to test penal treatment programs in systematic fashion. The results of such studies were slow in coming, but by the early 1970s, several surveys of treatment studies had been published.[4] The results were disappointing, indeed. Although many offenders seemed to show improvement (that is, did not return to crime), this tended to occur as much among untreated as among treated individuals*—the treatment as such had little perceptible influence.[5]

Beyond these program failures, Francis Allen suggests, has come a loss of belief in human malleability.[6] Penal rehabilitationism requires the assumption that even the most recalcitrant seeming individuals can be made to change their characters, values, and habits through state-sponsored treatment efforts. This faith in human receptiveness to change has waned. Although crime and other forms of social deviance were plentiful in the past, their persistence in the face of elaborate and costly social and educational efforts has shaken our confidence. Perhaps people are not so easily remade—at least not those who lack the necessary mo-

---

*These pessimistic conclusions were confirmed by a 1979 report by the National Academy of Science's Panel on Research on Rehabilitative Techniques.

The panel report is set forth in Lee B. Sechrest, Susan O. White, and Elizabeth D. Brown, eds., *The Rehabilitation of Criminal Offenders: Problems and Prospects*, 3–118.

Recently, there have been occasional reported successes with particular treatment methods dealing with particular offender types. See Ted Palmer, "Treatment and the Role of Classification: A Review of the Basics." But no serious researcher has been willing to reassert the rehabilitationists' traditional claim that treatment can routinely be made to work for the bulk of criminal offenders.

In the face of discouraging evidence, a few writers have bravely maintained their optimism about the prospects of rehabilitative sentencing. See, for example, Francis T. Cullen and Karen Gilbert, *Reaffirming Rehabilitation*. But such sanguine attitudes have not been widespread among penologists.

Aside from questions of effectiveness, the fairness of rehabilitative sentencing has also been questioned. Andrew von Hirsch, *Doing Justice: The Choice of Punishments*, 127–128.

tivation. Certainly the state no longer appears so efficacious a remaker.

Was the traditional penal ethic, however, so exclusively *rehabilitative*? Certainly, treatment was an important element. But there was also a second component: predictive restraint. Sentencing and correctional officials were supposed to gauge not only individual offenders' treatment needs but also their likelihood of returning to crime. Redeemable offenders were to be treated (in the community, if possible), but those judged bad risks were to be confined.

In virtually every text extolling rehabilitation, this other element of predictive restraint was discernible.[7] The National Council on Crime and Delinquency's proposed Model Sentencing Act, notwithstanding its emphasis on community treatment, provided for prison terms up to *thirty years* for dangerous and untreatable felons.[8] A more representative document, the American Law Institute's Model Penal Code, authorized judges to commit offenders to prison whenever they found "[an] undue risk that . . . the defendent will commit another crime."[9] The prevailing American ideology was less purely rehabilitative than positivist — in the sense used by writers of the Italian positivist school such as Enrico Ferri and Raffaele Garofalo.[10] Its aim was to prevent further crimes by convicted offenders. When those crimes might be forestalled through rehabilitative efforts, treatment programs should be tried. But to the extent that the success of such programs was uncertain, the offenders who were bad risks could always be restrained.

The positivist ideology had such appeal, I believe, precisely because it offered both therapy and restraint. One did not have to assume all criminals were redeemable but could merely hope that some might be. Therapy could be tried on apparently amenable defendants, but always with a fail-safe: the offender who seemed unsuitable for or unresponsive to treatment could be separated from the community. The system's institutions were organized on this bet-hedging premise. Judges could place promising offenders on probation but imprison the poor risks. Parole boards could release good prisoners early, while denying release to potential troublemakers. Probation and parole agents could service their cooperative clients, while recommending revocation and imprisonment for clients who seemed headed back to crime. The ideology was suited perfectly to Americans' desire to have it both ways: to be optimistic about criminals' potential for improvement while simultaneously being "realistic" about their potential for future criminal activity.

Once the traditional rationale is thus understood, the reasons for its decline become less obvious. Perhaps rehabilitative efforts failed, but the art of prediction was not in quite such sorry shape. Techniques for forecasting criminality had been explored since the 1920s. Statistical prediction instruments had been developed, using a few simple facts about the offender's criminal record and social history. Such instruments achieved some success in identifying offenders having a higher than average incidence of recidivism.[11] Yes, the forecasting techniques were crude and prone to error (and their deficiencies will be discussed at length in later chapters). But they did not wholly fail in the way rehabilitative efforts appeared to: statistical prediction devices *did* pick out recidivists better than, say, random selection would. Had treatment programs performed as well as prediction instruments did, the results would have been considered quite encouraging. Yet in the late 1970s, the enthusiasm for predictive sentencing as well as for treatment declined markedly.

In part, prediction may have suffered from its close links with treatment. Forecasts about recidivism were often expressed in rehabilitative terms. The parole board, when deciding that a prisoner was a bad risk, would assert that he had not "progressed" enough toward cure. As doubts about curing criminality grew, they undermined faith in the associated predictive judgments.

The skepticism about prediction also had more substantial grounds. Civil libertarians began to worry about the tendency of forecasts of criminality to overpredict. Although statistical forecasting methods could identify groups of offenders having higher probabilities of recidivism, these methods showed a disturbing incidence of "false positives."* Many of those classified as potential recidivists were, in fact, not found to offend again.[12] The rate of false positives was particularly high when forecasting serious criminality—for example, violence. The majority of those designated as dangerous were persons who were *not* found to commit the predicted acts of violence when allowed to remain at large.

---

*Social scientists had long been aware of the tendency of predictions of rare events to produce a high incidence of false positives. Albert Rosen, as early as 1954, published a study pointing out the tendency toward overprediction in forecasts of suicide in mental hospitals ("Detection of Suicidal Patients: An Example of Some Limitations in the Prediction of Infrequent Events"). But it took more than another decade for criminologists to begin to measure systematically the false-positive rate in predictions of criminality, and to consider its moral implications.

Confining convicted individuals on the basis of erroneous attributions of future criminality seemed dubious justice.[13]

The false-positive issue did not much exercise more conservative thinkers, who were concerned primarily with enhancing the crime-preventive efficacy of sentencing. However, they had their own reasons for disenchantment with the predictive ethos in traditional positivism. The existing prediction studies addressed only individual risk: whether some defendants were more likely than others to commit further crimes. The positivist remedy was to confine the high-risk offenders. Such individualized responses, however, in no way assured that the sentencing system as a whole promoted the reduction of crime. What is the benefit of assuring that this defendant is restrained from offending again, if potential victims stand a possibly unaltered chance of being harmed by other criminals? The crime-control theorists began to feel that an effective system should give less emphasis to the criminal propensities of particular convicts and more to systemwide preventive effects. They thus drifted away from the positivists' individualized prediction theories and began to focus their interest on crime-control strategies that were addressed to potential offenders in general. Their attention turned, therefore, to general deterrence.

The General Deterrence School

The deterrence school had its heyday in the mid to late 1970s. Its principal exponents—James Q. Wilson,[14] Ernest van den Haag,[15] Richard Posner[16]—felt no compunction about emphasizing social control aims. Crime could effectively be reduced, they asserted, through sentencing policies aimed at intimidating potential offenders more efficiently.

This view drew heavily from economics and econometrics. Traditionally, criminal justice was thought to be in the competence of jurists, sociologists, and psychologists. Now, deterrence theorists began to argue that crime could usefully be viewed as a quasi-economic activity, whose frequency could be made to vary with the costs imposed on it.[17] Some of them wrote in a style reminiscent of economics texts.[18]

If one asks why the institution of punishment should exist at all, general deterrence may offer some useful answers. As the Norwegian legal scholar Johannes Andenaes notes, "it is still a fundamental fact of social life that the risk of unpleasant consequences

is a very strong motivational factor for most people in most situations."[19] Crime rates are admittedly high today, but they undoubtedly would be higher still if acts of theft, force, and fraud went
completely unpunished. One reason, or possible reason, for the existence of a system of criminal sanctions is that it deters—that is,
secures more compliance than there would be if no criminal penalties existed.*

The deterrence theorists wished to go further, however: to revive Bentham's sentencing calculus of two centuries earlier.[20] The
quantum of sentence was to be decided by weighing the deterrent
benefits of penalties against the "costs" of punishing. Punishment
prevents harm by deterring crimes; it also inflicts harm by making
punished offenders suffer and incurs additional costs through the
resources it absorbs. The proper sentence, supposedly, was the one
that yielded the optimum balance of aggregate benefits (crime prevented) over aggregate costs (the pain inflicted on offenders, and
the financial costs of the criminal justice system).[21]

Viewed from this perspective, the traditional positivist approach—of imprisoning potential recidivists while treating the
"good risks" mildly—was said to be inefficient. It created the hope
among prospective offenders that, if apprehended and convicted,
they might be among the more fortunate individuals deemed not
dangerous and thus punished lightly. A rational deterrence strategy would help ensure that *all* those convicted of major felonies
would receive a substantial punishment, thus eliminating this
hope of leniency. Standardized sentences, rather than individualized ones, were thus advocated.

Deterrence of crime would, supposedly, be supplemented by
incapacitative effects—but these effects likewise would be collective. It was James Q. Wilson who stressed this latter theme.[22]
Most major felonies, he asserted, are perpetrated by small numbers
of repeaters who, because of the large number of offenses they commit, sooner or later are caught and convicted. If prison sentences
(even of modest duration) were invariably imposed for such crimes,
this would remove from circulation the most frequently convicted
(and hence most active) felons for a portion of their criminal careers. As individual predictions would not be involved, there need
be no fear of overlooking actually dangerous convicts. Wilson pro-

---

*For fuller discussion of the role of deterrence in justifying the existence of
the criminal sanction, see chap. 5.

jected impressive results from such a strategy[23]—a reduction in the robbery rate of up to 20 percent.[24] One would not, he asserted, even have to resort to long prison terms. In a system with limited resources, the harsher prison terms are, the less likely it is that they would regularly be used.

The theory was well attuned to the law-and-order mood that had become strong in in the United States. To citizens fearful and angry about rising rates of serious crime, a strategy of intimidating potential criminals and incapacitating convicted criminals had undeniable attractions. In the flurry of legislative activity on sentencing during this era, Wilson's views and those of his colleagues were influential and frequently cited.

The Desert Theory

With the demise of traditional positivism, civil libertarians and others concerned about the fairness of the criminal justice system had to travel a longer route. For them, small improvements in positivist doctrine were not enough, and Posner's and Wilson's deterrence and incapacitation theories held little appeal. What they needed was a sentencing theory that gave a central, not peripheral, role to notions of equity and justice.

These concerns led to borrowings from a different discipline: moral philosophy. Hitherto, penologists, as practical men and women, had seldom felt compelled to consult that literature. But once sentencing came to be seen as a question of justice, perhaps the philosophers were worth attending to.

The philosophical literature proved useful in several ways. First, it supplied a principled critique of aggregate cost-benefit thinking about social issues. Writers such as John Rawls, Bernard Williams, and Nicholas Rescher showed how such thinking could lead to infringement of individual rights, when that served majority interests.[25] This gave the civil libertarians arguments for resisting the utilitarian calculus proposed by deterrence theorists. Second, the philosophers offered the notion of *desert*—of deserved punishments, proportionate to the blameworthiness of the criminal conduct. The notion of deserving or desert, far from being retrogressive or arcane, was an integral part of everyday moral judgments involving praise or blame.[26] Essays such as Herbert Morris's *Persons and Punishment* suggested how desert notions might provide principled limits on the state's punitive power,[27] and might treat those punished with more dignity than purely preventive policies would.

Interest in desert was also facilitated by the fact that this idea had not historically been the ideological property of the law-and-order right. Conservative theorists had, as I have mentioned, first been part of the positivist consensus and then had opted for deterrence. Desert—little explored hitherto by American penologists of any ideological stripe—was something of a tabula rasa in the United States.

The first movement in this direction might be dated to 1971, when the Quaker-sponsored Friends Service Committee published its report, *Struggle for Justice*.[28] The report recommended moderate, proportionate punishments, and opposed reliance on rehabilitative and predictive considerations in sentencing. Several other proposals, embodying a similar implicit sentencing philosophy, appeared in the ensuing years.[29]

The Friends Committee report, however, did not explicitly rely on the idea of desert as the basis for its proposals. That was left to subsequent writings, including a 1973 book entitled *Punishment and Desert* by the Australian philosopher John Kleinig;[30] and my own 1976 book, *Doing Justice: The Choice of Punishments*, published on behalf of the Committee for the Study of Incarceration. Since that time, discussions of the desert rationale have become prevalent in the American sentencing literature.[31]

The central organizing principle of sentencing, on this rationale, is that of "commensurate deserts." Sentences, according to this principle, are to be proportionate in their severity to the gravity of the defendant's criminal conduct. The criterion for deciding the quantum of punishment is retrospective: the seriousness of the violation the defendant has committed. Future-oriented considerations—the offender's need for treatment, his likelihood of offending again, the deterrent effect of his punishment on others—do not determine the comparative severity of penalties. In such a system, imprisonment, because of its severity, is visited only upon those convicted of serious felonies. For nonserious crimes, penalties less severe than imprisonment are to be used. The degree of intrusiveness of these nonprison sanctions is determined not by rehabilitative or predictive considerations but, again, by the degree of gravity of the criminal conduct. Warnings, limited deprivations of leisure time, and fines are among the sanctions that could be used.[32]

Advocates of the desert model opposed the use of individual prediction in sentencing as a matter of principle, not merely because of such forecasts' tendency to error. Their objection to predictive sentencing was simply that it led to undeserved punishments and would do so even if the false-positive rate could be reduced. The use of predictions, accurate or not, meant that those identified as future recidivists would be treated more severely than those not so identified, not because of differences in the blameworthiness of their past conduct, but because of crimes they supposedly would commit in future. It was felt that punishment, as a blaming institution, was warranted only for past culpable choices and could not justly be levied for future conduct. Unless the person actually made the wrongful choice he was predicted to make, he ought not be condemned for that choice—and hence should not suffer punishment for it.[33]

The literature on desert in the United States, like the counterpart literature in Scandinavia, has emphasized moderation in punishment levels. *Doing Justice* recommended penalties well below the prevailing American severity levels,[34] as did comparable texts.[35]

The desert philosophy has considerably influenced sentencing policy in several American jurisdictions.[36] Oregon, for example, adopted legislation that required the state parole board to set standards for duration of imprisonment and provided that the primary objective of those standards should be "punishment which is commensurate with the seriousness of the prisoner's criminal conduct."[37] Minnesota established a sentencing commission to set guidelines for judicial sentencing decisions, and that body's guidelines explicitly purport to reflect a desert rationale in modified form.[38] The state of Washington likewise established a sentencing commission that has issued similar guidelines.[39]

The relations between the two schools of thought was, at best, one of mutual wariness. The deterrence theorists castigated desert advocates for being insufficiently concerned with the practical business of crime control. The latter, in reply, were disturbed by the moral implications of the Wilson-Posner-van den Haag view. That view, they complained, looks at aggregates—how much total harm a given type of crime does, and how much total suffering must be inflicted on offenders in order to reduce its incidence. Any such aggregate cost-benefit comparisons will tend to bypass questions of justice. If moderate, uniform sentencing policies fail to work, the deterrence theory might well support harsher or less uniform ones.[40]

Nevertheless, the two theories had certain points of convergence in practice. One common theme was limitation of sentencing discretion. There should be more standardization of punishments, and explicit rules specifying or recommending the quantities of those penalties.

The other common thesis was that punishments should depend on the gravity of crimes, with prison sentences reserved chiefly for the more serious felonies. For desert advocates, this was a matter of principle. Only those convicted of the most reprehensible conduct deserved the severe sanction of imprisonment. For deterrence theorists, more practical reasons were decisive. In a system having limited resources, the first priority should be to prevent offenses that cause the greatest social harm.

An uneasy alliance between the two schools of thought was thus possible—albeit by no means inevitable.* A state could develop sentencing guidelines recommending imprisonment primarily for serious offenses. Such a system would attract the support of desert theorists on grounds of justice, and of deterrence theorists as *a* way of ensuring the deterrence of crime.[41] Disagreement over theory did not necessarily result in disagreement over actual sentencing policy.

The Emergence of Selective Incapacitation

This uneasy alliance between desert and crime-control advocates began to deteriorate in the early 1980s, as the latter lost faith in the deterrence model and began to shift their allegiance back to strategies of individualized prediction.

---

*In some jurisdictions, deterrence advocates supported legislatively prescribed mandatory minimum sentences as a way of ensuring that those convicted of specified felonies would get at least a given amount of time in prison. Desert advocates objected to such a strategy as unfair, because it left insufficient room for sentence reduction where there were legitimate mitigating circumstances, and did not restrict judges' discretion to overpunish: to impose prison terms far in excess of the prescribed minimums. These disagreements reflected the tension between desert theorists' concern with equity and deterrence theorists' preoccupation with crime control.

THE DECLINE OF THE DETERRENCE MODEL

As scholars scrutinized the deterrence model for sentencing, its evidentiary problems became apparent. To determine sentences on the basis of their general deterrent effects, one needs information on how the rates of various crimes are affected by changes in penalties. Little reliable information of this sort was obtainable. Although there is reason to believe that some form of penalty deters better than none, scant capacity exists for measuring the magnitude of deterrent effects. Deterrence typically is gauged by varying the penalty and tracing the effect on the crime rate. The crime rate, however, is affected not only by the penalty level but also by a host of other factors—the likelihood of criminals being apprehended for crimes they commit; demographic changes; changes in economic conditions; and increases or decreases in racial or intergroup tensions. Techniques for identifying and controlling for these other variables remained, at best, rudimentary.[42]

Similar evidentiary difficulties plagued Wilson's collective incapacitation hypothesis. That depended largely on estimates of the average rates at which offenders commit crimes. The crime-preventive payoff appeared to be substantial when those rates were assumed to be high, and much more modest when those rates were assumed lower. Little or no empirical evidence, however, was available to support any given estimates of those rates.[43]

These problems were documented in detail by a panel of well-known criminologists and econometricians chaired by Alfred Blumstein, and sponsored by the National Academy of Sciences. After surveying the available research, the Blumstein panel found that little was known about the magnitude of deterrent or collective incapacitation effects.[44] Wilson, the most prominent former proponent of such strategies, signed the panel's 1978 report. The report was circulated widely among criminologists and marked the beginning of the decline in influence of the deterrence/collective incapacitation model for sentencing. As faith in that model declined, interest in individual prediction began to revive. What was needed was new evidence that showed progress in the predictive art. Studies purporting to show such progress were not long in coming.

THE RECENT SELECTIVE INCAPACITATION LITERATURE

In the early 1980s, several researchers undertook studies of criminal careers. The research suggested a skewed distribution of

offense rates. While most of the individuals studied were only occasional criminals, a few appeared to offend with startling frequency.
Some convicted robbers reported committing as many as fifty to a
hundred robberies per year.[45] Why not, then, concentrate on identifying and isolating the high-frequency offenders?

One study in particular adopted this strategy. Dr. Peter
Greenwood of the RAND Corporation developed a prediction instrument for identifying high-frequency robbers, based on interviews with incarcerated robbers in three jurisdictions.[46] His instrument, Greenwood asserted, could be employed to identify,
select out, and confine the potential high-rate serious offenders.
Greenwood termed the strategy one of "selective incapacitation"*
—and that term has since become part of penologists' vocabulary.

Greenwood made a number of strong claims in his report.
First, his seven-factor prediction scale was, he asserted, capable of
spotting potential high-frequency robbers with considerable accuracy.[47] Second, the prediction instrument, if applied in sentencing
decisions, was capable of reducing the overall incidence of robberies. Greenwood set forth calculations purporting to show a possible
15 percent reduction in aggregate number of robberies in California.[48] Last, the strategy did not require an increase in the number
of persons incarcerated. Greenwood calculated that his promised
reduction in California robberies could be achieved while simultaneously lowering the prison population by 5 percent.[49] It sounded
most impressive: an accurate prediction instrument, capable of reducing crime without increasing the total number of offenders incarcerated—thus dealing with the threefold problem of overprediction, violent crime, and prison overcrowding!

Other researchers were not so sanguine. Jan and Marcia
Chaiken, also RAND Corporation researchers, constructed a similar prediction instrument from the same data base as Greenwood's.
They warned, however, that the false-positive rate was disturbingly high and that the prediction factors would lose their forecasting utility when official data about offenders rather than self-
reports were used.[50] However, the Chaikens' caveats tended to be
ignored in the widespread publicity that attended publication of
the Greenwood study.

The crime-control theorists—those former advocates of deterrence and collective incapacitation strategies—seized upon selec-

*The term was first used in 1975 by David Greenberg ("The Incapacitative
Effect of Imprisonment: Some Estimates"), but it is Peter Greenwood who has made
it well known, and the term has become identified with his proposed strategy.

tive incapacitation. In his revised 1983 edition of *Thinking about Crime*, Wilson reports Greenwood's results with virtually no reservations and urges the use of such prediction strategies in sentencing.[51] His account of the benefits of selective incapacitation is hardly less optimistic than his earlier claims. Wilson's colleague, Mark Moore, has written a book purporting to show that selective incapacitation can be ethical as well as effective.[52] The Reagan administration's Department of Justice has provided vigorous advocacy. Only one well-known conservative penologist, Ernest van den Haag, has withheld his endorsement of the idea.*

Given the preoccupations of these theorists, their response is understandable. With the loss of faith in deterrence and collective incapacitation, they had no other crime-control technique to adopt. Moreover, Greenwood had addressed their main former objection to predictive sentencing: its lack of apparent impact on crime rates. If his calculations were correct, selective incapacitation would have a considerable impact on the incidence of serious crimes. And (important to fiscal conservatives) it could do so without large outlays for the construction of new prisons. Puzzling only is the uncritical quality of the response. After these writers' disappointment with deterrence strategies, their unreserved enthusiasm for selective incapacitation seems to represent, truly, the triumph of hope over experience.

THE CONFLICT OF THE TWO RATIONALES

The emergence of selective incapacitation exacerbates the potential conflict between justice and crime-control aims in sentencing. Whereas desert theory requires the sentence to be based on the seriousness of the criminal conduct, selective incapacitation makes risk determinative. Risk is measured, in prediction schemes such as Greenwood's, by such factors as the offender's age when first convicted, and his employment and drug history. As these factors have no visible bearing on the blameworthiness of the defendant's choices, desert advocates can hardly support their use in sentencing.

The conflict between the two rationales is illustrated in a passage from Wilson's latest book. After espousing selective incapacitation, Wilson now seeks to limit (albeit not eliminate) the influence of the gravity of the criminal conduct in determination of the

---

*Professor van den Haag has recently expressed his concern about the potential loss of deterrence from selective incapacitation strategies. See Ernest van den Haag, "Thinking about Crime Again."

sentence. Within broad retributive limits, offenders committing *less* serious crimes or having *less* lengthy records should receive longer prison terms when they are worse risks. In his words:

> Sentencing would be shaped, though not rigidly determined, by sentencing guidelines that take into account not only the gravity of the offense and the prior conviction record of the accused, but also the full criminal history, including the juvenile record and the involvement, if any, of the accused with drug abuse. The outer bounds of judicial discretion would be shaped by society's judgment as to what constitutes a just and fair penalty for a given offense; within those bounds, sentencing would be designed to reduce crime by giving longer sentences to high-rate offenders (even when convicted of a less serious offense) and shorter sentences to low-rate offenders (even if the offense in question is somewhat more serious).[53]

No desert theorist can feel comfortable with such a strategy of giving harsher punishments to those whose criminal conduct is *less* reprehensible. The two leading conceptions in sentencing today, desert and selective incapacitation, apparently lead to divergent sentencing policies.

Past or Future Crimes: The Topic of This Book

Faced with such a conflict, it becomes tempting to "solve" the problem by simply blending the two rationales. One takes a dose of desert and adds a dose of prediction. The quotation from Wilson seems to reflect that approach: selective incapacitation is permissible within unspecified desert constraints. A simple blending, however, is not a principled solution. One must ask whether it is *fair* to rely on individual predictions, even within limits. If so, how wide should the limits be? Should the system's principal emphasis be on desert or shift to selective incapacitation?

This book addresses desert and selective incapacitation in sentencing policy.* It reexamines the case for desert, considers the

---

*By giving so much attention to selective incapacitation, I do not mean to suggest that it is the only conceivable crime control strategy. Deterrence and rehabilitation were historical alternatives: were new and more positive research findings to emerge, they might require renewed attention. However, today's crime-

case for predictive sentencing, and attempts to identify the extent and depth of the tensions between the two conceptions. Let me briefly sketch the book's outline.

The Desert Rationale. It has been nearly a decade since the publication of *Doing Justice*. When that work appeared, the notion of desert had hardly been discussed in the sentencing literature. Much of the book was devoted to attempting to outline a coherent desert theory. Since then, the idea of penal desert has been both furiously attacked and vehemently defended in our profession. The time has come to take a second look at the main elements of the desert rationale, to see how well conceptions developed a decade ago have survived this debate, and how much they require rethinking and reformulation. This will be the topic of part II of the book, chapters 3 through 5.

How Much Punishment Is Deserved? As ideas of proportionality and desert become more familiar to penologists, the question of how much punishment is deserved comes to the forefront. The desert model is helpful to sentencing policymakers only if it can provide guidance in deciding the actual quanta of punishments. This "how much?" question is addressed in part III, chapters 6 through 8.

Selective Incapacitation. Next, I turn to sentencing based on dangerousness. Has it become possible to spot dangerous criminals more accurately than before? Has it been demonstrated that selective incapacitation is capable of reducing the aggregate incidence of serious crimes? Is such a strategy especially capable of reducing prison overcrowding? Have any new or better answers been offered to moral doubts about sentencing convicted criminals for their expected future crimes? How just would a hybrid system be, one that permitted selective incapacitation within certain limits? My aim in part IV, chapters 9 through 12, is to see whether the case for individual prediction in sentencing is currently any stronger than it was in the past.

Toward a Synthesis of Past and Future Finally, in chapters 13 through 15, I discuss the question of synthesizing past and fu-

---

control concerns and today's research focus on selective incapacitation. That is why I choose it to compare with desert.

ture: whether there are any alternate crime-control strategies that conflict less sharply with the requirements of desert than selective incapacitation would. In this connection, I examine an incapacitation strategy that focuses on categories of crime, rather than on particular offenders.

CHAPTER 2

Sentencing Guidelines

Sentencing guidelines, in penologists' terminology, refer to standards that prescribe normally recommended penalties, given relevant facts about the offense and the offender's history. Guidelines are numerical and specific: they prescribe definite amounts (or ranges) of punishments. Judges are expected to invoke the prescribed penalties (or remain within the prescribed ranges), unless they give reasons for deviation.

Although they agree on little else, American advocates of desert and of selective incapacitation generally favor sentencing guidelines. The desert theorists consider guidelines useful to make sentences comport properly with the gravity of crimes.[1] The proponents of selective incapacitation want guidelines to assure that sentencing judges will use the new predictive instruments.[2] What advocates of the two viewpoints disagree about is the content of the guidelines—whether the guidelines should emphasize the gravity of crimes or the estimated risk posed by defendants. The salient differences between the two theories can therefore be illustrated through the differences in their resulting guidelines.

The Sentencing Commission and Grid

To elucidate the theoretical issues in this book, I shall show how they bear on the drawing of the *in-out* line on a *sentencing grid* in guidelines written by a *sentencing commission*. For readers unfamiliar with these terms, let me explain them, in reverse order.

THE SENTENCING COMMISSION

Detailed standards for sentencing are a relatively new development. Traditional American positivists supported sweeping discretion, to permit the sentencer to suit the sentence to the particular offender's need for treatment and risk of recidivism. Typically, American statutes set only maximum penalties, and judges could choose almost any sentence within the (usually high) statutory maximums. There were few other limits placed on sentencing judges' discretion, and almost no guidance provided for the exercise of that discretion. As positivism declined, however, so did faith in such broad decision-making powers. Uncontrolled sentencing authority, it came to be felt, meant disparity and sentencing practices not governed by considered policy. Starting in the early 1970s, interest in standards for controlling sentencing decisions grew markedly.[3]

During this past decade of experimentation with sentencing standards, a variety of standard setters have been tried: the legislature, the judiciary, the parole board, and the sentencing commission.[4] The first three rulemakers have, generally, proven less than satisfactory. Legislatures, when writing specific norms for sentencing, have tended to become embroiled in law-and-order politics.[5] The judiciary, when willing to draft sentencing standards at all, has been wont to rely on past sentencing practice and to avoid controversial issues of policy.[6] Parole boards have occasionally drafted coherent standards for parole release decisions but cannot regulate judges' decisions about whether or not to imprison.[7]

These difficulties have made the fourth alternative, the sentencing commission, seem attractive. The idea of a sentencing commission was originally suggested in 1972 by a federal judge and former law professor, Marvin E. Frankel.[8] The legislature, he proposed, should establish a rule-making agency: a sentencing commission, consisting of a small number of members nominated by the jurisdiction's chief executive, and backed by a full-time professional staff. The commission would be granted authority to prescribe guidelines for sentences. Judges would ordinarily be required to observe the guidelines, and departures would be subject to appellate review.

The guidelines would be prescriptive, not merely reflective of past sentencing practice. The commission's main function would be to make considered, explicit policy decisions about what the basis of sentencing ought to be.[9] The commission could have time to devote to the development of that policy and, not being elective, might not be under excessive pressure to adopt posturing stances of toughness.

Minnesota was the first state to implement the idea of a sentencing commission. The Minnesota legislature created the state's Sentencing Guidelines Commission in 1978, and the commission completed its guidelines in the beginning of 1980.[10] The guidelines, which purport to implement a "modified" desert rationale,[11]* had considerable impact on sentencing practice in the state.† They have also elicited extensive interest and comment outside the state.

Two other jurisdictions, Washington and Pennsylvania, established sentencing commissions shortly after Minnesota. Washington's guidelines[12] became effective in 1982—and have a format and rationale similar to Minnesota's. Pennsylvania has had more difficulty. Its commission's initial guidelines were rejected by the state legislature in 1981, and the commission had to increase the severity of the guidelines and dilute their constraints on judicial discretion in order to survive legislative scrutiny.[13] Some other jurisdictions have since been experimenting with sentencing commissions, with varying apparent prospects for success.[14]

To illustrate the various issues herein, I shall refer to a hypothetical sentencing commission, located in an imaginary jurisdiction. The commission, I assume, is weighing which sentencing rationale to adopt and considering how its choice of rationale affects the content of the guidelines.

THE SENTENCING GRID AND THE "IN-OUT" LINE

Several sentencing commissions, including Minnesota's and Washington's, have employed a sentencing grid. This is a two-dimensional table that sets forth the normally recommended sentences or ranges of sentence.‡ The vertical axis of the grid repre-

---

*For further discussion of the rationale, and of some of the problems, of the Minnesota guidelines, see my "Constructing Guidelines for Sentencing: The Critical Choices for the Minnesota Sentencing Guidelines Commission."

†See Appendix 2 for discussion of the early successes, and some current difficulties, in implementation of the Minnesota guidelines.

‡Credit for the invention of the grid belongs to two criminal justice researchers, Leslie Wilkins and Don Gottfredson. They developed this device in the early 1970s for use by the United States Parole Commission in its parole release guidelines. For an account of those guidelines' development, see Don M. Gottfredson, Leslie T. Wilkins, and Peter B. Hoffman, *Guidelines for Parole and Sentencing: A Policy Control Method*, chap. 1.

sents the "offense score." That score rates the seriousness of the crime of which the offender currently stands convicted on a numerical rating scale, say, from 1 to 10. The horizontal axis is the "offender score," representing relevant aspects of the offender's history. The offender score might, as in Minnesota and Washington rate the extent of the defendant's previous criminal record.[15] Alternatively, the offender score might, as in the United States Parole Commission's paroling guidelines, be a statistical prediction index.* Which of these two scoring methods is preferable depends, as we shall see, on the rationale selected for the guidelines by the commission. The grid format is shown in figure 2.1.

The cells in the sentencing grid represent the normally recommended sentences or sentence ranges. Suppose, for example, an offender is convicted of felony X, having had two similar prior convictions. The commission will have rated the seriousness of various crimes. Let us suppose it considered felony X fairly serious, and assigned it a seriousness rating of 7 on a ten-point scale. That means the offender has an offense score of 7. Suppose the grid's offender score measures the criminal history, and that two prior felony convictions rate a score of 2. The normally recommended sentence will then be found by locating the cell on the grid applicable to these offense and offender scores. The cell might prescribe a prison sentence of (say) thirty-six to forty-two months, as shown in figure 2.2. This means the offender ordinarily should receive a prison sentence somewhere between thirty-six and forty-two months. However, the judge would be permitted to depart from the range if he finds aggravating or mitigating circumstances present, and explains his reasons. For this purpose, the guidelines may furnish a list of aggravating and mitigating factors that warrant such departures.[16]

On the grid will be a so-called in-out line. It separates the cells prescribing terms of imprisonment from the cells prescribing lesser penalties. A simple example is shown in figure 2.3. In this example, the line is affected by both the offense and offender scores. It is not yet clear, however, which rationale this sample line reflects—if, indeed, any coherent one.

The Minnesota commission made the drawing of the in-out

---

*The United States Parole Commission's guidelines use an offense-seriousness score as the vertical axis and a prediction score as the horizontal. In the commission's grid, the vertical axis influences dispositions somewhat more than the horizontal. See Gottfredson, Wilkins, and Hoffman, *Guidelines for Parole and Sentencing,* chaps. 2, 3, and 4.

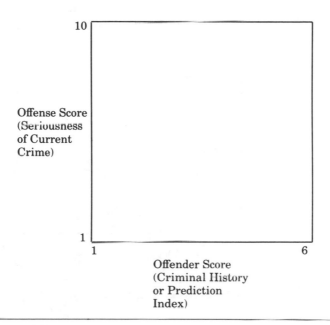

FIGURE 2.1. **The Sentencing Grid**

line its critical decision. The slope of the line would reflect the rationale of the guidelines. A relatively flat line emphasizing the seriousness of the offender's current crime, the commission asserted, would suggest a desert rationale, whereas a steeper line, emphasizing his prior criminal history, would indicate a more predictive orientation. Ultimately, the commission chose what it termed a "modified" desert line: flat for most offenders, but steep for offenders with lengthy criminal histories.[17]

Having done so elsewhere,[18] I shall not here examine the merits of the Minnesota commission's particular solution for the slope of its in-out line. What is of interest for present purposes is the commission's technique: utilizing a particular rationale

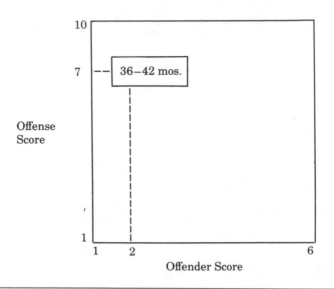

FIGURE 2.2. **Cells in the Sentencing Grid**

—emphasizing desert or prediction—to determine the slope and elevation of the in-out line on the sentencing grid.* In the chapters that follow, the reader will see in-out lines of various slopes and elevations, designed to elucidate and compare the major sentencing theories.

A NOTE ON IMPRISONMENT

The sentencing grid, as developed in Minnesota and elsewhere, uses imprisonment as its most severe sanction. The grid is supposed to provide guidance on which convicted offenders are to be imprisoned, and for how long.

On an incapacitation theory, the use of imprisonment is easily explained: the prison prevents offenders from being able to com-

*This useful modeling technique was developed by the Minnesota Sentencing Commission's former research director and current executive director, Kay A. Knapp.

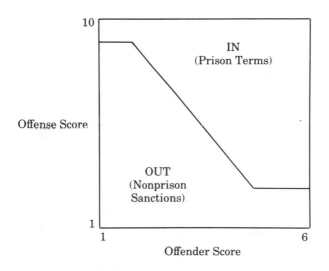

FIGURE 2.3. **Sample In-Out Line**

mit further crimes while confined, at least against members of the outside community. Alternative incapacitants, such as exile or house arrest, may be impracticable for a variety of reasons.

A desert theory, however, does not specify the mode of punishment, it only addresses its degree of severity. For serious crimes, the theory does not necessarily call for imprisonment rather than some other conceivable penalty of comparable severity. Why, then, utilize imprisonment? An important reason is the absence of an acceptable alternative.[19] The pains and abuses of imprisonment are well documented. But what other *severe* penalty could there be? Imprisonment, at least, can be regulated with respect to its duration. The very costliness of the prison is some disincentive to its use. Severe penalties of other hypothetical kinds seem still more repellent.* The sentencing grid should certainly

*One penologist has, amazingly enough, proposed a return to corporal punishment (Graeme Newman, *Just and Painful: A Case for the Corporal Punishment of Criminals*). His arguments for replacing the prison with electroschock give, unin-

prescribe alternative, nonprison sanctions of a less severe nature for less heinous crimes. But as the penalty reserved for the worst offenses, I see little other choice than the prison.*

Imprisonment, in American legal practice, is a sentence in a *state* facility for a term in excess of a year. This means that nonprison sanctions would include terms of a year or less in a county jail. It is a debatable question whether the in-out line should address the use versus nonuse of *imprisonment* as thus defined, or should address, more broadly, the use or nonuse of incarceration for any period in any facility.[20] Minnesota adopted the former approach,[21] and I shall follow it for illustrative purposes in this book. State imprisonment is the sanction that is most visible, most costly, and involves the greatest intrusion into the offender's life.† It thus makes sense, in my judgment, first to establish standards regulating the use of this sanction. When that is done, supplementary standards will be needed for sanctions below the in-out line. These should prescribe when jail terms are permissible and when other, lesser sanctions are called for.††

Guidelines: Implementation or Illustration?

Are sentencing guidelines really a good idea? As their use has spread in the United States, so has the debate over their value.[22]

Despite blanket assertions sometimes heard about the failure or success of sentencing standards,[23] no such generalizations are tenable. Some states' standards are meant to increase the severity

---

tentionally, a persuasive case for retaining imprisonment as the system's severe penalty. The sanctions he proposes would be almost impossible to regulate effectively; their cheapness would be a great incentive to increased use; and their assault upon the offender's personal integrity would be still greater than that of imprisonment. For a valuable discussion of such issues, see Jeffrie G. Murphy, "Cruel and Unusual Punishments."

*A further question is whether imprisonment can be justified by its incapacitative effects, in preference to another hypothetical severe sanction for serious crimes. In *Doing Justice* (112), I suggested so, provided the extent of imprisonment's use was governed by desert principles. I touch again on this topic in chapter 13, when discussing "categorial" incapacitation.

†Save, of course, for the death penalty, which I shall not be treating as a sentencing alternative and which I oppose on principle, on grounds ably discussed in Murphy's article, "Cruel and Unusual Punishments."

††The Minnesota sentencing commission is authorized by statute to develop such supplementary standards but has not yet done so.

of sentences, others are not. Some are drafted with care and others are not. Some have strong enforcement mechanisms and others do not. How successfully standards can regulate sentencing discretion depends on such factors, which vary from jurisdiction to jurisdiction.[24]

More interesting is the question of whether there is any alternative way of setting explicit sentencing policy, other than having numerical guidelines that prescribe definite quanta or ranges of punishments. There is at least one alternative, and it has been tried in some European countries: the adoption of statutory principles for sentencing.

The use of statutory sentencing principles requires that the principles be coherent and not mutually contradictory. If several principles in potential conflict with one another are stated, little is accomplished.* One European country has, however, adopted a reasonably coherent statement: Finland. In 1976, the Finnish Criminal Code was amended to add the following provision:

> The punishment shall be measured so that it is in just proportion to the harm and risk involved in the offense and to the [degree of] guilt of the offender manifested in the offense."[25]

This paragraph has a consistent rationale: it focuses on past crimes, and requires that penalties be proportionate to the gravity of the criminal conduct. In Sweden, a similar effort is under way. A government-appointed study commission, the Committee on Prison Sanctions, is now drafting for the Swedish Parliament's consideration amendments to the penal code setting forth principles of sentencing. Those draft principles are a more elaborate version of the Finnish provisions, and likewise emphasize penalties proportionate to the gravity of the defendant's criminal conduct.[26]

---

*An example of potentially conflicting principles is found in the German Penal Code. Paragraph 46 of the code is an amalgam of two separate drafts, written by drafters having different penal philosophies, and it reads as follows: "The [degree of] guilt of the offender shall be the basis for measurement of the sentence. However, the expected effect of the sentence on the future life and conduct of the actor are to be taken into account." The problem should be apparent. The first quoted sentence appears to reflect a desert philosophy and focuses on past crimes—on the seriousness of the offender's criminal acts. The second quoted sentence focuses on future crimes—seemingly, on predictive and rehabilitative considerations. The paragraph does not clearly explain the relative priorities to be given to these ideas, although it might be read as suggesting that the first be primary. For the statute and a bibliography on its possible conflict of aims, see Karl Lackner, ed., *Strafgesetzbuch mit Erläuterungen*, § 46 and commentary at 216–219. See also Winfried Hassemer, *Einführung in die Grundlagen des Strafrechts*, 270 ff.

Is this Scandinavian sentencing principles approach "better" or "worse" than the American-style numerical sentencing guidelines? Much depends on where it is attempted. Finland and Sweden happen to have strong legalist traditions. Judges feel themselves closely bound by the letter and legislative history of statutes, and their sentencing decisions are closely scrutinized by appellate courts. This environment may give a carefully worded statement of principles considerable potential for impact. But even if the adoption of sentencing principles were to prove useful in these countries, it might not prove useful in the United States, with its very different penal traditions.

For the purposes of the present book, however, we do not need to decide when and under what circumstances numerical sentencing guidelines would be preferable to general sentencing principles, or vice versa. The sentencing grid, even if not actually implemented, remains useful as a heuristic device—a way of illustrating the critical issues of sentencing rationale. By using the grid, and drawing the in-out line at various slopes and elevations, one can illuminate the various issues concerning deservedness and dangerousness that are the subject of this book.

The grid would be useful for these illustrative purposes, even were a decision ultimately made not to adopt numerical guidelines. In January 1984, I had occasion to testify before a working group of the Swedish Committee on Prison Sanctions in regard to its proposals for statutory sentencing principles. In that context, no one expected numerical guidelines to be adopted. Yet I used a hypothetical sentencing grid in my presentation of the various issues involved in the working group's draft principles, including the issue of previous convictions. This use of the grid appears to have been considered helpful by the group.

I therefore shall sidestep the current debate in the United States over the value and success of numerical sentencing guidelines—for that topic merits a book in itself. My purpose here is to examine the aims of sentencing policy, and I wish to use the sentencing grid to elucidate these issues.

PART II

The Conception of Desert

LET ME BEGIN with the conception of sentencing that focuses on past crimes—the desert rationale. I shall be concerned in this part with the general theory of desert in sentencing, and will examine three questions that have prompted debate during recent years. The first is about the justification for the commensurate-deserts principle: *why* should punishments be proportionate to the gravity of offenses? The second concerns the extent to which that principle constrains the choice of sentence: is desert a "determining" or only a "limiting" principle? The third question addresses the justification for the criminal sanction's existence: why should there be a sanction that visits censure on violators? I dealt with the last question in *Doing Justice*, but my present answer is somewhat at variance with that suggested therein.■

CHAPTER 3

Why Punish
Proportionately?

The central principle of a desert rationale for sentencing is commensurability. Sentences should be proportionate in their severity to the gravity of offenders' criminal conduct. The criterion for deciding quanta of punishments should, according to this principle, be retrospective and focus on the blameworthiness of the defendant's actions. Prospective considerations—the effect of the penalty on the future behavior of the defendant or other potential offenders—should not determine the comparative severity of penalties.

It might be useful to begin the discussion of desert by reviewing the justification for this principle. Why should proportionate penalties be inflicted? A variety of possible justifications has been suggested, some based on crime prevention, and others based instead on fairness grounds. It is my view that only the latter can provide a firm basis for the principle.

Beccaria and Bentham's Deterrence Argument

The first systematic defense of the principle of proportionate sanctions was utilitarian. It was given two hundred years ago by Cesare Beccaria[1] and Jeremy Bentham.[2] They advocated a tariff of graded penalties—based on objectives of crime prevention, especially general deterrence. When people commit crimes, they argued, it is preferable that they commit lesser rather than greater ones. Hence, the state should grade its prescribed sanctions according to the seriousness of the offense, so that potential offenders would (if they offend at all) be induced to prefer petty thefts over burglaries, and burglaries over violent crimes. Failure to observe the principle of proportionality in punishing would result in a misdirected structure of disincentives. Offenders would as soon commit grave as lesser crimes.[3]

Beccaria and Bentham's argument for proportionate sanctions has resurfaced in the writings of some modern American deterrence theorists, such as Ernest van den Haag.[4] It has serious deficiencies, however. One of its difficulties has been touched upon already in chapter 1—our very limited knowledge of deterrent effects. To decide sentencing policy on the basis of deterrence, one needs to be able to gauge how much the rates of various crimes are affected by changes in penalties. We are still far from having reliable information of this sort.[5]

Bentham and Beccaria's argument for proportionality assumes, for example, a high degree of (to use economists' language) "cross-elasticity" among rates for various crimes. The crime rate for one type of offense is assumed to be influenced not only by its punishment but by the punishment for alternative crimes. Hence, offenders might switch toward more serious crimes unless punishments were scaled according to the seriousness of crimes. But for all we know, cross-elasticity may be weak or nonexistent. We simply cannot judge with any degree of confidence how the burglary rate might be affected by increases or decreases in comparative punishments for other, more serious offenses such as robbery.

Even if cross-elasticity were successfully confirmed, this theory would leave the proportionality principle weak and prone to exceptions. Deterrence might require that penalties be *on average* scaled in some approximate relationship to the gravity of crimes. But it might well permit exceptions—for example, the imposition of exemplary punishments on a selected few individuals in order to intimidate others more efficiently. (Van den Haag, for example, has not hesitated to propose such special measures, despite his general advocacy of the Beccaria-Bentham theory.)[6] When the proportionality principle is thus defended—when its basis is said to be crime-preventive efficacy and nothing more—then it loses its status as an independent ethical requirement and can be subject to whatever dilutions seem needed in the name of crime control.

The Inhibition-Reinforcement Argument

European penologists, even when utilitarian in general outlook, have tended to recognize the limitations of deterrence as a guide to sentencing policy. As an alternative, they have stressed the role of punishment as a reinforcer of citizens' internal inhibitions against crime. The criminal sanction, Johannes Andenaes has pointed out, is a "concrete expression of society's disapproval" of criminal acts, and thereby "creates conscious and unconscious inhibitions against crime."[7]

This norm-reinforcing function is sometimes said to provide the basis for the principle of proportionality. The noted German legal theorist Claus Roxin contends, for example, that a penalty structure in which penalties are kept commensurate with the gravity of crimes will be perceived as more just, and being so perceived, will better strengthen citizens' self-restraint and respect for law.[8] Disproportionate sanctions are said to risk weakening the moral influence of the penalty structure.

Plausible as this argument sounds, it troubles me. The idea ultimately remains one of crime prevention. It involves the assertion that if one punishes proportionately, the citizenry's moral inhibitions will be reinforced, which in turn will enable the criminal law to carry out its crime-restraining role more successfully.

The question that naturally comes to mind is: how does one know? There is little or no reliable evidence on how much punishment reinforces law-abiding attitudes, and (as Andenaes himself has recognized)[9] the link may be weak and tenuous. If we know so little about how and to what extent punishment reinforces conscientious self-restraint, that is a frail basis for the idea of proportionate sanctions.

We could, of course, seek further evidence. Although direct evidence would be difficult to obtain, a variety of psychological experiments could be devised that would explore the causal connections between punishment and the formation of moral inhibitions. But what if the results of these experiments were no more encouraging than the rehabilitation research of past decades? What if the experiments suggested that proportionate punishments appeared no more successful in promoting self-restraint and respect for law among the citizenry than punishments that ignored the proportionality principle? If the basis of proportionality is its presumed pedagogical influence, and if such research fails to confirm the existence of this influence, proportionality then would rest on weak empirical foundations; it would become, like rehabilitative punishment, merely another penal strategy unsupported by evidence. And even were the research less discouraging, such a line of reasoning does not account for our sense that proportionality is not just a prudential but an ethical principle. We feel that there is something wrong, not simply counterproductive in the long run, about inflicting punishments that are not fairly commensurate with the gravity of offenses. That sense of the wrongfulness cannot be explained merely by arguing that proportionality influences citizens' attitudes in such a way as to reinforce the inclination to law-abidingness.

A further problem has been suggested by Andenaes's Norwegian colleague, Nils Christie.[10] If the theory is that proportionate sanctions foster values of law-abidingness, Christie asks: Why not strive instead to foster other values? Why not relax the constraints of proportionality in order to create a system that emphasizes compromise, reconciliation, and conflict resolution? It is far from obvious that the latter values are any less important to a cohesive, well-ordered society.

The Argument from the Condemnatory Implications of Punishment

The principle of commensurate deserts does not, in my judgment, rest on crime-prevention considerations at all. It is, instead, grounded on the blaming character of punishment.*

Desert, customarily, refers to certain kinds of reasons for a favorable or unfavorable response to someone. The reasons are those concerning the good or bad qualities of his deeds. Someone may be said to deserve something pleasant by virtue of his distinguished contributions, or undesired by virtue of his poor work or bad acts. The concept is not directed toward the future: by saying that A deserves x, one is not asserting that he (or someone else, or society in

*I first sketched this condemnation argument in *Doing Justice*, 71–74. It is distinct, however, from the proposed retributive justification for the existence of punishment that I discuss elsewhere in that book (ibid., 47–48). I no longer subscribe to the latter theory, for reasons explained in chap. 5.

general) will necessarily be better off if he gets *x*. Rather, the concept is retrospectively oriented. One is saying that *x* is A's due because of the quality of what he has done.[11]

In trying to decide what is just, one frequently must choose among competing possible criteria of justice. When speaking of economic justice, for example, one must choose whether desert, or need, or some other criterion is appropriate. What makes this choice so difficult, and so controversial, is that economic goods, on their face, provide no clue about which criterion of justice is preferable. There is nothing about material wealth per se that makes readily apparent whether justice requires it be distributed according to who has merited it, or according to who most needs it, or according to utilitarian criteria of optimum aggregate satisfaction.

There are, however, certain institutions that by their very nature connote approbation or disapprobation. Prime examples are grades, prizes, and punishments. If one establishes such things at all, then they ought, given their implications of praise or blame, to be distributed according to the degree of praiseworthiness or blameworthiness of the actor's conduct.*

Take punishment in particular. Punishing someone consists of doing something painful or unpleasant to him, because he has purportedly committed a wrong, under circumstances and in a manner that conveys disapprobation of the offender for his wrong. Treating the person punished as a wrongdoer, as the philosopher Richard Wasserstrom has pointed out, is central to the idea of punishment.[12] If one asks why punishment ought to be apportioned to the gravity of the criminal conduct, therefore, the answer is not that this would create the optimum deterrent or pedagogical influence, for it may or may not do so. The requirement of proportionate punishment is, instead, derived directly from the censuring implications of the criminal sanction. Once one has created an institution with the condemnatory connotations that punishment has, then it is a requirement of justice, not merely of efficient law enforcement, to punish offenders according to the degree of reprehen-

---

*One can, of course, debate the criteria for praiseworthiness or blameworthiness. Consider school grades. Most American schools grade students according to the quality of their academic work. Given that criterion, students whose work is superior should receive the superior grades. So-called progressive schools use a different grading criterion, namely, the amount of effort expended by the student on his or her work. Still other schools might conceivably adopt different performance criteria. But the principle remains the same: those students who have best satisfied the applicable criteria deserve the best ratings (assuming students are graded at all).

sibleness of their conduct. Disproportionate punishments are unjust not because they are ineffectual or possibly counterproductive, but because the state purports to condemn the actor for his conduct and yet visits more or less censure on him than the gravity of that conduct warrants.

A few comments about this condemnation-based justification for proportionality are in order. It makes clear that the principle of proportionality does not rest on factual claims that commensurability in punishment enhances the crime-preventive utility of the system. Suppose we were to discover evidence that proportionate punishments were no more effective a deterrent than, and perhaps not as effective as, disproportionate ones. Suppose, further, that new psychological evidence suggested that formal penal sanctions, whether proportionate or not, contributed little to the development of people's inhibitions against predatory conduct. Would such evidence mean that one properly could ignore the requirements of proportionality? Certainly not. As long as the state continues to respond to violence, theft, or fraud, or similarly noxious conduct through the institution of the criminal sanction, it is necessarily treating those whom it punishes as wrongdoers and condemning them for their conduct. If it thus condemns, then the severity of the state's response ought to reflect the degree of blameworthiness, that is, the gravity, of actors' conduct.

This argument uses a commonly understood concept, employed in everyday life: the notion of censure. The idea is that once one has established a condemnatory institution to respond to criminal acts, one ought then to allocate its sanctions in a manner that comports with the reprehensibleness of those acts. The argument does not presuppose the idea of requiting evil for evil, or other arcane notions that have sometimes surfaced in the literature of retribution.[13]

This account of proportionality also puts us in a better position to answer Nils Christie's query, whether we might respond to crime in a manner that fosters "other values," such as reconciliation.[14] If one has established the criminal sanction, one has created an institution that condemns criminal behavior and should allocate punishments accordingly. It is unfair, once the institution of punishment is in place, to shift in an eclectic fashion between condemnatory and noncondemnatory responses: to mediate when the parties are prepared to talk to one another, but punish otherwise. Such nonpunitive responses to wrongdoing are inappropriate when others who have committed no more blameworthy acts continue to face being punished. Were one serious about giving Christie's "other values" precedence, one would have to devise a nonpunitive response for the whole universe of behavior with which the criminal sanction now deals.[15]

My account of proportionality thus far is incomplete in two respects. First, I have not yet explained the nature of the proportionality principle's requirements. Is proportionality only a limit on permissible punishments? Or is it a principle that determines actual quanta of penalties? Or is it a combination of both? That will be the subject of the next chapter.

Second, my account assumes that punishment—that is, a condemnatory sanction—justifiably exists. The argument for proportionality has been stated in conditional form: *if* the institution of punishment with its censuring implications has been established, then penalties ought to be apportioned to the blameworthiness of the criminal conduct. This leaves the justification for the institution of punishment still to be explained. Why should the state respond to crime with a condemnatory sanction, rather than with disincentives to criminal behavior that have no blaming overtones? I shall address that question in chapter 5.

CHAPTER 4

Proportionality: Determining or Limiting?

Much of the debate over the idea of penal desert in the last decade has concerned the degree to which it constrains the choice of sanctions. Retributivists are said to assert that desert alone can guide the fixing of penalties. Others—including the distinguished penologist Norval Morris—disagree and claim that desert is no more than a limit. My view is that the proper role of desert is actually more complex than either contention suggests.

Professor Morris's position is one he calls "limiting retributivism"[1]—a mixed model somewhere between strict retributivism and pure penal utilitarianism. Desert, he contends, supplies only the upper and lower bounds within which a penalty can justly be levied; inside these bounds, crime prevention concerns (e.g., deterrent and predictive considerations)[2] should be decisive. Desert thus properly can serve only as a limiting, not a determining principle. In his words:

> Desert is not a defining principle; it is a limiting principle. The concept of "just desert" sets the maximum and minimum of the sentence that may be imposed for any offense and helps to define the punishment relationships between offenses; it does not give any more fine-tuning to the appropriate sentence than that. The fine-tuning is to be done on utilitarian principles.[3]

The reason desert is only limiting, Morris argues, is that none of us have an idea precisely how much punishment is deserved for any category of offense. We can grasp only what would be manifestly disproportionate in lenience or severity. As he puts it:

> When we say a punishment is deserved, we rarely mean it is precisely appropriate in the sense that a deterrent punishment could in principle be. Rather we mean that it is not undeserved; that it is neither too lenient nor too severe; that it neither sentimentally understates the wickedness or harmfulness of the crime nor inflicts excessive pain or deprivation on the criminal in relation to the wickedness or harmfulness of his crime. It is not part of the utilitarian calculus . . . The concept of desert defines relationships between crimes and punishments on a continuum between the unduly lenient and the excessively punitive within which the just sentence may be determined on other grounds.[4]

Since desert is only a limit, Morris continues, the sentencer is not obligated to impose equal sentences on equally deserving (or rather, undeserving) criminals. Cases that are alike in respect to the blameworthiness of defendants' conduct may be treated *unlike* where necessary for utilitarian ends—provided none of those disparate punishments become grossly disproportionate to the degree of iniquity of the crime.[5]

When one asks whether desert is limiting or determining, however, it is necessary to specify: *limiting or determining for what purpose?* It is essential to distinguish between *ordinal* and *cardinal* magnitudes of punishment, that is, between (1) the question of how crimes should be punished relative to each other, and (2) the question of what absolute levels of severity should be chosen to anchor the penalty scale.* To view desert as a determining principle in deciding comparative punishments does not commit one to the claim that it is determinative also for deciding the overall degree of punitiveness or lenience of the system.

For desert theory, this distinction is crucial. Desert should be treated as a determining principle in deciding *ordinal* magnitudes. But it becomes only a limiting principle in deciding the system's *cardinal* dimensions of severity. Let me explain.

---

*Other writers on desert theory have explored the ordinal/cardinal distinction. See, for example, Hugo Adam Bedau, "Classification-Based Sentencing: Some Conceptual and Ethical Problems."

Ordinal Magnitudes: Desert as Determining

The issue of ordinal magnitudes concerns how a crime should be punished compared to similar criminal acts, and compared to other crimes of a more or less serious nature. Proportionality is a determining principle here: comparisons of the gravity of the criminal conduct should be decisive of relative severities of punishments. This involves meeting two requirements. The first is the requirement of *parity*. Persons whose criminal conduct* is equally serious should be punished equally. The second is the requirement of *rank ordering*. Penalties should be graded in severity so as to reflect gradations in relative seriousness of the conduct. These requirements preclude the resolution of questions of comparative punishment on grounds other than the blameworthiness of the offender's conduct. They preclude, for example, punishing a particular burglar more severely than other convicted burglars not because his particular crime is any worse, but because he is a worse risk, or because giving him a higher-than-usual punishment would make him a useful example to others.

To disregard these ordinal proportionality requirements, and treat desert as providing only limits in the manner Morris proposes, would ignore the censuring implications of punishment. Suppose one decides that, for a given species of crime, less than a years imprisonment is undeservedly lenient, and more than b years, undeservedly severe. Suppose one treats desert as supplying only those outer limits—that the sentence must fall somewhere between a and b—and then allows the disposition to be decided within these bounds on utilitarian grounds. This would allow two offenders, whose conduct is equally reprehensible but who are considered to present differering degrees of risk, to receive differing punishments. One may receive a punishment close to the lower limit, a, and the other may get a sentence at the upper limit, b. Through these different penalties, the two offenders would be visited with different amounts of implied censure, although the reprehensibleness of their conduct is the same. In fact, a defendant who commits a less serious crime may receive comparatively the greater penalty, if he is deemed to represent the higher risk.

---

*The extent to which criminal conduct, for this purpose, includes the defendant's earlier convictions will be addressed in chap. 7.

In his latest book, Professor Morris has dismissed such objections as merely circular—as "restat[ing] the conflict rather than resolv[ing] it against [Morris's] view."[6] But the argument is *not* circular. It can be stated in general terms thus:

1. Suppose X is an institution whose central defining features include the ascription of commendation or censure, so that the quantum of x distributed to any recipient connotes how much he is to be praised or blamed for his conduct.

2. It follows that a fair distribution of x should reflect recipients' comparative deserts—so that equally commendable or reprehensible conduct yields equal quantities of x, and so that those whose conduct is the more or the less praise- or blameworthy receive more or less x.

3. Therefore if one does not wish to distribute x according to recipients' comparative deserts, one needs to make one of these two moves: (1) deny the premise: that is, show that institution X has no such essential praising or blaming features; or else (2) reconstitute institution X so that its praising or blaming implications are eliminated or diluted as much as possible.

Let me give a modest illustration. Each year, the School of Criminal Justice at Rutgers awards a certain number of fellowships and assistantships to graduate students. The fellowships are explicitly designated as awards and carry a stipend. The assistantships also carry a stipend, but involve working with faculty members and are not designated as awards. Because of the different character of these two institutions, our faculty uses different criteria to distribute them. The fellowships, by virtue of their character as awards, are distributed strictly according to desert—that is, according to the quality of the student's academic performance. The assistantships, however, are distributed according to more pragmatic criteria. Since they are jobs primarily, the student's experience in a faculty member's area of teaching and research is an influential factor. Were our faculty to propose distributing fellowships similarly, we would have to change their designation and character to make them less of an award and more of an employment.

Applying the point to punishment, the logic runs similarly. Desert theorists claim that punishment is essentially a condemnatory institution and, hence, that penalties should be distributed according to the degree of blameworthiness of the criminal conduct. In order to reflect blameworthiness, the system should observe the ordinal requirements of desert: to punish equally reprehensible criminal conduct equally, and to grade punishments so that their severity comports with the rank ordering of seriousness of crimes. To resist these conclusions, one needs to deny the premise, that is, to assert that punishment either (1) is not or (2) ought not to be a condemnatory institution.

Assertion (1), which denies that punishment essentially involves censure, seems implausible to me. The only perceptible difference between a tax and a fine, for example, resides in the condemnatory character of the fine—not in the material deprivation, which in both cases is money taken. I doubt Professor Morris would wish to deny the blaming nature of the institution of punishment.

Assertion (2) might be less implausible. Someone conceivably could argue that the censuring element in punishment is a historical relic, and that one should seek to reform the criminal sanction so as to make it a material disincentive against undesirable conduct, with few or no moralizing overtones.[7] One could argue, further, that downgrading the ordinal proportionality requirements is a step toward thus reconstituting the criminal sanction as a non-condemnatory response—to be taken along with other symbolic changes including, perhaps, eliminating morally laden terms such as innocence or guilt. This is not purely hypothetical. Juvenile justice reformers in the United States tried for years to recast the juvenile justice system so as to eliminate all traces of moral stigma. Yet I wonder if this route would have much attraction for Professor Morris, because it would lead to the elimination of even his outer desert limits.* I would certainly resist such a change. For reasons spelled out in the next chapter, I think it desirable that the criminal sanction retain its condemnatory character. If that character is retained, then I find it hard to understand how the ordinal desert requirments can be justly disregarded.

Morris's other argument, the reader will recall, has been that we can only recognize manifest *dis*proportion in punishment, and cannot meaningfully judge as proper any particular proportion between a crime and its punishment. Applied to the *ordinal* requirements of proportionality, this claim is unpersuasive. Judging par-

---

*Eliminating or downgrading the censure element in punishment would eliminate desert requirements *too* well. It would dispense not only with the need for parity and rank ordering in punishments but also with the desert requirement Morris does wish to keep—to wit, the cardinal proportionality principle barring manifest disproportion between crimes and their punishments. The civil commitment law has had no similar principle, as Morris recognizes, precisely because no moral stigma purports to be involved in its sanctions (Morris, *Madness and the Criminal Law*, 30).

ity and rank ordering in punishment involves making judgments about the comparative seriousness of crimes and the comparative onerousness of punishments. These rating judgments have their complexities, of which more will be spoken in chapter 6. Yet such assessments—of how harmful the conduct is, how culpable the actor has been, how painful the punishment is—have their roots in moral and practical judgments that ordinary persons make in everyday life. So long as some kind of rational judgment of seriousness and severity can be made, there is no insurmountable obstacle to determing whether the ordinal proportionality requirements are being met.

Cardinal Magnitudes: Desert as Limiting

Once one grades penalties according to the comparative seriousness of crimes, the scale as a whole still needs to be anchored. This issue, of anchoring the penalty scale by fixing the absolute severity levels for at least some crimes, is the issue of cardinal magnitude. It is here that desert can play only a limiting, not a determining role.

The intuitive reason why this is so is the greater difficulty of making cardinal desert judgments. Suppose one is trying to find the appropriate, deserved penalty for the crime of burglary. If one has already decided the penalties for some other crimes, then one can locate the burglary penalty by making comparative judgments: how much worse or more venial is burglary than those other crimes? But such judgments require a starting point, and the issue of cardinal magnitude deals with finding that starting point. There seems to be no crime for which one can readily perceive a specific quantum of punishment as the uniquely deserved one.

This intuition is confirmed when one considers the notion of censure that underlies the principle of commensurate deserts. Assessments of ordinal proportionality rest on familiar judgments of comparative blameworthiness. When judged in absolute rather than comparative terms, however, the censure expressed through penal deprivation is a convention, expressing so much disapprobation through given levels of severity. When a penalty scale has been devised to reflect the comparative gravity of crimes, altering that scale by making modest pro rata increases or decreases in all the prescribed sanctions would represent a change in that convention but not necessarily an infringement of cardinal proportionality.*

To say the link represents a convention, however, does not mean that all conventions are equally acceptable. When penal deprivation expresses disapprobation, the amount of that deprivation should bear some reasonable relationship to the disapproval intended to be expressed. This militates, for example, against more than a certain degree of inflation of the penalty scale as a whole. Suppose punishments on a scale were so much escalated that drastic penalties (say, those involving substantial periods of imprisonment) were visited even on offenses that rank low on the grid's seriousness scale. The objection is plain enough. Expressing the moderate degree of disapproval appropriate to such lesser offenses through such severe sanctions fails to accord respect to the person punished. The use of long prison terms as a symbol for lesser censure denigrates the importance of the defendant's right to liberty. Such sanctions imply that the defendant's liberty is of such slight importance that its prolonged deprivation is an appropriate symbol of modest blame. This means that the principle of proportionality provides some upper limit, albeit an imprecise one, on cardinal magnitudes. Similar arguments can be advanced to suggest that the principle also provides some lower bounds, that the scale ought not be so deflated that trivializing penalties are visited even on the most serious offenses.

The upshot is that commensurate deserts is, indeed, a limiting but not a defining principle where cardinal magnitudes are concerned. If it is only limiting, that opens the way for other considerations to affect the choice of magnitude of scale. What those other considerations might be is discussed in chapters 8 and 13.

Once, however, the magnitude and anchoring points of the scale have been chosen (with whatever uncertainties this choice involves), then the *internal* scaling requirements of proportionality—the ordinal requirements—become binding. The impre-

---

*Kleinig (*Punishment and Desert*, 124) has taken a different view, that desert can determine cardinal magnitudes. The scale, he argues, should be anchored by "reserv[ing] the mildest punishment we can reasonably give for the least serious wrong, the most severe punishment for the most wicked deed, and scale other wrongs and punishments in between." This may be *a* permissible solution, but it is not the only possible one. Why, for example, not truncate the scale at the top, so that the worst crime receives a substantial punishment but one considerably less severe than the most that could humanely be inflicted on the wrongdoer? If his solution is not unique, then it is, as I suggest, a matter of convention whether to adopt his solution or such an alternative. A fuller critique of Kleinig's solution is set forth in Don E. Scheid, *Theories of Legal Punishment*, 173–182.

cision of cardinal proportionality is not a warrant for infringing these principles of comparative scaling.

At one point in his recent book, Morris argues as though it were.[8] He quotes a passage of mine where I am speaking of how a sentencing commission might decide the elevation of the in-out line on its sentencing grid.[9] I state that cardinal proportionality calls for severe punishments (imprisonment) for the grave crimes; requires milder punishments for lesser violations; but is not precise enough to determine where, among the intermediate crimes, the prison sanction should begin to be invoked. Hence, I suggest, the rulemaker might invoke nondesert considerations to decide this latter issue. Morris siezes upon this statement as suggesting some kind of inconsistency with a desert orientation; in his words: "Professor von Hirsch would thus allow utilitarian considerations within desert constraints to guide a sentencing commission but would deny them to a judge. I don't see why, except to protect the elegance of his thesis or the robe of the judge."[10]

My point has nothing to do with theoretical or sartorial elegance. It has to do with the difference between ordinality and cardinality. A sentencing commission, within the limits of cardinal proportionality, might anchor the penalty scale by deciding to locate the elevation of the in-out line slightly higher or lower on the sentencing grid. But once the scale has been so anchored, then desert requires that parity be observed among crimes of a given degree of seriousness—and that comparatively more or less serious crimes be ranked higher or lower on the scale. Even though I have no precise amount in mind as the absolute deserved penalty for burglary, I am still entitled to insist on parity in the punishment of burglars, and on the rank-ordering of other crimes in proper proportion to the penalty decided upon for burglary.

How much guidance will my theory give? The cardinal limits will necessarily be imprecise. But the model calls for considerably more specificity in deciding ordinal magnitudes. To meet the requirements of parity and rank ordering, crimes have to be graded according to their seriousness; normally recommended penalties assigned to those gradations; and deviations from those penalties permitted only in special circumstances related to the harm or culpability of the offender's conduct. This will not, in pure theory, provide for a unique set of solutions since (given the merely limiting nature of the cardinal requirements) the penalty scale as a whole could be toughened or made milder to a degree while the relative proportions among punishments are held constant. But in practice, such a theory can provide considerable guidance to rulemakers. A sentencing commission usually will not have all that much leeway in increasing or scaling down aggregate severity levels, before it encounters limits on the availability of prison resources,* on one hand, and political constraints on reducing severities, on the other. Where the commission's power resides, and where it needs the guidance, is in resolving questions of relative severity, and in determining how much to emphasize the gravity of the criminal conduct versus how much weight to give other factors. It is precisely on this issue of relative severities that the desert theory, with its strong ordinal requirements,can be so helpful.

---

*For discussion of the legitimacy of considering the availability of correctional resources, see chap. 8.

CHAPTER 5

Why Punish at All?

My arguments in the last two chapters—about the rationale for the commensurate-deserts principle and about the ordinal and cardinal scaling requirements of that principle—have relied heavily on the condemnatory features of the institution of punishment. Those arguments rest on the assumptions that the state (1) should establish an official sanction against victimizing and other wrongful behavior, which (2) involves the visitation of censure or condemnation on the perpetrators. Let us consider the justification of these two assumptions.

Why Not Abolish Criminal Punishment?

It might be useful to begin by thinking about abolishing criminal punishment altogether, and asking what the possible objections might be. Nils Christie, in his latest book on punishment,[1] has urged that we seriously consider abolition. With suitable (and rather fundamental) changes in the political and social structure, he argues, we could begin responding to what is now called crime in nonpunitive ways: by mediating between victim and aggressor; perhaps, giving some formal expression of sorrow over the commission of the act.[2] In such a system, one might not have to be concerned about actors' desert because blame is not being levied.

Would such a purely nonpunitive response make sense? Arguably, it could for minor infractions. The boundary between civil and criminal law has been historically conditioned, and we might live with a system that dealt with petty offenses through mediation or compensation. But the case seems otherwise for the more sub-stantial crimes, the acts of force or theft that visit or threaten substantial harm on their victims. There, a purely nonpunitive re-sponse is open to two prima facie objections.

First, the threat of painful consequences appears needed to keep the more blatant forms of noxious behavior within tolerable limits. If we ask—not how much punishment should be levied on those convicted—but whether criminal behavior should ever be pe-nalized, surely one possible reason is that doing so helps prevent such behavior. The available evidence for punishment's preventive effects, and the common-sense case for those effects, is most per-suasive when one compares the consequences of punishing with those of not punishing at all.[3] Were one merely to try to mediate between criminals and their victims, and visit no painful conse-quences, it seems likely that victimizing conduct would become so prevalent as to make life nasty and brutish, indeed.

Second, when victimizing acts have been committed, a re-sponse that fails to condemn the actor scarcely seems morally ade-quate. The acts of intentional harm with which the criminal law centrally deals are acts that we justifiably consider wrong. If they are wrong, and if perpetrators may properly be held respons-ible, then a sanction that embodies censure, as punishment does, is warranted.

There appear thus to be two main considerations undergird-ing the criminal sanction: crime prevention and reprobation for wrongdoing. These grounds for punishment each need closer scrutiny.

Can Reprobation
Be Derived from Prevention?

Let me begin in reverse order, with reprobation. Is the cen-sure element in punishment derivable from larger crime-preven-tion aims, or does it have independent justification? A Finnish col-league, Klaus Mäkelä, has argued for the former view, of basing the censure on preventive aims.[4] It was pointed out a quarter of a century ago, by H.L.A. Hart, that one can use the notion of crime prevention to explain the existence of punishment without being compelled to rely on it to decide how much to punish.[5] Mäkelä uses Hart's distinction for his own account, as follows:

1. Punishment's existence is justified on crime-prevention grounds—because it helps discourage certain undesirable behavior. It does so primarily because of its inhibition-strengthening features. Through its censuring implications, punishment helps reinforce people's sense of the wrongfulness of criminal behavior and hence strengthens their inhibitions against committing crimes. Punishment should have its condemnatory features in order to perform this inhibition-reinforcing function.

2. Once punishment is established, it should in fairness be distributed among convicted offenders consistently with its condemnatory implications. Therefore, the rules on how much to punish should be governed by normative judgments about desert. Notice he does not suggest that proportionate punishments will necessarily be more effective in reducing crime than disproportionate ones. Prevention is being relied upon, instead, at a logically prior step in the argument, of explaining why punishment should exist at all.* The account is thus similar to one that might naturally be used to explain academic grades. If one asks why good students should get high grades, the answer is retrospective and desert oriented. Since high grades symbolize approval for good performance, they are deserved by those (and only those) who have earned them through the quality of their work. But if one asks why a school or university should grade students at all, that answer could nevertheless be forward looking and utilitarian: grades are an incentive for better work.

From the point of view of practical sentencing policy, Mäkelä's view makes him a desert theorist. Most policymakers are likely to assume that the institution of the criminal sanction is unavoidable, however it might be explained theoretically. They will wish chiefly to understand the principles concerning how much to punish, as these govern sentencing policy. To assert, as this theory does, that desert should control the distribution of punishments among convicted offenders, makes desert principles (not crime-prevention aims) paramount for such practical policy judgments. Nevertheless, the justification for punishment's existence

---

*In an unpublished lecture, Bernard Williams has suggested a similar two-tiered concept, relying on crime prevention to explain punishment's existence and desert to govern its distribution. Williams's lecture was presented at a colloquium on punishment and desert, held under the auspices of the Rutgers University School of Criminal Justice, at Sterling Forest Conference Center, Tuxedo, N.Y., 19–21 November 1978. See also Walter Moberley, *The Ethics of Punishment.*

remains an important philosophical question. Can the reprobative features of punishment be fully accounted for by ideas of crime prevention, as the foregoing theory asserts? Such an explanation leaves me skeptical for several reasons.

We have (once again) the evidentiary question. There is good reason, as I have said, for thinking that a system of punishments prevents criminal behavior better than no punishment would. But how much do we really know about the psychic mechanisms by which the threat to punish influences people's behavior? One important reason why most people desist from committing crimes is that they believe victimizing behavior to be wrong. But do we really know how important the formal criminal sanction is in forming or reinforcing such moral attitudes? Might not people's sense of the wrongfulness of such conduct stem predominantly from other social sources and from their own capacities for moral reasoning? Might not the preventive utility of the criminal sanction depend more on its intimidating than on its moralizing effects? Without answers to these questions (or at least satisfactory methods of seeking answers), I find it hard to place great confidence in the proposition that the condemnatory features of punishment can be justified on preventive grounds.

These are worrisome doubts for Mäkelä's theory. They suggest that, conceivably, some kind of nonblaming official disincentive against what is now called criminal behavior might suffice. To the extent that the case for having a condemnatory sanction is weakened, that also undermines the argument for having deserved, proportionate sanctions. Arguably, a system of nonblaming disincentives might be distributed without regard to degree of fault.

I doubt that the censuring elements in the criminal sanction can be given a purely instrumentalist explanation. Condemning people for the wrongful acts they commit is part of having a morality that holds people responsible for their behavior. When a misdeed has been committed, one judges the actor adversely for having committed the wrongful deed. Given that adverse judgment, one expresses one's disapprobation of the actor for his act—which is what censuring is about. One would withhold the expression of disapprobation only if one had special reasons for not reproving the actor: for example, if one doubted that this particular person could properly be held responsible ("you can't really blame him, he didn't know what was at stake"), or if one doubted one's authority to confront the actor ("I can't say anything, he's not *my* colleague").

The expression of disapprobation may (or may not) influence the moral attitudes of third persons, but any such pedagogical effect is derived from the role of censure in expressing the moral judgments of the speaker himself. Why should I permit my moral attitudes to be influenced by the fact that A censures B for a misdeed? It is because it brings to my attention the fact that A has judged B's behavior to be reprehensible. To the extent that I respect A's judgment, the condemnation may reinforce my own sense of the inappropriateness of the conduct. It should have this effect, however, only if I have reason to believe that A is censuring B as an authentic expression of moral standards he believes in and is prepared to defend, and not merely as a way of influencing my attitudes. Were I to think that A was not particularly indignant about B's conduct, and was reproving him simply to influence third parties such as myself, I should surely be less impressed.*

Criminal punishment is inflicted by the state, not by private individuals, but a similar logic applies. The role of punishment in reinforcing law-abiding citizens' moral inhibitions must derive from the more fundamental role of expressing judgments about the wrongfulness of certain conduct. Why should anybody take his or her moral clues from the criminal law? The answer has to be that the penal law embodies a considered judgment that the punished behavior is wrong, and that people should take that judgment into account in forming their own standards of right and wrong.

Reprobation as an Independent Justifying Element

My account of the institution of punishment thus runs differently. An official response to victimizing conduct should serve two

---

*One might wish to inquire further into the logic of censure. When one judges an act to be wrong, why confront the actor with one's disapproval, rather than keeping silent or merely communicating one's displeasure about the actor to others? The starting point for such an inquiry would be P. F. Strawson's remarkable essay, "Freedom and Resentment." He argues that the capacity to respond to wrongdoing by disapproval, censure, and the like is an integral part of treating persons as moral agents rather than as mere subjects to be controlled.

An adequate theory of censure, in my view, will need to account for its character as *moral* judgment: the judgment it reflects that the actor has done wrong, and that the censurer is entitled to visit his disapprobation. I do not think purely subjectivist explanations—those that focus merely on others' negative feelings toward the actor, or the social functions of such feelings—are satisfactory. Compare, e.g., J. L. Mackie, "Morality and the Retributive Emotions."

distinct purposes: (1) to discourage conduct of that sort, and (2) to express disapproval of the conduct and its perpetrators. Punishment has its two salient features—the imposition of hard treatment and the visitation of censure*—in order to serve these dual purposes. By threatening unpleasant consequences, one hopes to discourage criminal conduct. By imposing those consequences in a solemn, condemnatory fashion, the state registers disapprobation of such conduct on behalf of its citizens.

The disapproving element of the response cannot be collapsed into the preventive element, as can be seen from the following *Gedankenexperiment*. Suppose someone were to propose (as was once attempted for juvenile crimes) that the state should penalize adult criminal conduct in as morally neutral a way as possible. Deprivations would be visited on those who commit the conduct, but the state would avoid any expressed or implied claim that there was anything wrong with the perpetrator's acts. What objections are there to such a proposal? The preventionist would object that it would lead to more criminal behavior. Once the state no longer condemned the prohibited conduct, people's inhibitions against such conduct would weaken—and hence they would become more inclined to commit crimes. But any such slacking of inhibitions (at least where *malum in se* crimes of violence, theft, and fraud are concerned) would hardly be likely to take place right away, since people's common moral attitudes would for a time remain supported by numerous social institutions other than the criminal sanction. The preventionist would have to argue that, although such a measure is not immediately objectionable, it would have long-run ill effects, diluting punishment's preventive efficacy.

I would assert, however, that the proposal is immediately obnoxious, regardless of its supposed long-run effects, because it is a

---

*The distinction between the elements of "hard treatment" and censure in punishment is described by Joel Feinberg in his essay, "The Expressive Function of Punishment."

The two elements interact: being imprisoned is so painful not only because of the loss of liberty but because the loss is a symbol of obloquy. Nevertheless, the two elements are separable for purposes of analysis, as Feinberg points out. In his words, "Reprobation is itself painful, whether or not accompanied by further hard treatment, and hard treatment, such as fine or imprisonment, because of its conventional symbolism, can itself be reprobatory. Still, we can conceive of ritualistic condemnation unaccompanied by any *further* hard treatment, and of inflictions and deprivations which, because of different symbolic conventions, have no reprobative force" (98).

morally inappropriate response. The core conduct with which the criminal law deals is wrongful conduct—conduct that violates the rights of other persons. If the state is to carry out the authoritative response to such conduct—as it must if it visits any kind of sanction upon its perpetrators—then it should do so in a manner that testifies to the recognition that the conduct is wrong. To respond in a morally neutral fashion, to treat the conduct merely as a source of costs to the perpetrator, is objectionable because it fails to provide this recognition. This would, among other things, depreciate the importance of the rights that had been infringed upon by the criminal conduct.[6] Such an objection would be incomprehensible were general prevention the only basis for the criminal sanction.

What difference would my view make? It means that the case for having a condemnatory sanction does not depend on how effective the institution of criminal punishment is in molding public morality. I do not wish to deny that the criminal sanction *may* well have collateral usefulness in reinforcing people's sense of the wrongfulness of criminal behavior. My own belief is that punishment probably has this effect, at least to some extent. I am only saying that it is not easy to *demonstrate* that punishment has this function, and that such a demonstration is not necessary in order to justify a condemnatory response to crime.

Must this condemnatory response take the form of punishment—involving as it does the deliberate infliction of material deprivations, as well as condemnation of the offender? Had punishment *no* usefulness in preventing crime, there should (as I shall argue next) not be a criminal sanction. In that unlikely event, however, we should devise other ways for giving authoritative expression to judgments of censure, only those would no longer be linked to the purposeful infliction of material loss. On the other hand, if one is convinced, as I am, that the imposition by the state of painful consequences *is* necessary to discourage victimizing conduct, then the case for having that sanction embody condemnation does not rest on further empirical proof of the condemnation's instrumental utility. Even if we failed to discover evidence confirming that the criminal sanction reinforces people's desire to be law-abiding (rather than merely intimidating them through its hard treatment of convicted offenders), the sanction still should express blame as an embodiment of moral judgments about criminal conduct.

Crime Prevention and
Treating Persons as Ends

This brings us to the other ground for the criminal sanction, crime prevention. The hard treatment element in punishment, I am suggesting, is warranted for preventive reasons: to discourage offending. A system of penalties is needed in order to prevent victimizing and other noxious conduct from reaching intolerable levels. Had punishment no preventive value, the suffering it inflicts would be unwarranted.

This claim, that punishment is justified at least in part on preventive grounds, is hardly novel.[7] It raises important ethical questions, however, about treating persons as ends. A crime-preventive justification assumes that convicted offenders should suffer loss of their liberty or other rights, in order that the rest of us be protected from crime. How can argument be consistent with the idea that each person (even an offender) has value in himself—and should not be used just as a means to benefit others? How can that argument be accepted, without having to concede the legitimacy of all kinds of other practices whose only justification is their preventive utility?

The idea of treating persons as ends, not merely means, scarcely needs introduction. A central tenet of Kantian ethics,* it has received much attention in contemporary moral philosophy.[8] When applied in social and legal ethics, it entails the notion that an individual's fundamental rights ought not be sacrificed solely to serve other persons' interests.[9]

Utilitarian justifications for intrusive social institutions are

---

*Kant expresses the idea in his second categorical imperative, as follows: "Act in such a way that you always treat humanity, whether in your own person or in the person of any other, never simply as a means, but always at the same time as an end." (*Groundwork of the Metaphysic of Morals*, 96).

Two theories of Kant's ought not to be confused. First, he had a general moral theory, of which this imperative is part, stressing the idea of respecting the value and integrity of persons. It is this theory, with its emphasis on individual rights, that has been so influential in modern ethical thinking. What I am discussing here is whether and to what extent the institution of punishment can be squared with such a general moral conception.

Kant also had his own retributive theory of punishment, expressed in various cryptic statements throughout his writings. As we will see below, this theory has been subjected to various quite different interpretations. One can be a Kantian in the larger sense of wanting to treat individuals as ends in themselves, without subscribing to the details of his view of punishment.

problematic, because they appear to involve just such sacrifice. A is to be deprived of his freedom of movement or other fundamental rights, in order that B and C be less exposed to risk of one or another type of harm. If individuals are seen as the basic moral units in a society, then sacrificing one individual for the good of others raises questions of justice.

Those questions present themselves in drastic form when one is speaking of institutions that impose major deprivations on individuals who have committed no prohibited act at all. Such institutions include quarantine, conscription, and the like—which restrict persons' fundamental liberties on account of facts about themselves over which they have no control: their medical condition in the case of quarantine,* their age and sex in the case of conscription. The individual cannot even avoid the interference with his liberty by complying with a rule. His interests are sacrificed so that the rest of us may be safeguarded from contagion, military threat, or other risks.

Writers such as Hart have emphasized that the criminal law is not so threatening to individuals as this, because it presupposes volition on the offender's part.[10] The requirement that the offender commit a prohibited act, and the requirements of criminal intent, ensure that individuals can protect themselves against criminal liability by choosing to comply with the prohibition.†

A volition requirement, however, does not fully solve the problem of sacrifice of the individual's interests. It alone could still permit prohibitions of unlimited scope, violation of which (if done voluntarily) would lead to painful sanctions. The individual may still complain that his freedom of action is being unduly restricted: his own choices and interests are not being respected.

In the case of punishment, this last problem is alleviated through the sanction's condemnatory features. Through those features, punishment is linked with wrongdoing. In principle, if not

---

*Quarantine laws sometimes give the appearance of requiring a voluntary act. The individual who has a contagious disease is called upon to appear "voluntarily" for diagnosis, treatment, and possible segregation—and is subject to involuntary confinement only if he refuses to appear. However, the "voluntary" hospitalization under these circumstances already involves loss of the subject's freedom of movement; and the facts that trigger the requirement of "voluntary appearance" are medical facts over which the person has no control. For discussion of quarantine, see Ferdinand D. Schoeman, "On Incapacitating the Dangerous."

†Although some strict-liability offenses continue to exist to some extent in the criminal law, there has been considerable support for restricting or eliminating such liability. See American Law Institute, *Model Penal Code* § 2.05.

always in practice, there should be a wrongful act—one that properly should evoke censure—before punishment may be levied. The link to wrongdoing should help limit the reach of the criminal law. Not all conduct that appears to the state to be worth discouraging is the appropriate subject for punishment. To criminalize conduct, a case needs to be made that the behavior is somehow reprehensible.

In a pluralistic society such as ours, there is plenty of room for disagreement over what is reprehensible. Current debates over the propriety of criminalizing drug use, prostitution, and a variety of other conduct on the borders of the criminal law, reflect these disagreements. But even so, the blaming implications of punishment create a significant constraint: before conduct is criminalized, it should be shown why the behavior is not only socially undesirable but wrong for an individual to commit.* The case for condemning the behavior as wrong is made easily only in a limited number of areas: victimizing conduct with which the criminal law traditionally has dealt; breaches of public or private fiduciary relationships; certain kinds of grossly negligent acts; and, perhaps, the deliberate injury to certain collectively held interests in tolerable living conditions (pollution offenses and suchlike). Outside of these familiar areas, it becomes progressively harder to argue that the conduct is wrong, even if it might be worth discouraging in order to achieve various social or economic policies; and hence, it becomes increasingly difficult to show why the conduct is an appropriate subject for criminal prohibitions.

Fragile as these limitations may be, they help answer the concern about unrestricted intrusion into individual choice. The state's criminal prohibitions should be aimed at wrongful acts— principally, those that the individual should have refrained from committing even in the absence of the state's prohibition. He thus cannot so readily complain that his proper ambit of choice is not being respected. Prohibiting robbery is not a matter of restricting

---

*David Richards thus has argued for the decriminalization of prostitution, on grounds that the conduct is not wrong when subjected to careful moral scrutiny (*Sex, Drugs, Death and the Law*, chap. 3).

To treat wrongdoing as a prerequisite for punishment does not require one to criminalize all possibly wrongful behavior, for there also are other principles for limiting the scope of the criminal law. One is the familiar principle that purely self-destructive behavior ought ordinarily not be penalized, in view of the value a free society should place on personal autonomy. For a valuable discussion of the relationship of such limiting principles to the idea of wrongdoing, see Neil McCormick, *Legal Right and Social Democracy*, chap. 2.

the robber's legitimate choices merely to serve majority interests. Robbery is an act that ought not be committed, regardless of its legal prohibition.

Traditional Retributive Justifications

The criminal law, then, can partially be justified by nonutilitarian notions. The censure embodied in punishment (as well as, to some degree, the underlying prohibitions) can be supported by moral arguments rather than by appeals purely to societal interests. What remains, however, is the problem of accounting for the element of material deprivation, of "hard treatment," in punishment. Why should the offender suffer that deprivation, rather than only being censured? On this issue, my argument has been consequentialist: the deprivation element in punishment helps prevent crime. The person is being made to suffer, rather than only being censured, in order to help safeguard others.

Are there any alternative justifications that would not be consequentialist? Purportedly, yes—the various traditional retributive justifications meant to show that a wrongdoer deserves not only condemnation but hard treatment. One such line of argument is the benefits-and-burdens theory, which I relied upon in *Doing Justice* to explain punishment's hard treatment element.[11] The idea, which derives from the writings of Herbert Morris[12] and Jeffrie Murphy,[13] is that the hard treatment offsets the "advantage" the offender obtained over law-abiding persons by not constraining his actions.* I stated it thus in *Doing Justice*:

> To realize their own freedom . . . members of society have the reciprocal obligation to limit their behavior so as not to interfere with the freedom of others. When someone infringes another's rights, he gains an unfair advantage over all others in

*Murphy attributes the argument to Kant. In an interesting recent article, however, (Kant's Retributivism") Don E. Scheid questions this attribution, and argues that Kant's penal theory has substantial consequentialist elements. In Kant's actual view, Scheid argues, "The general justifying aim of the institution of punishment is crime control (or, more immediately, special and general deterrence), which is also essentially the general aim of the state, that is, guaranteeing all individuals against unjust infringements [by offenders] of their liberties. Questions of how punishments are to be allotted are determined within the institution of punishment by the retributivist principles. Punishing criminals so as to achieve crime control does not run afoul of the injunction against using persons as mere means because punishments are allotted according to the retributivist principles, and these guarantee that each is treated with the respect due him as a person" (275).

the society—since he has failed to constrain his own behavior while benefiting from other persons' forbearance from interfering with his rights. The punishment—by imposing a counterbalancing disadvantage on the violator—restores the equilibrium: after having undergone the punishment, the violator ceases to be at advantage over his non-violating fellows. (This righting-of-the-balance is not a matter of preventing future crimes. Aside from any concern with prospective criminality, it is the violator's *past* crime that placed him in a position of advantage over others, and it is that advantage which the punishment would eliminate.[14]

I have since come to doubt the force of this and similar arguments. They seem to suffer from three kinds of problems. First, they require a heroic belief in the justice of the underlying social arrangements. Unless it is in fact true that our social and political systems have succeeded in providing for mutual benefits for all members including any criminal offender, then the offender has not necessarily gained from others' law-abiding behavior. As Hugo Adam Bedau states the point, "justifying punishment in this way relies upon a general theory of social justice, rather than upon any narrower principle of retributive justice."[15] Must the legitimacy of the institution of punishment depend on the existence of larger social arrangements that are absolutely fair? Arguably, no. The actor certainly may be worthy of censure—even in an imperfect social system—if, for example, he victimizes someone who is in no way responsible for those social inequities.*

Second, even in an ostensibly just social system, the sense in which committing a crime constitutes an "advantage" and its punishment an offsetting "disadvantage" tends to be elusive when subjected to closer analysis. Many crimes do not, in any literal sense, provide advantage to their perpetrators—so that one would have to contend that the act of disregarding mutually beneficial rules *itself* constitutes the advantage.[16] Punishment, unlike compensation, does not in any literal sense restore the fair distribution of social benefits that the wrongful act has disrupted. This means, again, that the benefits-and-burdens argument would have

---

*Were .those social evils great enough, and were the state sufficiently involved in the propagation of those evils, one might wish to challenge the state's authority to perform *any* of its functions—whether it be punishing, taxing, or whatever. Short of this, however, it is not obvious why the existence of *some* social or economic inequities must destroy the legitimacy of punishment in all its potential applications. Compare, *Doing Justice*, chap. 17.

to be bolstered by wholehearted social contract theory in order to be sustainable.

Even if the benefits-and-burdens theory were correct—that *something* needs to befall the offender who has gained an unfair advantage over law-abiding persons by infringing upon mutually beneficial rules—it is not obvious that the "something" need be the hard treatment involved in punishment. Suppose the offender were formally censured and also required to compensate the victim. Why is this "disadvantage" not sufficient to satisfy the benefits-and-burdens theory?[17] Yet one can (in fact, I have already in this chapter) suggest a justification for the censuring element in punishment without resorting to that theory.

Finally, the arcaneness of the benefits-and-burdens theory (and of various other retributive arguments of a similar nature)* troubles me. It seems easier to accept the institution of punishment than to understand and accept the premises these theories propose as the basis for punishment. My present explanation rests on simpler ideas. Prevention explains why the state should impose painful material consequences on victimizing conduct. Reprobation for wrongdoing explains why that sanction should take a condemnatory form. These two ideas of prevention and reprobation cannot be collapsed into one another. Both ideas are used in practical and moral discourse in everyday life.

I also think it is preferable to have a general justification for the criminal sanction that is expressly consequentialist in part. This makes the warrant for the existence of punishment dependent on that institution's having significant crime-preventive benefits. According to a wholly deontological rationale, punishment would have to be preserved even if it were found to have no preventive utility. To avoid this conclusion, I was compelled to argue in *Doing Justice* that while the benefits-and-burdens argument was the *pro*

---

*Herbert Morris has recently put forward a paternalistic theory of punishment—that punishment morally benefits the offender himself by confronting him with the wrongfulness of his conduct. ("A Paternalistic Theory of Punishment"; see also, Jean Hampton, "The Moral Education Theory Punishment"). Robert Nozick has argued for punishment on grounds that it "connects" the offender with the proper values (*Philosophical Explanations*, 363–397). Both theories have troublesome obscurities. On Herbert Morris's view, even were one to accept his argument that punishment morally benefits the transgressor, it is not clear why the state is entitled to impose such benefits against the offender's wishes. The strong paternalism needed to accept this argument seems still more difficult to defend then punishment itself. Nozick's account suffers from the lack of clarity of his concept of "connecting," and the difficulty of understanding why the connection between wrongdoers and good values should be effected.

tanto reason for having a penal system, the absence of preventive utility could be a countervailing reason for its abolition in order to reduce suffering.[18] My present view—that the affirmative justification for punishment rests in part on its preventive utility—surely has the virtue of greater simplicity.

This limited use of consequentialist arguments does not, I think, concede too much. When an intrusive institution is grounded *solely* on its social benefits, serious concerns are raised about treating individuals as means only. We should, for example, then feel morally uncomfortable about the institution of medical quarantine. The individual quarantined has done no wrong—in fact, may have done nothing to contract the disease—and the only justification for depriving him or her of his liberty is the interest the rest of us have in preserving *our* health. If the institution of quarantine must exist, then its problematic fairness should be recognized—and its scope stringently restricted. Punishment, on my account, does not similarly rest solely on its social benefits.

One final word on this subject. My use of crime-preventive arguments herein does not, it should be clear, lead to utilitarianism in the distribution of penalties. The condemnatory element in punishment has, on my view, an independent justifying role. It is the condemnatory element that requires punishments to be distributed according to offenders' degree of fault. That brings us to our next topic: gauging degrees of fault.

PART III

How Much Punishment Is Deserved?

A THEORY OF sentencing, to be adequate, should be capable of providing meaningful guidance to a rule-making body assigned the task of writing sentencing guidelines. The theory need not supply automatic or unique solutions, but should help the rulemakers to narrow the options. The question is whether desert theory, the conceptual basis of which has just been explored, is capable of providing such practical guidance. In this part, I shall suggest how it is.

Perplexities over gauging deserved punishments have centered on three major issues: (1) How the seriousness of crimes should be rated; (2) What weight (if any) should be given the offender's record of earlier convictions; and (3) How a penalty scale can be "anchored." I will consider these issues in turn.■

CHAPTER 6

Gauging the Seriousness of Crimes

A desert rationale makes punishments depend on seriousness of crimes. How can one judge seriousness?

When I first became interested in sentencing policy a decade and a half ago, not much attention had been paid to the concept of seriousness. At the time, that was hardly surprising: positivism was only beginning to be questioned, and on that view sentence was determined by the offender's treatability and risk. Since that time, however, penal desert has come to the forefront and its chief criterion is the seriousness of crimes. One would expect a great deal of discussion of the concept of seriousness, yet that has not developed.[1] Why not?

Seriousness has seemed at once too complex and too uncontroversial. Conceptually, the subject looks formidable. When philosophers have had such difficulty supplying criteria for judging right from wrong, how can anyone devise criteria for judging the *degree* of wrongfulness of criminal behavior? Moreover, criminal conduct is so varied. Different crimes injure different interests of victims, and some crimes involve no identifiable victims at all. How can such incommensurables be compared within a single dimension of seriousness?

In practical terms, on the other hand, the work of gauging crimes' seriousness has proceeded straightforwardly enough. In the three states where sentencing commissions have written guidelines—Minnesota, Washington, and Pennsylvania—those commissions succeeded in developing grading scales and assigning seriousness gradations to a wide variety of offenses.[2] While the process was time cosuming, each commission did obtain a consensus among its members on the seriousness ratings—and those ratings did not encounter widespread professional or public criticism. The Pennsylvania Sentencing Commission, for example, created an elaborate numerical ranking scale for offense-seriousness.[3] The rankings were developed through explicit criteria for assessing criminal harms, and involved subcategorization of such broad offense categories as robbery and burglary.[4] When the commission made its proposed guidelines public at the end of 1980, there was much outcry over their other features—and the legislature eventually rejected the guidelines on the grounds that penalties were too lenient, and the guideline ranges too narrow. A year later, the commission submitted, and the legislature let survive, revised guidelines of greater apparent severity and range width.[5] Nevertheless, the original system for grading seriousness was largely preserved: amid all the controversy, that aspect of the Pennsylvania commission's work generated little attention.[6] This does not mean that the sentencing commissions have solved the problems of grading seriousness, but only that the grading efforts have not proven to be their most troublesome task. As long as the issue of seriousness generated so little practical disagreement, there has not been much incentive to explore it in depth.

The Components of Seriousness: Harm and Culpability

Let me begin where I left off in *Doing Justice*, with the two major components of seriousness: harm and culpability.[7] Harm refers to the injury done or risked by the criminal act.* Culpability refers to the factors of intent, motive, and circumstance that determine how much the offender should be held accountable for his act. Culpability, in turn, affects the assessment of harm. The conse-

---

*The risk involved in a criminal act concerns *past* conduct and is germane to desert. When someone drives recklessly, but is lucky enough to not hit anyone, his conduct is harmful because it exposes others to hazards of death or severe injury. That hazard is created by his choice to drive as he did.

The risk of recidivism is different. It concerns future crimes, which someone *might* commit after being sentenced. His past choice does not create this risk. When the person speeds and is caught, his act may have endangered others at the time. But to endanger persons in future, he must recidivate—that is, must *decide* to get into his car and speed again. His risk of recidivism does not affect his deserts, as it concerns the likelihood of his possible future choices, not the possible consequences of his past choices.

quences that should be considered in gauging the harmfulness of an act should be those that can fairly be attributed to the actor's choice. This militates, for example, against including in harm the unforeseeable consequences of the act, or the consequences wrought by other independent actors who happen to choose similar actions.[8] Shoplifting is not rendered serious by the large number of persons who commit this crime and by the aggregate economic injury done, for no shoplifter has control over the number of other persons who choose to engage in this conduct.

Assuming these are the components of seriousness, how can crimes be rated? Marvin Wolfgang has suggested relying on empirical studies of the public's perceptions of the gravity of offenses.[9] Thorsten Sellin and he stimulated such research with their 1964 survey of perceptions of seriousness.[10] There have been numerous follow-up studies,[11] including a large recent survey directed by Wolfgang himself on the basis of National Crime Survey data.[12] These studies provide the persons surveyed with brief descriptions of a wide variety of crimes and ask them to rate those offenses in their seriousness on a numerical rating scale. The studies show that people from different walks of life tend to rate the gravity of common criminal acts similarly, and confirm that judgments of seriousness are not matters about which there is likely to be hopeless disagreement.* When a sentencing commission develops its rankings of seriousness, such studies may also be helpful in providing information about how ordinary people rank criminal conduct—so that the commission is at least aware of the extent to which its judgments of seriousness coincide with or diverge from popular conceptions.

I do not think, however, that ratings of seriousness for sentencing can simply be derived, without further analysis, from such surveys. The harmfulness of criminal conduct, Richard Sparks has pointed out,[13] is determined not by what people *think* the consequences are, but by what they really are. People may believe that burglaries entail a greater likelihood of violence than in fact they do, and think that white-collar crimes have fewer injurious effects than they in fact have. To the extent the public lacks accurate information, its perception of harm may be based on factual error.

Sparks has proposed that the assessment of the harm-element

---

*There has, however, been continuing debate among criminologists concerning the extent of the consensus these studies actually show. See, Terance D. Miethe, "Types of Consensus in Public Evaluations of Crime: An Illustration of Strategies for Measuring 'Consensus'."

in crimes should rely not on opinion surveys but on empirical studies of the type and degree of injury associated with various types of offenses.[14] Traditional victimization studies have been more concerned with measuring the frequency of criminal acts than with detailing their injurious consequences.[15] While such studies provide some data about the short-term effects of being victimized (e.g., the type and extent of property loss, personal injury, and loss of earnings), a more systematic inquiry into short- and longer-term consequences is needed. More important, victimization studies need to be analyzed (as they have not systematically been to date), from the point of view of how they may be brought to bear on the assessment of harm.

Such empirical inquiry into criminal harm must be supplemented by value judgments, however. Different crimes injure different interests. Car theft involves a substantial loss of property; armed robbery usually entails much less money lost, but a threat to the person's life. Most of us would rate car theft as much less serious than robbery, because we consider the interest in personal safety to be more important than that in common items of property. But more thought is needed on *why* we assign these priorities. There also remains the other comparably important element in seriousness: the offender's culpability for the acts he commits. How, then, can such value judgments be made?

Harm:
The Ranking of Interests

Let us consider harm, first. How can the importance of different interests be compared for the purpose of assessing harm? To simplify the discussion, let us address two generic interests: physical integrity and property. A great many common crimes involve invasion of either of these two generic interests, or both.

It is sometimes said that there is no objective way of gauging the importance of the interests infringed by criminal conduct, because those interests depend upon culturally conditioned beliefs about what is most worth preserving in life. Of course they depend on such beliefs, why not? A primitive society, for example, might well place a higher value on property and a lower one on physical integrity than we do. If goods are scarce, that may make theft all the more heinous. If the family rather than the individual is seen as the most valued moral unit of the society, and if a premium is also put on the virtue of self-defense, then personal assaults may seem less reprehensible than they do to us. But this should scarcely by surprising, as grading enterprises invariably reflect more fundamental value preferences. When a university grades its students' academic performance, the grading system perforce will reflect this society's underlying intellectual culture. It will typically be assumed that the quality of the student's work is what counts, not the degree of his or her effort; that comprehension on the student's part is more to be valued than rote memory. These choices are not inevitable. Another society might make them differently, but that does not mean that we are incapable of making intelligible grading judgments which reflect *our* intellectual values.

Two matters, however, do complicate the grading task. First, one cannot simply declare certain generic interests to be paramount. It is sometimes asserted that physical integrity is more important than property, but that cannot always be the case. Most of us would rather suffer a common assault than be swindled out of our life savings. Personal and property harms can vary in seriousness, and we need a theory of harms that can account for those variations.

Second, our culture is pluralistic. A free society, moreover, is one in which individuals *should* be entitled to decide for themselves what interests are most important in their lives.[16] We want a theory of harm, in other words, that makes allowance for differences in how people value the worth of life's goods. How, in such a pluralistic system, can one achieve a consistent ranking of the relative importance of interests for the purpose of rating crimes?

The philosophical literature may provide guidance. Joel Feinberg has sketched a theory of harms in his 1984 book, *Harm to Others*,[17] building upon earlier work by John Kleinig[18] and Nicholas Rescher.[19] Feinberg developed his theory for the purpose of deciding which kinds of conduct should be made criminal at all. His ideas, however, can be carried over to the rating of harm for sentencing purposes.

SERIOUS HARMS: INVASIONS OF "WELFARE INTERESTS"

Feinberg begins with the concept of "welfare interests."[20] These are the interests that persons need satisfied in order to have any significant capacity to choose and order their way of living.

They provide, in his words, "the generalized means to the advancement of [a person's] more ulterior interests."[21]* When these interests are destroyed or threatened, the person is foreclosed from almost any tolerable mode of life he might wish to pursue. The attraction of the concept of a welfare interest lies precisely in its pluralism. It is designed to identify high-priority interests in a manner that offers a wide scope for individuals to define their own ends.

Up to a certain point, both physical integrity and property constitute welfare interests. That point, Feinberg suggests, is defined by a tolerable minimum of these two generic interests.[22] Why there is a welfare interest in physical integrity should be fairly obvious. A person needs a certain minimum of physical well-being in order to proceed about his business. If denied this minimum, he is impeded from pursuing virtually any aims of his choice. Whether one wants to be a philosopher, miser, or rock star, that obviously cannot be done if one is dead, and is much more difficult to do if one is physically incapacitated.

It should be similarly apparent why a welfare interest in property exists. A person requires a certain tolerable minimum of economic support in order to pursue his plans; when stripped of his means of livelihood, he is virtually debilitated. It is, however, only a limited subclass of property offenses that characteristically threaten this welfare interest. Theft of a person's life savings may do so, but routine larcenies clearly do not.

We have, then, identified two welfare interests, one physical and one economic. Harms that invade these welfare interests should be classified as serious harms. Crimes should be classified as serious—located high on the vertical scale of the sentencing grid—when (given the requisite degree of culpability) they inflict, or substantially threaten to inflict, such harms. This should include major violent offenses such as murder, aggravated assault,

---

*Feinberg (in *Harm to Others*, 37) describes welfare interests more fully as follows: "These are interests in conditions that are generalized means to a great variety of possible goals and whose joint realization, in the absence of very special circumstances, is necessary for the achievement of more ultimate aims. In one way, then, they are the very most important interests a person has, and cry out for protection, for without their fulfillment, a person is lost. . . . These minimal and nonultimate goods can be called a person's 'welfare interests.' When they are blocked or damaged, a person is very seriously harmed indeed, for in that case his more ultimate aspirations are defeated too; whereas setbacks to a higher [and more particular] goal do not to the same degree inflict damage on the whole network of his interests."

and armed robbery, and certain economic crimes that characteristically deprive persons of their basic means of support.

A further question is whether one of these two welfare interests is more important than the other. Does the personal safety interest outrank the livelihood interest? Feinberg suggests not, because of the interdependence of the various welfare interests.[23] If one is in glowing health but becomes destitute, one still cannot pursue any desired goals; neither is it likely that one will remain in good health for long. However, the criminal law has treated the violent offenses as *the* most serious, more so even than the worst property crimes. This can be accounted for, I think, on the basis of the degree of irreversibility of the intrusions involved. As a rough generalization, gross physical intrusions tend to be the less easily remediable. If deprived of one's means of support, one can be compensated or try to take up a new livelihood; if one is a victim of mayhem, recovery of lost functions may be impossible. It is harder to grow back one's arm that one's savings.

INTERMEDIATE HARMS: INVASION OF "SECURITY INTERESTS"

Feinberg's next category is what he calls "a security interest, cushioning a welfare interest."[24] Beyond the bare minimum of health and economic well-being required to make any meaningful choices, a person needs a certain additional safety margin. Without that margin, the person may barely be able to function but must live in acute anxiety and discomfort.

Consider living an existence—as many do in deteriorated neighborhoods—where one is periodically beaten or has one's home ransacked. One can subsist in such an environment, in a way one cannot if grievously wounded or rendered homeless. But the quality of one's existence deteriorates, because one lacks a reasonable margin of security above the bare minimum provided by the welfare interests of which I have spoken. Such intrusions into one's physical integrity and the integrity of one's place of abode, threaten that margin of security. Violations of these security interests should be considered to be harms of the next level of importance—that is, intermediate harms. Crimes that (with the requisite degree of culpability) inflict or threaten this type of harm should be classified as of intermediate seriousness. These would include substantial (but not potentially lethal) assaults and certain types of residential burglary as well.

LESSER HARMS: "ACCUMULATIVE" INTERESTS

Beyond the basic interests just described, people pursue and seek to accumulate the various good things of life. An enjoyable existence involves these various pursuits, be they of goods, leisure, or whatever. These constitute people's "accumulative" interests, as Feinberg calls them.[25] Invasions of these interests should be deemed less serious than invasions of welfare or security interests. Crimes involving these accumulative interests should rank lower on the sentencing grid's seriousness scale. Common theft offenses, for example, typically and foreseeably deprive the victim neither of his minimum livelihood nor of the margin of security above that minimum. They invade his accumulative interests.

Thus far, I have addressed only physical integrity and property. Other generic interests that criminal conduct may involve—in privacy, reputation, or whatever—need also be considered. There, the same questions need to be asked. To what extent does any portion of that generic interest qualify as a welfare interest—one that must be satisfied in order to exercise a significant choice of life goals? To what extent does it qualify as a security interest providing a margin of safety for any welfare interests? What I have attempted is to suggest the direction in which the analysis might proceed.

In rating harms, it will be essential to distinguish standard from special cases. The general classifications and ratings of harms must be fashioned by reference to the standard case. These harm ratings (together with certain judgments concerning culpability) should yield the gradations of offense-seriousness for the sentencing grid. Harm in exceptional cases bears upon aggravation and mitigation, and concerns departures from the grid ranges. Suppose the offender breaks the victim's little finger. It is sometimes claimed one cannot determine the harmfulness of that act, because it depends on whether the victim is a stockbroker or a concert pianist. But it is possible to determine how important the loss of the small finger *normally* is to welfare or security interests in health or livelihood, and then to deal with the concert pianist as a special case.*

I have presented only a sketch. Demonstrating the workabil-

---

*Even if one found the pianist was harmed more because his livelihood depended on his hands, the culpability question would remain: whether the offender should have foreseen that contingency.

ity of my suggested harm criteria would require the systematic application of those criteria to a variety of offenses to see how much guidance they supply. But even if they fail to prove illuminating, their failure may suggest other, more fruitful approaches. In any event, we need also develop a supplemental account of harms not involving individual victims (such as corruption or tax evasion).

Rating harmfulness involves *judgment*. Since the definitions of the welfare or security interests are couched in general and imprecise terms, one can expect some disagreement about whether and to what extent a given type of criminal act infringes on such interests. But such imprecision almost inevitably exists in grading situations: grading is typically a judgmental exercise in which the graders utilize general criteria that guide but do not automatically determine the rating decision. The individual graders may differ in the ratings they assign, but the differences seldom are pervasive enough to cast doubt on the grading enterprise.

Culpability

The concept of culpability has received extensive attention in the substantive criminal law. Every law student must read about criminal fault—about the requirements of criminal intent and the doctrines of excuse.[26] In sentencing, however, the concept has hardly been studied. There are four main kinds of situations where the issue of the offender's culpability arises in a sentencing context. Three have analogies in the substantive law; the fourth does not.

There is, first, the principle that the gravity of conduct varies with whether the actor's behavior was *purposeful, knowing, reckless,* or *negligent.** This quadruple distinction, set forth in the

*For nonlawyers, these distinctions can be summarized as follows: A does x *purposely* if it is his conscious object to bring about x. If Smith sets about to kill Jones and does so, this is a purposeful killing. A does x *knowingly* if he knows his act will accomplish x whether or not accomplishing it was the objective of his undertaking. If Smith sets about to rob a bank and shoots Jones at point-blank range while trying to escape, that is a knowing act: Smith's objective was to get the money not to kill anyone, but he kills Jones knowing that this is what he is doing or almost certain to do by his act of pulling the trigger. A does x *recklessly* if he consciously disregards a substantial and unjustifiable risk that x will occur. If Smith rolls the boulder down the mountain aware that this may well kill or maim someone, and it hits Jones and kills him, this is reckless homicide—whether or not he wished anyone to die or was certain they would. A does x *negligently* when he carelessly disregards such a risk without necessarily knowing he is doing so. If Smith dislodges the boulder without thinking whether anyone might be below, this may be negligent homicide if the rock strikes Jones—even if Smith had not the slightest desire to

Model Penal Code and familiar to lawyers,[27] bears on the extent to which the actor has committed himself to the bringing about of his act.

Well established as these distinctions are, they have not been made full use of for sentencing purposes. Statutory definitions of specific offenses often lump several of these degrees of fault together. The Model Penal Code, for example, defines an aggravated assault as any infliction (or attempted infliction) of serious bodily harm, regardless of whether done purposely, knowingly, or recklessly.[28] Most state laws similarly combine degrees of fault in offense definitions, if they define these degrees at all. Sentencing guidelines seldom attempt to provide different dispositions for knowing, purposeful, or reckless conduct, where such distinctions are missing in the statutory offense definitions.[29]

Michael Tonry has called for a general recodification of offense definitions.[30] Although broad and loose definitions may have suited the rehabilitatively and predictively oriented approach of traditional American positivism, he argues, they are unsuitable for a system whose sentencing structure seeks to base dispositions on the gravity of criminal conduct. Offense definitions need to be made more precise, and part of that recodification should be fuller use of the distinction in degrees of fault.[31]

Second, in the substantive law, necessity and duress are established excuses.[32] In the law of homicide, provocation by the victim reduces the degree of the offense from murder to manslaughter.[33] Little attention has been paid, however, to the analogues of these excuses as claims-in-extenuation for sentencing. Even if the conduct does not meet the requirements of complete exculpation on grounds of necessity or duress, the person who breaks the law is less reprehensible if he faced risk of injury from third persons or from natural causes had he complied. Even where homicide is not involved, provocation should be treated as grounds for mitigating the severity of the sentence.[34] These are situations where the action is deemed less reprehensible, because the external circumstances make it so much more onerous for a person to comply with the law. Some sentencing schemes recognize these kinds of extenuation. The Minnesota sentencing guidelines, for example, make it a mitigating circumstance when the victim "was an aggressor in the incident," or if the offender "participated under circumstances

---

hurt anyone and had no thought his action would do so. Despite his awareness of the risk, he acted negligently if he should have been aware.

of coercion or duress."[35] What is needed, however, is a fuller exploration of the basis, scope, and limits of such claims.*

Third, the insanity defense likewise has its sentencing analogue. It is the situation of "half madness," where the defendant has not qualified for complete exculpation but nevertheless was suffering from a significant degree of mental disturbance when he committed the act.[36] Here, the actor is less blameworthy because his own psychic disabilities significantly diminished his capacity to comprehend and be guided by the law's requirements. The Minnesota guidelines recognize the principle by making it a mitigating circumstance justifying departure from the guideline ranges that "the defendant, because of . . . mental impairment, lacked substantial capacity for judgment when the offense was committed."[37] The Washington guidelines contain a similar provision.[38] But again, the scope and limits of this claim-in-extenuation need fuller inquiry.

A final issue concerns the defendant's motives. Criminals sometimes commit crimes for reasons perceived as less than, or more than, commonly reprehensible. Stock examples are the offender who commits the law violation as a matter of conscience or to benefit others, and the offender who inflicts injury for no perceptible benefit even to himself, but apparently out of sheer spite. Judges are wont to consider such motives in their sentences, but the question (which has received little attention) is whether they should.†

Despite the need for theorists to do more homework on the subject of culpability, the subject is not beyond comprehension today. The first of the four areas concerns well-established distinctions in degrees of fault. The next three areas—because they deal with exceptional situations—concern the definition of mitigating or aggravating circumstances, rather than the seriousness ratings

---

*The German Penal Code also recognizes other excuses, such as mistake of law, when the actor was not at fault for the mistake; and excessive force in self-defense under conditions of "confusion, fear or alarm" (Strafgesetzbuch § 17,33). It needs to be examined whether the sentencing law should recognize the analogies to these excuses—for example, for the actor who acts in ignorance of the law where that ignorance was only partially his own fault.

†There has been considerable discussion of the issue of civil disobedience. It has, however, emphasized the question whether an individual is obligated to obey a law he believes to be wrong, rather than the question whether the sentencer should treat disobedience as less reprehensible because motivated by conscience. A useful discussion of the philosophical issues can be found in Richard Wasserstrom, "The Obligation to Obey the Law." See also, Ronald Dworkin, *Taking Rights Seriously*, chap. 8.

to be given to crime categories for the sentencing grid. Of these three, two have analogies in the substantive law of excuses; serious uncertainty exists only in the last area, of motive. A sentencing rulemaker should have no difficulty in scaling reckless conduct below purposeful and in providing for reduced sanctions for the partially coerced or the provoked.

Grading Seriousness in Practice: What Can a Rulemaker Do?

I have identified a number of empirical and theoretical issues concerning seriousness that would benefit from further inquiry. More data need to be developed on the harmful consequences of various types of crimes. My suggested criteria for ranking interests need further theoretical scrutiny. The idea of culpability likewise requires more analysis.

While such inquiries are under way, what can a rulemaker do? I think that a rulemaking body can take a number of practical steps that will enable it to formulate a workable, if not perfect, seriousness scale for use in its guidelines. At least so far as typical crimes of theft, force, and fraud are concerned, one can develop a rough assessment of their consequences using the legal definition of the crime and available common knowledge of its probable effects. One can also make commonsense moral judgments about the relative importance of the rights and interests that different crimes invade. One can grade culpability at least according to whether intentional, reckless, or negligent conduct is involved. When a rule-making agency constructs a seriousness scale, therefore, the question is what steps would facilitate making such judgments. I suggest that the following four steps would be useful.

1. The seriousness of crimes should be graded explicitly in the guidelines. Several guideline systems (including, as I noted earlier,[39] the guidelines written by the Minnesota, Washington, and Pennsylvania sentencing commissions) have numerical seriousness grades. Other systems have no rankings, however. California simply assigns a presumptive penalty to each of the various statutory offense categories, without expressly grading the seriousness of those crimes.[40] An explicit seriousness scale helps compel the rulemaker to consider whether its proposed penalties comport with its judgment of the comparative gravity of offenses.

2. The rule-making body should make its own conscientious judgment of gravity. It should not borrow the grading system from somewhere else. Some jurisdictions adopted preexisting statutory felony classes as the offense rankings for their sentencing guidelines or rules.[41] The trouble is that those statutory gradations were designed for a wholly different purpose, namely, for defining the maximum permissible penalty for the worst possible case of a given crime. Another form of borrowing would base ratings on popular perceptions of seriousness as derived from opinion survey research. The difficulty of relying on such surveys, as I have just pointed out, is that they impede the making of a reasoned judgment. The surveys to date simply ask people to rate the gravity of crimes, without asking them to explain their judgments or holding those explanations up to critical scrutiny. The Minnesota, Washington, and Pennsylvania commissions made their own judgments of seriousness.[42]

3. The rule-making body should subject itself to the discipline of providing explicit reasons for its rankings. This has seldom been attempted in systematic fashion in sentencing rules developed to date. The Minnesota sentencing commission's technique for rating seriousness, for example, consisted of having each commission member rate offenses according to his or her best judgment of seriousness, and then resolving disagreements in ratings through discussion among the commission members.[43] This procedure ensures that reasons are given in disputed cases, but no discussion ensues when members initially agree on the rating assigned to a crime. Reasons should be discussed and given for *each* seriousness ranking that is assigned.

4. The reasons given for rankings should, to the extent feasible, be based on a *systematic* rationale. Seriousness, as noted above, depends both on harmfulness and culpability. One could begin by looking at harmfulness—holding the culpability variable constant for the moment, by considering only intentional crimes and their forseeable consequences. The rule-making body could rate such intentional conduct generically, according to its members' judgment of the relative importance of rights or interests threatened by the conduct. It might, for example, tentatively adopt generic criteria, giving the highest ranking to conduct that inflicts grave physical injury, the next highest to conduct that visits loss of economic livelihood, and so forth. In making those judgments, the commission could establish its own criteria.[44] Or, if it wished to be more ambitious, it could draw on such theory as exists, including

the tenative ideas sketched earlier in this chapter. Once such general criteria have been established, they could be used in assigning provisional seriousness ratings to the various statutory crime categories. Those results could then be compared with the ratings that were assigned by members of the rule-making body using their unaided common-sense judgments. Where the formally derived and intuitive ratings diverged, the members could debate those cases and give reasons for the rating eventually decided upon. A procedure of this kind was used by Pennsylvania's commission.* The advantage is that it provides some kind of systematic rationale for the rankings and allows the rule-making body to take a closer critical look at those ratings that depart from the rationale that it has tentatively adopted.

This simple procedure will not automatically produce agreement—nor could any other rating procedure, however sophisticated it were to become. Rating crimes is ultimately a matter of making value judgments, on which persons reasonably may differ. Those judgments can, however, be supported and guided through the giving of reasons and through debate. The purpose of procedures just outlined is to provide a structure for rating crimes' gravity that encourages the giving of reasons in systematic fashion.

---

*Originally, the commission appointed a subcommittee to rank offenses. The subcommittee adopted a ten-point ranking system and assigned offenses numerical seriousness ratings according to its members' intuitive sense of the wrongfulness of the behaviors.

As a result, certain offenses—particularly burglary—received intermediate seriousness ratings, although the legislature had previously assigned them a high statutory classification for purposes of setting the statutory maximums. One of the members of the full commission questioned whether the subcommittee's rankings conflicted with the legislative intent.

The matter was submitted to a consultant (the present author) who suggested that—rather than following the statutory classification automatically—those classifications be examined to see if any rationale or general principles emerged. The consultant and commission staff examined the statutory classifications, derived a few simple principles for gauging harm and culpability, and then assigned proposed seriousness rankings to offenses, based on those principles. These rankings were then submitted to the commission, which compared them with the subcommittee's earlier rankings and adopted final ratings of its own that were incorporated into the proposed 1980 guidelines.

CHAPTER 7

Previous Convictions

Most penal systems impose less punishment on first offenders than on those who have previous convictions. Should this be so? If so, how much less?

In a future-oriented theory of sentencing, the practice of treating first offenders differently is easy enough to explain. Most prediction studies indicate that first offenders are less likely to return to crime than offenders with criminal records (or at least, with certain kinds of criminal records).[1] The presence or absence of previous convictions would be relevant to the determination of sentence on grounds of risk. A desert theory, however, is not concerned with risk. Unless the first offender *deserves* less punishment, he should be penalized the same as the recidivist.

In *Doing Justice*, I maintained that offenders' prior criminal records bear on their deserts. A first offender, I argued, merits reduced punishment; he does not deserve full measure of condemnation for his criminal act when he has not been previously convicted.[2] Other desert theorists have disagreed. George Fletcher[3] and Richard Singer[4] have maintained that the presence or absence of earlier convictions is irrelevant to a convicted criminal's deserts. The person has been punished already for his previous convictions, and hence those convictions should not affect the quantum of the deserved punishment for his current crime.

The issue of prior criminality is critical to a desert-based theory of sentencing, because it influences the structure of the penalty scale so much. If the prior record is irrelevant, then penalties can be ranked unidimensionally to reflect the comparative seriousness of offenders' current crimes. If it is relevant, a two-dimensional grid is required, in which penalties are ordered to reflect not only the gravity of the current act but the extent of the criminal record as well. It then becomes essential to decide how much weight the record should carry. Should the emphasis remain on the current crime, or should it shift primarily to the record? I shall argue in this chapter for primary but not exclusive emphasis on the current offense.

Explanations Directed to the Present Act

To support the claim that prior convictions are germane to an offender's deserts, the argument might be made that those convictions alter the seriousness of the present act for which he is being sentenced. A burglary, one might say, is made less serious when committed by a first offender, or is made more serious when committed by a recidivist.

I espoused this kind of view in *Doing Justice*. My thesis addressed the offender's culpability. His culpability in committing his most recent crime, I contended, is altered by the existence or nonexistence of a record of previous convictions.

> The reason for treating the first offense as less serious is . . . that repetition alters the degree of culpability that may be ascribed to the offender. In assessing a first offender's culpability, it ought to be borne in mind that he was, at the time he committed the crime, only one of a large audience to whom the law impersonally addressed its prohibitions. His first conviction, however, should call dramatically and personally to his attention that the behavior is condemned. A repetition of the offense following that conviction may be regarded as more culpable, since he persisted in the behavior after having been forcefully censured for it through his prior punishment.[5]

The theory is that prior convictions affect the offender's consciousness of wrongdoing when he commits his current crime.

Does this argument have merit? Some, perhaps. The offender's degree of awareness of wrongdoing *is* germane to his moral culpability for his act, and could be considered as such in gauging the seriousness of crimes for sentencing purposes. Although ignorance of a legal prohibition usually is not an excuse in the substantive criminal law,[6] this strict doctrine need not necessarily be carried over into the sentencing law. The fact that the offender has been personally and explicitly warned against conduct beforehand bears on the question of his awareness.* Having been previously convicted and punished serves as a kind of warning.

The difficulty with the argument is that, were it accepted, it would only establish that prior convictions are an item of evidence—to be considered along with other evidence—in judging the offender's culpability for his current crime. Inferences about culpability based on the offender's criminal record could be contradicted by other evidence. The first offender, while new to the criminal process, may have been personally warned by friends or the authorities against committing the act. The repeater may have been convicted before but for a wholly different kind of crime—and thus may not have been conscious of wrongdoing with respect to his current criminal act. This theory does not support a rule that makes the record per se a basis for altered punishments.

Alternatively it might be claimed that prior convictions alter the harm done by the present act. Obviously, they do not affect the act's direct consequences or risks. But someone might argue that repeating the offense introduces another kind of "harm," namely, defiance of the law. The repeater, arguably, flouts the law in particularly outrageous fashion and such defiance is an evil in itself.

Two kinds of objections can be made to this argument. The first parallels what I have just said about culpability: repeating an offense can at most be evidence of greater defiance, not proof per se of it. The second and more fundamental objection is to the idea of defiance as something reprehensible in itself; as George Fletcher points out:

> I would argue that, in a liberal society, defiance should not constitute a wrong that justifiably enhances the punishment a recidivist deserves. . . . In some social contexts, such as the family, the military, or a football team, those in authority might regard it as justified to respond to threatened defiance with a penalty greater than that otherwise thought appropriate for the offense already committed. . . . But do we want to conceptualize civil society in this way? . . . A society that respects individuality and diverse purposes hardly stands in

*For a discussion of ignorance of law as a culpability-reducing factor at the sentencing stage, see Martin Wasik, "Excuses at the Sentencing Stage." On the issue of being personally warned before the act, Fletcher ("The Recidivist Premium," 59) cites the principle in Jewish law that an assassin is subject to capital punishment only if, immediately prior to the killing, two people warn him against doing so and he disregards the warning.

analogy to organizations devoted to specific goals, such as winning a war or a game.[7]

One need not necessarily adopt Fletcher's definition of a liberal society in order to see the force of his assertion. A defiance theory, he is pointing out, makes the treatment of recidivists depend on a particular (and rather authoritarian) political doctrine that treats insubordination to state power as a wrong aside from any any injury resulting from the criminal act itself. Not all of us would wish to accept such a doctrine (I, for one, do not find it particularly appealing). It would be preferable if the issue of first offenders versus recidivists could be resolved without resort to such a contentious political doctrine.

Explanations Directed to the Criminal Career

Why not look, instead, to the offender's career? There are contexts in everyday life where we address the merit or demerit of a person's career as a whole. A prime example of career-desert is provided by the prizes for distinguished research that some universities periodically offer. The chairmen of various departments nominate candidates, whose names (and curricula vitae) go to a university committee. After weighing the recommendations, the committee chooses for the award a few individuals whose work is thought to show signal distinction.

Such judgments, however, have a different logic than the criminal law as presently constituted. The prize is not *for* any particular work, but relates to the recipient's entire output. Nominees are not (as they are in essay competitions) required to submit any new product. A nominee's most recent efforts may be given little weight, or may even be discounted entirely by the judges, if his or her earlier contributions are considered more significant.

The criminal law is structured otherwise. The actor is punished *for* a particular crime—that for which he now stands convicted. The substantive criminal law defines, classifies, and prohibits *crimes*. (A career-oriented system would classify *persons* according to the frequency and gravity of their offending. It would make habitual offender statutes the archetype of the law, rather than its exception.) Existing trial and sentencing procedures are well suited to determine the offender's guilt or innocence for the current crime and perhaps, to evaluate extenuating and aggravating circumstances surrounding that crime. Without fundamental procedural changes, however, the criminal process does not have the capacity to inquire into the degree of demerit of a person's whole criminal career with care and discrimination.*

Would it be desirable to try to reshape the criminal law so as to emphasize criminal careers rather than crimes? I think not. The advantage of a criminal law that focuses primarily on crimes is that it provides a comprehensible valuation of conduct. What chiefly counts is what was done, not who did it. The penal sanction thus furnishes a reasonably clear public expression of the blameworthiness of conduct. If that conduct is serious, the condemnation is severe—thereby recognizing the importance of the rights of the victimized (see chapter 5).

A career-based system would make the law's public valuation of conduct much more diffuse. The focus would no longer be on what was done but, rather, on who did it and on what his record was. It is true that the rulemaker would have to rate the gravity of crimes in order to set standards about criminal careers. But the punishment—the expression of condemnation that is the product of such reckonings—would vary independently of the current act, depending on the prior record. As a result, the criminal sanction could no longer so clearly testify to the recognition of the wrongfulness of the conduct, and to the significance of the rights that had been infringed.

An Alternative Explanation

If we reject explanations based purely either on the present act, or on the career, what is left? In an essay written in 1981,[8] I sketched an alternative: a theory of desert that is primarily oriented toward the present crime, but qualified to a limited extent by considerations related to prior conduct. Let me describe and comment upon this account.

A punishment (like any other judgment of censure or reproof for an act) connotes that the act was wrong, and expresses disap-

---

*Evaluating a criminal's "career-desert" would call for *in-depth* information about the past crimes for which he was convicted. One would, for example, need full information about any aggravating or mitigating circumstances that had been found to exist with respect to any such prior crime. Existing sentencing procedures and record-keeping methods are not remotely capable of establishing such facts.

probation of the actor for that wrong. Although the basis for the condemnation is wrongful conduct, the disapprobation is addressed to the actor. One visits censure or reproof on people, not acts—and it is this feature that makes prior misconduct relevant to an actor's deserts.

When a person commits a misdeed in everyday life and faces the opprobrium of friends, associates, or colleagues, he may plead that the misconduct was uncharacteristic of his previous behavior. He may use such language as "I'm sorry, I don't know what got into me—it's not been like me to do that kind of thing." What this plea addresses is the inference from the judgment about the wrong-fulness of the act to the disapprobation directed at the person for the conduct. The actor is pleading in self-extenuation that though this act was wrong, he should not suffer the full measure of oblo-quy for it because it was out of keeping with the standards of behavior he has observed in the past. He is suggesting that the moral quality of this act should not be used fully in the judgment of him, because it was uncharacteristic for him. The plea, by its manifest logic, carries its greatest force when the actor has not committed the misconduct before, and it loses force progressively with each repetition.

To understand the plea, one must grasp the role played by disapproval of the person in judgments of reproof or censure. One is not using the actor's misdeed merely as the occasion to express moral distaste for the conduct. (That might involve a wholly different kind of response, where one bemoaned the fact that the act occurred, expressed special sympathy for the victim, but paid no special attention to the wrongdoer.) Instead, one is singling out the offender for unfavorable attention. So long as censure or reproof is thought to address only the act, the plea will be incomprehensible. Why should past acts have any bearing on the moral quality of a distinct act, occurring now?

The plea cannot, therefore, be explained in terms of culpability factors associated with the present act, such as lack of full knowledge of the consequences of the conduct, or possible (mistaken) beliefs that the conduct was justifiable. Someone who commits misconduct of a certain kind may concede that the act clearly was wrong; that he was fully aware of the consequences; and that there were no other specific mitigating circumstances. Yet he still may claim, as grounds for reducing the disapprobation he receives, that the act was a first misstep which was out of keeping with what otherwise had been his practice. The plea, let me reiterate, addresses not the moral quality of the act but the inference from the quality of that act—which is assertedly atypical of his past conduct*—to the judgment of disapproval of the actor.

The plea does not, however, go to the other extreme of breaking the nexus between the current act and the judgment of censure, and of calling for a judgment of the actor's entire career. It presupposes that the person is being judged for his present conduct; that he is not to be relieved from all disapprobation, but only to receive somewhat less, if the misstep is his first. Career-desert judgments are different. If the person's other achievements and virtues are sufficiently impressive, he may deserve praise rather than censure, because those other achievements and graces outweigh the present misdeed in the assessment of his whole merit.

The plea thus reflects a complex set of judgments that can be described neither purely in terms of the present act nor purely in terms of the career of the actor. The primary focus is on the present act, because the actor is being censured for this conduct. Any such censure, however, entails disapprobation directed at the actor himself. His claim is that this disapprobation of him should be dampened somewhat because the act was out of keeping with his previous behavior. The judgment focuses chiefly on the present act but is qualified to a limited extent by judgments addressed to the actor's past.

So much for the plea's logical structure. The next question is: *Why* disapprove less of the first offender? Although it would be wonderful if people's moral inhibitions were strong enough to keep them from wrongdoing at all times, we know that even the self-control of those who ordinarily refrain from misconduct may fail in a moment of weakness or willfulness. We wish to condemn the person for his act but accord him some respect for the fact that his

---

*To speak of the act as "atypical" or "uncharacteristic" does *not* make the first offender's plea a prediction. Speaking of behavior as "characteristic" or "uncharacteristic" has two distinct uses: one is predictive; the other supports the quite different, retrospective purpose of supporting judgments about an actor's deserts. Consider the assertion that Professor Z is characteristically or habitually late for class. The assertion has a predictive use, as when a student tells others that they need not hurry to arrive at the scheduled beginning of his classes. But the assertion may also be used in making judgments about Z's deserts: his habitual lateness may be grounds for judging him as deserving scant praise as a teacher, and such judgments may be made even after he has retired or left the university. For an analysis of the logic of dispositional statements, see Stuart Hampshire, "Dispositions."

inhibitions against wrongdoing have functioned on previous occasions, and show some sympathy for the all-too-human frailty that can lead someone to such a lapse. This we do by showing a reduced disapproval of him for his first misdeed.

The somewhat muted disapproval that the actor gets on the first occasion is still blame. It confronts the person with the wrongfulness of the conduct and others' disapprobation of him for that conduct. The remonstrance should give the person the opportunity to reconsider, reflect on the propriety of his conduct, and decide whether he should pursue a different course. This not a matter of giving the actor notice that the act was wrong. He ought to have been aware of that already, and may well have been aware. His misdeed may have been the result not of ignorance but of having at the moment placed his own needs or inclinations above the requirements of doing right. The point is that fallible humans are capable of acting thus in a moment of unwisdom; that the adverse judgment of others gives the person the opportunity to reflect on his conduct.

Nor is the judgment predictive or rehabilitative in nature. It is not a matter of muting one's response because one thinks it unlikely that the actor will repeat the act, or because one thinks that a scaled-down response will return the actor most effectively to the straight and narrow. Were that the logic, some first offenders would get the benefit of the scaled-down condemnation and other first offenders would not—depending on the assessment of particular actors' likelihood of repetition and of their sensitivity to the censuring judgments of others. (Those forecasts might, in turn, depend on a variety of facts about an actor, such as the incentives he apparently has to repeat the conduct, and the degree of contrition that he shows.) Rather than trying to foretell which actors will or will not repeat the offense, the idea is that every actor is at first entitled to some scaling down of the disapprobation directed toward him.

Underlying these ideas are certain assumptions about how stringently or tolerantly persons ought to be judged. When allowing the actor a partial respite from censure on the first occasion, we are showing a limited degree of tolerance for wrongdoing.*

---

*By tolerance, I mean the willingness to discount wrongdoing to some extent in deciding how much disapproval the person deserves for his acts. Tolerance, in other words, is something that is exercised in determining the level of response that is deemed deserved. This concept is to be distinguished from mercy—which involves the notion of punishing or disapproving less than a person is thought to merit, for a variety of reasons. See Claudia Card, "On Mercy."

That tolerance is granted on the grounds that some sympathy is due human beings for their fallibility and their exposure to pressures and temptations—and some respect is owed their capacity, as moral agents, to reflect on the censure of others. The temporary nature of the tolerance—the fact that it diminishes (and is eventually wholly withdrawn) with repetitions—is critical. This assures that, ultimately, people are held fully accountable for their misdeeds, as any conception of desert requires.

In the criminal law, such a scaled-down response for first offenders seems particularly appropriate. If a partial and temporary tolerance for human frailty is called for anywhere, it surely is for a mode of reproof so onerous as criminal punishment—one that is so public, has such lasting stigma, and can be accompanied by so much material deprivation. The law is also well suited to formalizing such judgments. Who qualifies for first-offender status can be defined—as someone who has not previously been convicted.* The size of the punishment discount for the first offender can be specified, as can the number of repetitions that must occur before the discount is lost entirely. Let us, then, turn to these subjects.

Prior Convictions on the Sentencing Grid

To illustrate how my proposed treatment of prior convictions would affect the sentencing structure, we should make use of the sentencing grid described in chapter 2. Let us examine specifically how the prior criminal record should affect the slope of the in-out line on the grid.† That line, as the reader will recall, demarcates prison sanctions from other, less severe penalties. The extent of the criminal record can be expressed by the horizontal axis of the grid.

Consider, first, a hypothetical scheme that reflects the Fletcher-Singer view of desert, in which only the seriousness of the current crime would count. Here, the in-out line would be flat. All crimes above a specified level of seriousness would receive terms of imprisonment (albeit of varying durations depending on how grave

---

*For discussion of why only previous *convictions* should be considered, and not alleged but unadjudicated prior offenses, see chap. 11.

†I focus on the in-out line to simplify the illustration. The rulemaker would also need to address the further issue of how durations of confinement should be affected by the criminal record for those cells in the grid above the in-out line.

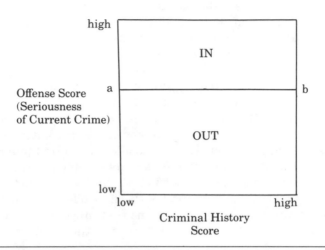

FIGURE 7.1. **In-Out Line in Desert Model, Disregarding Prior Criminality**

those crimes were), and all crimes below that level would incur a nonprison sanction. This is shown in figure 7.1.

How would a scheme reflecting my own view differ? Clearly, the in-out line could no longer be flat, as the criminal record would be permitted to play some role. On the other hand, my view calls for continued principal reliance on the seriousness of the current offense and allows only a limited penalty discount for first offenders compared to recidivists. Thus the in-out line cannot be steeply sloped, for we still wish to place much the greater weight on the current offense. The result is shown schematically in figure 7.2. Putting this into words: when one is a first offender, a somewhat more serious offense is required to send one to prison. As one's record accumulates, the first-offense discount is progressively lost, and a somewhat less reprehensible offense will warrant a prison sanction. However, the punishment differential between first offenders and recidivists is not nearly so large as that between minor and se-

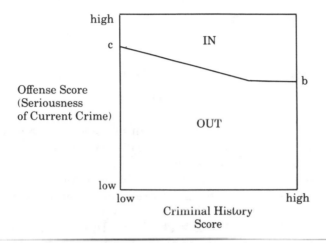

FIGURE 7.2. **In-Out Line in Desert Model,
Utilizing Prior Criminality**

rious current crimes. The in-out line is thus gradually rather than steeply sloped.*

How many repetitions may occur before the discount is lost entirely? I have no ready answer, as this seems a matter of judgment even in everyday acts of censure. Although I have called it a "first-offender discount" for convenient reference, my account has suggested the discount is gradually lost. After a certain number of repetitions, however, the plea will have been spent entirely and the offender should get his full measure of punishment. If, after that, the actor commits further repetitions, he should not get any more severe a response. There simply would be no extenuation,

---

*Figure 7.2 is somewhat of a simplification. The line would actually have a stepwise rather than linear appearance, since the grid is arrayed in cells and the criminal history score would have numbered gradations. Those steps might be somewhat higher on the left or the right of the grid, depending on how quickly the punishment discount is lost as one accumulates prior convictions. The figure is intended only to illustrate the principle—of a sloped, but only moderately sloped line.

and the person would be punished as before. Were it permissible to keep increasing the response with each subsequent repetition, even minor offenses could eventually receive very severe punishments with a sufficient number of repetitions. The in-out line should thus be hinged, as shown by figure 7.2: while sloping moderately downward on the left, it should become flat near the right for offenders having the highest criminal history scores.*

Less Punishment for First Offenders Versus More for Recidivists?

Desert theorists have been arguing over whether consideration of previous criminality constitutes a discount in punishment for first offenders, or a premium for recidivists. I have described it as a discount. Fletcher and Singer assert that any such adjustment constitutes a recidivist premium.[9] The argument may be reminiscent, to the skeptical reader, of James Thurber's anecdote in *The Thirteen Clocks*.[10] The lame Duke of Coffin Castle asked visitors to describe his legs. If the unwary guest said one leg was shorter than the other, the wicked Duke killed him and fed him to the geese—because the correct answer, according to the Duke, was that one leg was *longer* than the other. Can any better sense be made of the "less versus more" issue here?

Without an outside reference point, *greater* and *less* are purely comparative terms. A is less than B, if B is greater than A. Thus, one cannot say whether we are speaking of a discount or a premium unless we introduce a reference point—namely, how a crime would be punished in the absence of any consideration of prior record.†

In my 1981 essay,[11] I thought I had defined such a reference point. It would be the Fletcher-Singer scheme described in figure

---

*This discussion has omitted two other issues: the quality of the criminal record and its "decay." It has been my view that the seriousness as well as the number of prior convictions should be reflected in the criminal history score; and that the record should decay so that an offender's convictions many years earlier carry reduced weight. For discussion of these issues, see my article, "Desert and Previous Convictions in Sentencing," 615–617.

†In his story, Thurber actually introduces a reference point. The reader is told that the Duke's legs had been once the same length, but that the right one had outgrown the left because as a boy he had used it so much "place-kicking pups and punting kittens." So His Grace had it right if one knew his history. The left leg was normal and the kicking leg had grown to abnormal size. However, the hapless visitor could not have known the Duke's history when asked the fatal question.

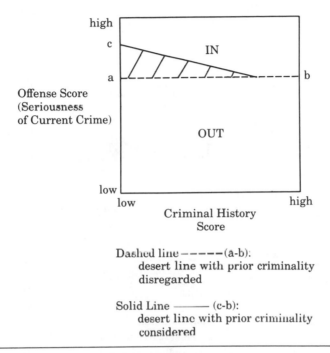

Offense Score
(Seriousness
of Current Crime)

Dashed line ─ ─ ─ ─ ─ (a-b):
    desert line with prior criminality
    disregarded

Solid Line ──────── (c-b):
    desert line with prior criminality
    considered

FIGURE 7.3. **The First-Offender Discount**

7.1, where prior criminal history was disregarded. My proposed treatment of criminal history *reduced* the severity of punishments, I said, because a first offender would be punished somewhat less than he would have been on a hypothetical sentencing scale that was blind to prior convictions; but a recidivist would be punished no more than he would have been on such a priors-blind model. This is shown in figure 7.3, with the shaded area constituting the first-offender discount.

The difficulty is that the reference point is less clear than figure 7.3 indicates. A desert rationale can offer reasonably definite

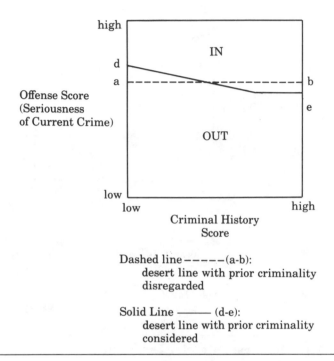

Dashed line — — — — —(a-b):
  desert line with prior criminality
  disregarded

Solid Line ——— (d-e):
  desert line with prior criminality
  considered

FIGURE 7.4. **Overlap between Desert Lines**

judgments of comparative severity. One thus can confidently say that a first offender should receive less punishment than a recidivist, but that this punishment differential should only be a modest one. However, *cardinal* desert judgments are not so exact, as I pointed out in chapter 4 and will elaborate in chapter 8. On desert grounds alone, we may have no unique elevation on the sentencing grid at which to anchor the hypothetical desert line that ignored prior convictions, shown in figure 7.3 as the dotted (a-b) line.[12] We therefore lack a clear enough reference point to be able to say whether the sloping line reflecting my own view constitutes a discount or a premium.

Where does this leave us? The treatment of first offenders can be conceptualized as a discount, as I have done herein. However, when one operationalizes a desert system in a sentencing grid, it will not be certain whether a premium or discount is involved. My sloped desert line may represent either somewhat less punishment for first offenders, or somewhat more for recidivists, compared with what could conceivably be envisioned in a scheme that is blind to prior convictions. Or else it could represent something in between, as shown in figure 7.4. This final figure describes a situation where first offenders are punished somewhat less, and recidivists somewhat more, than they would be in a system that ignored prior convictions.

What remains important, however, is that the adjustment for prior criminal record be a limited one—so that the primary emphasis of the grid is on the seriousness of the current crime. Instead of continuing to argue whether the differential between first offenders and recidivists constitutes a discount or premium, we should concentrate on keeping the size of the differential within proper bounds. By bearing this in mind, we can consider as suspect on desert grounds the provisions in many of today's laws that impose large disparities between the treatment of first offenders and recidivists.*

---

*Habitual offender laws typically impose very long prison terms, or even life imprisonment, for third conviction of routine felonies. Some determinate-sentencing laws also provide for large enhancements in the punishment of recidivists. This is true, for example, of the California Determinate Sentence Law. See Andrew von Hirsch and Julia M. Mueller, "California's Determinate Sentencing Law: An Analysis of Its Structure," 286–291. From what I have said in this chapter, it should be evident that I do *not* support such drastic measures for repeat offenders.

CHAPTER 8

Anchoring the Penalty Scale

By addressing the seriousness of crimes and the role of the prior criminal record, the rulemaker can decide issues of comparative severity. Punishments can be ordered to reflect the gravity of defendants' current crimes and to give (a limited) cognizance to their prior convictions. What remains, however, is the question of anchoring the penalty scale as a whole. Anchoring points are needed that begin to establish the levels of severity appropriate for given degrees of blameworthiness. Otherwise, the crime-seriousness rankings and the punishment scale will "float" independently of each other.

The Constraints
of Cardinal Proportionality

Anchoring the penalty scale involves the issue of *cardinal* proportionality, discussed in chapter 4. Even where penalties on a scale have been ranked in the order of crimes' seriousness, the scale may infringe cardinal proportionality if its overall severities are sufficiently inflated or deflated. A scale so inflated that it visits extensive deprivations of liberty on lesser criminal conduct is objectionable, because it overstates the blame for that conduct or else undervalues the importance of the rights of which the defendant is being deprived. To imprison criminals even for routine thefts would necessitate either treating such acts as more seriously reprehensible than they are; or else treating the defendant's liberty (inappropriately) as so unimportant that its deprivation can serve as an expression of lesser censure.[1] Similar reasoning will support objections to deflating the penalty scale so much that serious crimes are visited with mild punishments.

It is important here to recall the difference between cardinal and ordinal proportionality. In deciding comparative punishments, desert is a determining principle: it fixes the ordering of penalties on the sentencing grid. However, when seeking anchoring points— the issue of cardinal proportionality—desert provides only limits.

To illustrate, let us return to our hypothetical sentencing grid. The commission has established its grid, and begins constructing its penalty scale by drawing the in-out line between prison and nonprison sanctions. Having already decided the slope of the line by the ordinal desert considerations discussed in the preceding chapter, the commission must next decide the elevation of this line—how near the top or bottom of the grid the line should be. Since no other quanta of punishments have yet been fixed for purposes of comparison, deciding the line's elevation becomes a matter of anchoring the penalty scale. We are therefore looking for cardinal proportionality limits on raising or lowering the line.

On the grid, the cardinal proportionality limits can be represented by two bands, an upper and a lower. The upper band delineates serious crimes for which the severe penalty of imprisonment is manifestly deserved,* and any lesser penalty would be disproportionately lenient. The lower band delineates the lesser crimes for which imprisonment is plainly excessive. In between are the intermediate crimes. Included in the upper band are crimes that invade welfare interests and involve a high degree of culpability (see chapter 6). Included in the lower band are crimes that invade only accumulative interests (again, see chapter 6). The bands are shown as the shaded areas in figure 8.1. The in-out line must be drawn somewhere between the two shaded areas so as to impose the severe sanction (imprisonment) for the serious crimes and to avoid it for the lesser offenses.

The problem will be to decide where, between these upper and lower bounds of cardinality, the in-out line should be fixed. Should it be closer to (but not touching) the upper shaded area? Or closer to the lower shaded area? Or somewhere in between, among the crimes of intermediate seriousness? Cardinal desert considerations

---

*I am assuming that imprisonment represents the system's severe penalty, for reasons discussed in chap. 2.

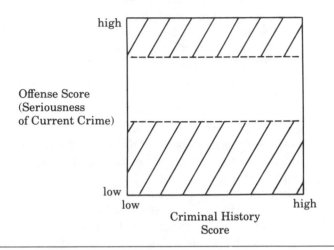

FIGURE 8.1. **Limitations of Cardinal Proportionality**

alone do not suffice to decide this matter, since the condemnatory "coinage" of punishment—that is, how much censure is expressed through given levels of penal deprivation—is in part a convention, as discussed in chapter 4. It thus seems necessary to invoke non-desert considerations. Which ones?

Crime-Control Considerations

Should crime prevention be introduced to decide the elevation of the in-out line? Some crime-control strategies have to be ruled out because they would violate ordinal proportionality—that is, they would upset the internal ordering of penalties on the scale. This obviously would be true of an exemplary deterrence strategy, of picking some but not other offenders convicted of a given type of crime for enhanced *in terroram* punishment. A selective incapacitation strategy would likewise violate the ordinal proportionality requirements, for reasons I shall detail in chapters 11 and 12, below.

Certain other crime-control strategies, however, might meet the requirements of ordinal proportionality—if they involved only pro-rata adjustments in punishments throughout the scale, and did not disturb the comparative ordering of punishments. Provided such adjustments did not inflate or deflate the scale as a whole unduly, they would also be consistent with cardinal desert limits.

What strategies might these be? One possibility, discussed in *Doing Justice*, might be to adjust penalties proportionately throughout the scale for the purpose of enhancing deterrent effectiveness.[2] Given the limitations of our knowledge, however, I doubt we could rely on deterrence in this fashion. Currently, we have difficulty enough gauging the deterrent effects of penalties for particular offense categories. We are very far from being able to take the further step of judging the *systemwide* deterrent impact of raising or lowering the severity of the entire penalty scale a few notches.[3]

Could incapacitation be approached similarly? That is, could one devise an incapacitation strategy that did not call for the differential punishment of offenders convicted of similar criminal acts? In chapter 13, I shall examine that possibility: that is, consider whether and to what extent "categorial" incapacitation (as I shall term it) might be helpful in deciding the elevation of the in-out line, without infringing upon ordinal proportionality requirements. But for the moment, the requisite data are not sufficient.

Availability of Penal Resources

What other considerations might be used? The Minnesota sentencing guidelines set a helpful precedent: they rely on the availability of penal resources. In determining the aggregate amount of imprisonment prescribed by the standards, Minnesota's sentencing commission took the state's existing prison capacities into account.[4]

Why consider prison resources, as Minnesota did? There are good moral and practical reasons why imprisonment as prescribed by the guidelines should not exceed the available prison space. The moral reason is that it simply is wrong to sentence people to over-crowded prisons: excessive crowding makes prisons unfit for human habitation. The practical reason is that the guidelines cannot be implemented as written—and would sooner or later have to be evaded—if their full application were seriously to overtax prison resources.[5]

Reliance on prison capacity seems sensible enough in Minnesota, which happens historically to have shown moderation in the construction and use of prisons.[6] But in jurisdictions where that is not the case, such reliance could lead to less satisfactory results. What of jurisdictions that have been prodigal or frugal in the extreme about the use of prisons? If availability of resources is relied upon in such places, the majority of felony offenders or almost none of them could be imprisoned as a result.

Considerations of resource availability could be combined, however, with normative judgments about cardinal proportionality.[7] Drawing the in-out line on the basis of availability of prison resources* would be only the first step. Then, the rule-making body would examine whether the line, thus tentatively located, is consistent with cardinal proportionality constraints.

Suppose the state has extremely little prison space that meets constitutional standards. In that event, an in-out line drawn on the basis of existing prison resources would have to be crowded high into the upper portion of the grid, as shown in figure 8.2. This line would be unacceptable. By impinging on the upper shaded area of the grid, it transgresses cardinal proportionality. The line is so high that serious crimes, deserving of severe punishment, will not be penalized by imprisonment and will instead receive lesser sanctions. The sentencing commission should recommend the funding of additional prison space, so as to bring down the in-out line to below the shaded area.†

Suppose, conversely, the jurisdiction has historically relied

---

*When the commission considers prison capacity, it should develop its own explicit criteria for rating the capacity of the system's prisons. Historically, the capacity of prisons has been rated by the correctional agencies themselves and has proven a plastic concept—with those agencies periodically altering their capacity estimates to reflect the public posture they wished to take. See Michael Sherman and Gordon Hawkins, *Imprisonment in America: Choosing the Future*, 28–32.

†Conceivably, the commission might offer two grids. One, representing the desired state of affairs, would show the elevation of the in-out line were the requisite prison facilities provided. The other would allocate the use of imprisonment given present, insufficient prison space.

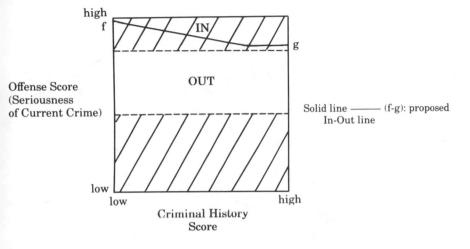

FIGURE 8.2. **Example of Excessively Lenient In-Out Line: More Prison Capacity Needed**

heavily on imprisonment and has extensive prison facilities. In that event, an in-out line drawn on the basis of available space might drop far down on the grid, as shown on figure 8.3. This in-out line is likewise unacceptable: it violates cardinal proportionality by impinging on the lower shaded area. The line is placed so far down that lesser offenses would be punished by the severe sanction of imprisonment. In this situation, justice would require a less-than-full use of available prison space, thus raising the in-out line above the shaded area. The commission should write guidelines that call for less aggregate imprisonment than existing institutional capacity permits.

Suppose, finally, the situation is similar to Minnesota's. Lo-

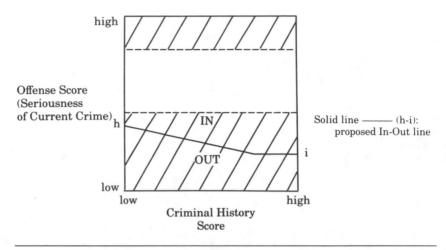

FIGURE 8.3. **Example of Excessively Severe In-Out Line: Prison Capacity Should Be Reduced**

cating the in-out line on the basis of available prison space would place it between the two shaded areas, as shown on figure 8.4. In that event, the rulemaker would not be violating cardinal-proportionality constraints by relying on resource availability for deciding the elevation of the in-out line. Pragmatic as some of the reasons for considering prison capacity are, the result does not conflict with a principled solution. By fixing the elevation of the line between the shaded areas, the rulemaker is anchoring the scale consistently with cardinal proportionality limits. And by making the line slope gently rather than steeply, it is observing the more definite ordinal proportionality requirements.

Does this provide a unique solution? Manifestly, it does not. The in-out line in figure 8.4 could be raised or lowered somewhat without impinging on the prohibited shaded areas. But as a practical matter, making a case for raising or lowering the line in this

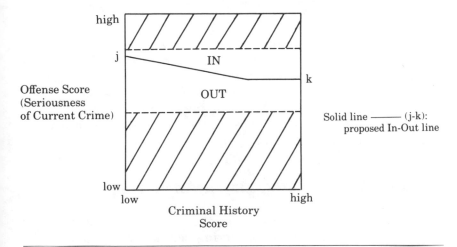

FIGURE 8.4. **Example of Acceptable In-Out Line: Retain Current Prison Capacity**

fashion will not be so easy. The high cost of prison space would militate against lowering the line and thus sending many more people to prison.* Assuring the political acceptability of the guidelines will militate against raising the line and thus making the system still more lenient. There is likely to be less ambiguity about the decision in practice than in theory.

Would a more definite solution to anchoring the in-out line ever be possible? In some conceivable circumstances, yes. Suppose a practical opportunity existed for raising or lowering the line— that is, there were both funds available for increasing prison space, and the political feasibility for reducing prison space by closing

---

*How much cost is a disencentive to expanding prison commitments will vary, however, with the criminal justice politics of the jurisdiction. For discussion, see James Jacobs, "The Politics of Prison Expansion."

some facilities down. Suppose also that the properly relevant crime prevention concerns provided no guidance—in the sense that moving the line up or down would not, to our knowledge, significantly affect the scale's preventive effects.* The principle of least restriction would then apply: the state has the obligation of keeping the suffering of offenders to the minimum consistent with its penal objectives, and bears the burden of justifying why a given level of intrusion, and not a lesser one, is called for.[8] The cardinal-proportionality limit constitutes grounds for keeping the in-out line out of the upper shaded area. But no reason has been provided, in this scenario, for allowing the line to fall any distance below that limit. In these hypothetical circumstances, the line should be located just below the upper shaded area.

Concluding Thoughts on Anchoring

It should be emphasized that the foregoing reasoning holds only for decisions about the anchoring points of the penalty scale. Once the decision about the appropriate elevation for the in-out line has been made (with whatever imprecision and even arbitrariness that decision may involve) the rule-making body becomes bound by the much more definite internal scaling requirements of desert—that is, by the requirements of ordinal proportionality. The imprecision involved in deciding the elevation of the in-out line would not justify tilting up the slope of that line so that desert considerations no longer govern the comparative ordering of penalties.

The present and the two previous chapters should suggest that deciding how much punishment is deserved is not an impossible task. True, there is no uniquely correct solution to anchoring the penalty scale. True also, the scaling of seriousness involves theoretical issues concerning harm and culpability that need further exploration. But a responsible rule-making body can in a reasoned practical fashion assign ratings to the seriousness of crimes. It can give the limited weight to prior criminality that desert warrants. And it can fix the anchoring points of a scale—for example, the elevation of the in-out line in the sentencing grid—within cardinal proportionality constraints, taking the availabil-

---

*How certain kinds of crime-control concerns might affect the line's elevation, were there the requisite information, is discussed in chaps. 13 and 14.

ity of correctional resources into account. None of these decisions can be precise, but they can be rational in the sense of being coherent and backed by reasons based on a general conception of deserved punishment.

PART IV

Selective Incapacitation

SENTENCING ON GROUNDS of potential future criminality has been a familiar notion in criminal justice. Proponents of the traditional positivist penal ethic long held that, while curable offenders should be treated, those who are bad risks should be identified and isolated from society. Only during the last decade and a half were significant doubts raised about the accuracy of predictions of dangerousness and about the justice of predictively based punishments.

Quite recently, however, predictive sentencing has attracted renewed interest in penological writing and research. The new focus is on offenders thought likely to commit serious crimes with high frequency, instead of on recidivists in general. The strategy has been given a new name: "selective incapacitation." Important advances are said to have been made in the technology of identifying high-risk offenders. Selective incapacitation, when applied in sentencing policy, is claimed to be capable of decreasing the aggregate incidence of serious crime, without increasing the number of offenders incarcerated. The strategy is also said by its proponents to be "fair"—to be consistent with requirements of desert insofar as those are deemed worth taking seriously.

This part is devoted to examining these claims. In chapter 9, I examine the efficacy of the new prediction techniques, to see what progress, if any, has been made in the ability to identify prospective recidivists. In chapter 10, I scrutinize recent claims that selective incapacitation is capable of reducing rates of serious crime and of solving problems of prison overcrowding. The final chapters of this part, 11 and 12, discuss the ethics of selective incapacitation.■

CHAPTER 9

Predictive Efficacy*

Traditional Prediction Methods

Statistical prediction of criminality has had a sixty-year history in this country. Hart and Warner, in the 1920s, fashioned tables for forecasting parole success.[1] In the next decade, the prediction scales for juvenile delinquency devised by Sheldon and Eleanor Glueck attracted worldwide notice.[2] After World War II, researchers developed prediction methods further and put them into use. The California Base Expectancy Score, a scale for predicting parole success or failure, was used extensively in parole and classification decisions in the 1960s.[3] A similar scale was adopted in 1972 by the United States Parole Commission as part of its guideline grid.[4]

The studies used essentially the same method, with varying degrees of sophistication.[5] The research began with the collection of various data about a sample of offenders—including subjects' crimes, criminal records, employment, and social histories. Using bivariate or multivariate statistics, the researcher then examined which of these factors were associated with subsequent recidivism and to what extent they were. (Recidivism was usually measured by reconvictions or parole revocations.) A predictive index was then constructed. The index utilized those factors that showed the

---

*The material in this chapter and the next is derived in part from an article Don Gottfredson and I coauthored in 1983 on selective incapacitation research, and is used with his kind permission, "Selective Incapacitation: Some Queries about Research Design and Equity." For a valuable further analysis, see Jacqueline Cohen, "Incapacitation as a Strategy for Crime Control: Possibilities and Pitfalls," 1–55.

strongest degree of association with recidivism, after eliminating items that were too strongly correlated with each other to add much predictive benefit.

Once the prediction index was constructed, the next, and crucial, step was its validation. The index was tried out on a new sample of offenders to see how well it identified the recidivists. This indicated whether the association found between the predictor variables and subsequent criminal conduct was merely an idiosyncracy of the original sample, or would hold up for successive groups of offenders.

The traditional forecasting studies tended to show that a few familiar predictor items—the offender's criminal history, employment, and drug habits—could be combined to identify subgroups of offenders who were bad risks—that is, who had a higher incidence of offending again than convicted offenders generally.[6] Examination of the studies revealed, however, that the association between the predictor variables and subsequent recidivism was a weak one. The percentage of variability in offender conduct accounted for by the predictive factors was modest. When multivariate statistics were used, the variability explained by all of an index's predictive factors combined was in the order of only 15 to 30 percent.[7] With such limited associations, a high rate of error could be expected and was found to occur.

The error was of two types. The first type of error was that of failing to identify persons who subsequently *did* return to crime. Even though the predictive instruments spotted some recidivists, they missed others. The rate of false negatives (that is, persons mistakenly identified as nonrecidivists) was substantial.[8]

Still more disturbing was the reverse kind of error: *over*prediction of recidivism. In order to spot any appreciable number of actual recidivists, the prediction instruments produced a much larger number of false positives—that is, persons mistakenly predicted to be recidivists.[9] The rate of false positives was particularly high in forecasts of serious criminality. John Monahan, in a 1981 study,[10] compared the results of six major studies that tested the accuracy of clinical and statistical forecasts of violence. In those studies, the rate of false positives tended to be 60 percent or more: of every three persons classified as potentially violent, two were *not* found to commit the predicted acts of violence. This problem was difficult to remedy, because it stemmed from the comparative rarity of the conduct to be forecasted. Serious crimes tend to be statistically infrequent events. The rarer the event, the greater will be the tendency to overpredict.

Trying to alleviate the false-negatives problem aggravated the overprediction problem, and vice versa. If the researcher wished to identify a larger fraction of the actual recidivists, he or she could lower the "cutting line" in the predictive instrument— that is, make the definition of being a bad risk more inclusive. This, however, sharply increased the already high incidence of false positives. Conversely, if the researcher wanted to reduce the number of false positives, the cutting line could be raised and the definition of dangerousness narrowed. This, however, meant missing a still greater number of actual recidivists.[11]

In the late 1970s these findings, as they became known, diminished enthusiasm for using individualized prediction in sentencing. The significant numbers of false negatives discouraged law-and-order advocates who wanted effective protection against recidivist criminality. The embarrassingly high incidence of false positives disturbed those with civil libertarian sympathies. It scarcely seemed just to deprive people of their liberty for anticipated crimes, when most would not commit those crimes.[12]

Selective Incapacitation: The RAND Studies

Now, however, a new variety of predictive sentencing is being developed: selective incapacitation. The most elaborate selective incapacitation studies to date are two companion RAND Corporation studies, based on the same sample of incarcerated offenders. One of these is Peter Greenwood's study, mentioned in chapter 1, which has reported extraordinary successes.[13] The other RAND study, by Jan and Marcia Chaiken,[14] utilizes similar methods for constructing the predictive index, but its authors have been more cautious about the potential utility of the index.

FOCUS ON FREQUENCY AND TYPE OF OFFENDING

Earlier prediction studies sought to predict recidivism versus nonrecidivism. If the offender was convicted again or had his parole or probation revoked for a new crime, he counted as a failure; if he did not return to crime, he counted as a success. The number or type of the offender's subsequent crimes, if he offended again, were not considered.

The chief novelty of selective incapacitation is its emphasis on the type and frequency of predicted offenses. The new studies focus on future crimes of a more serious nature: robberies or other violent crimes. Moreover, the studies seek ways of identifying high-rate criminals, those who can be expected to commit numerous such crimes in the future. Greenwood speaks of "high-rate robbers," and the Chaikens of "violent predators."

THE RESEARCH DESIGN

The probability of being *convicted* of robbery or other serious crime is small: only a fraction of reported robberies result in conviction for that crime.* To identify high-rate offenders, therefore, one needs an indicator of subjects' rate of offending other than the number of convictions—one that more closely approximates their actual offense rates. The RAND studies relied on offenders' self-reports for this purpose.† The researchers asked a sample of incarcerated robbers how frequently they committed robberies in the past. Most reported low rates, but a small minority reported committing as many as 100 robberies per year.[15] Such self-reports were considered the best approximation of actual offense rates.

The RAND sample consisted of selected inmates in jails and prisons in California, Michigan, and Texas. The researchers asked offenders about their criminal records, employment, social, and drug histories. These items of information were treated as the predictor variables. Through the same questionnaire, prisoners' self-reports of the frequency with which they committed robberies were also obtained. The number of robberies reported was treated as the behavior to be predicted. The researchers then developed their

---

*Or more precisely, it is small in most American jurisdictions. In California, that probability is 3 percent for robbery, according to Greenwood's own figures (*Selective Incapacitation,* xvii).

†The reliance on self-reports raises problems of reliability. The research is not even focused on the behavior of the majority of respondents, unlike must self-report research in the social sciences. If it were, one could discount the risk of untruthfulness among some respondents. Instead, it concentrates on the behavior of those who report themselves to be a troublesome minority—it is the high-risk offenders that the instrument is meant to identify. It seems to be assumed that these individuals (like the homicidal Irish maiden in Tom Lehrer's famous song) are happy to wreak the worst mayhem but know that lying is a sin. Perhaps, persons who are supposedly so very lawless might be less than candid. Perhaps, also, many exaggerate their criminal activities to the interviewer in order to cast themselves as tough or macho. For fuller discussion, see Andrew von Hirsch and Don M. Gottfredson, "Selective Incapacitation," 18–21.

forecasting index by determining which "predictor" variables were associated with high self-reported rates of offending.

Such research is not prediction in the strict sense. The RAND studies all stem from a single questionnaire, and essentially are cross-tabulations—linking prisoners' reported personal histories with their reported criminal behavior. The Chaikens recognize this and call their study one of "*post*diction"; Greenwood does not and treats his study as though it were a true prediction method. The distinction between prediction and postdiction is important, because subjects' behavior patterns can change over time. To the extent of such change, the factors associated with earlier behavior will not predict *subsequent* behavior well.*

RESULTS OF THE RESEARCH: CAN WE PREDICT ANY BETTER?

What are the results of the RAND research, and how impressive are they?

Let us examine, first, the predictive factors that supposedly identify high-risk offenders. In the Greenwood study, those factors are similar to ones that have long been known associated with recidivism. They consist of the offender's criminal history, age at first involvement with criminal justice agencies, drug consumption, and employment history.† No novel indicia of future criminality are found here. The predictors identified in the Chaiken study

---

*Imagine a researcher seeking to predict the physical condition of pregnant women from self-reports of their symptoms during the ninth month of their pregnancy. Such predictions may be worthless for forecasting the women's health *after* the ninth month, for reasons I hardly need explain.

An offender's criminal career may not change as quickly or spectacularly as the course of a pregnancy, but the essential point remains. A criminal's robbery habits may fluctuate over time. He may have been uncharacteristically active during the period immediately preceding his incarceration, and placed himself at greater risk of arrest and conviction precisely because he was then most active. Moreover, an offender's criminal habits can change with age (or even, perhaps, with the experience of incarceration). To the extent such fluctuations occur, the factors associated with criminality in his earlier career will not be associated (or associated in the same degree) with the person's subsequent patterns of behavior. Thus, a postdictive index will not necessarily be useful as a predictor of later criminality. For changes of offense rates over time, see Neal Shover, "The Later Stages of Ordinary Property Offender Careers."

†The seven factors in Greenwood's prediction scale (*Selective Incapacitation*, 50) are:

1. Prior conviction for the instant offense type.
2. Incarceration for more than half of the preceding two years.
3. Conviction before the age of sixteen.
4. Time served in a state juvenile facility.

are not very different: they emphasize youthful violence and drug involvement.[16]

In earlier prediction studies, as we have seen, the association between the predictor variables and subsequent criminal behavior was rather weak. Does the new research disclose any stronger association? Unfortunately, it does not. The Chaiken study uses multiple regression analysis. This familiar statistical technique allows one to determine the percentage of variability in offender conduct that is explained by all predictor variables combined. The percentage reported* is 32 percent,[17] which is comparable to the performance of traditional prediction methods. Greenwood in his study uses simple bivariate statistics and does not calculate or report the efficiency of his predictive device. When those calculations were made on the basis of his reported data, however, they showed his scale to be comparable in efficiency to, but no improvement on, traditional statistical measures.[18] With so little of the variability in behavior accounted for, one can expect—and, indeed, does find—a high rate of false positives and a substantial incidence of false negatives.

Greenwood reports a strikingly low false-positive rate, in the order of only 4 percent.[19] He does this by treating as false positives only those offenders predicted to be high-rate offenders who had, in fact, the lowest reported rates—namely, the most extreme category of false positives. He fails to treat as false positives those predicted to be high-rate offenders who proved to have medium rates, although these also could receive longer incapacitative sentences under his own proposals.† When one asks what percentage

---

5. Drug use during the preceding two years.
6. Drug use as a juvenile.
7. Employment during less than 50 percent of the preceding two years.

Using this scale, he develops three categories: predicted low-rate, medium-rate, and high-rate offenders. The categories are defined as follows:

Offender Risk Category	Number of Factors Present
low	0–1
medium	2–3
high	4 or more

*In statistical terms, the R^2 for all predictor variables combined is 0.32.

†Greenwood's claims of being able to reduce the robbery rate substantially are based on a suggested policy of giving short jail terms to medium- and low-rate offenders, but very lengthy prison terms to high-rate offenders. On the basis of this policy, any person classified as a high-rate offender who shows medium or low robbery rates in fact is a false positive, since the prediction is not only false but also drastically affects the duration of the offender's sentence.

of supposedly high-rate offenders were thus erroneously classified, the false-positive rate shoots up. Of those offenders in his sample predicted by his index to be high-rate offenders, less than half in fact were so. The remainder showed medium or low rates. The false-positive rate was 56 percent,[20] which shows scant improvement over previous studies. The false-negative rate was also substantial. Of those predicted to be low- or medium-rate offenders, one-sixth (16 percent) showed high rates. In sum, Greenwood's technique for predicting potential robbers—even by his own data—shows little improvement in accuracy over forecasting methods of the past.

The Chaikens' study shows comparable error rates. The incidence of false positives remains high. Over 60 percent of those classified as high-rate robbers had lower rates or did not commit robberies at all.[21] But the Chaikens, to their credit, explicitly call attention to the large number of false positives, and assert that it raises ethical problems about the suitability of using their predictive index in sentencing decisions.[22]

SELF-REPORTED VERSUS OFFICIALLY REPORTED PREDICTORS

The use of prisoner self-reports as the basis of the RAND research creates a special problem: that of identifying predictive factors that are still predictors when official information about the offender's history is relied upon. It is one thing to find that high robbery rates are correlated with an offender's private admissions to an interviewer that he is an active drug user or has never held a steady job. It is quite another matter to use those factors in a forecasting index for sentencing purposes. That would require records or other available evidence that the offender *is,* indeed, a drug user or has been chronically unemployed. When one shifts from self-admitted drug consumption to officially reported drug use, the predictive utility of the factor may largely disappear.

Greenwood ignores this problem. He presents his seven predictive factors as though official reports about an offender's criminal record, employment, and drug history are predictive of high rates of robbery. But that is untrue, as the Chaikens found in a subsequent analysis of Greenwood's work.[23] Of the seven factors used in Greenwood's index, five either had no official records in the data or else proved to have no predictive usefulness when official data rather than offenders' own admissions to the researcher were used! If Greenwood's index were utilized in actual sentencing decisions, defendants would be unlikely to oblige the courts with accurate descriptions of their criminal and social histories. Thus if official records regarding such records and histories have no predictive value, the index is virtually worthless as it stands as a guide to sentencing decisions.

Prospects for Improvement

Selective incapacitation techniques, as exemplified by the RAND research, are thus not workable tools for sentencing as they stand. Even were one to accept the principle of predictively based sanctions, their problems of design and accuracy are too severe.* Greenwood, in effect, conceals these problems; the Chaikens admit them candidly and warn against treating their index as a readily usable sentencing technique.

Can one improve upon the RAND studies? Were enthusiasm the only requirement, one might have reason for optimism, since so vigorous a revival of interest in prediction methods is taking place. There exist, however, considerable obstacles to success.

A major source of difficulty will be that of making the predictions hold up, when official data of the kind a sentencing court has available is relied upon. The objective of selective incapacitation, as we saw, is to target the potential high-rate serious offenders and to distinguish them from a variety of lesser recidivists. Officially recorded information about offenders' adult and juvenile records make this distinction poorly. When the Chaikens analyzed their own data to see how well the high-risk offenders could be predicted from information existing in court records, the results were disappointing. The officially recorded facts —arrests, convictions, and meager data about the offender's personal history—did not demarcate the potential high-rate robbers from the potential burglars and thieves. The factors in their self-report study that had proved useful—such as early and extensive youthful violence, multiple drug use, and persistent unemployment—were *not* reflected in official records.[24] The Chaikens con-

---

*The recently organized Panel on Research on Criminal Careers, sponsored by the National Academy of Sciences and chaired by Professor Alfred Blumstein, has commissioned a reanalysis of the RAND data. The reanalysis, undertaken by Dr. Christy Visher, has highlighted a number of ways in which the ability to identify high-rate offenders would diminish when applied in a real sentencing context. See Christy A. Visher, "The RAND Second Inmate Survey: A Reanalysis."

clude that "most of the information that distinguishes high-rate robers from other incarcerated criminals cannot be found in records the criminal justice system readily has available."[25]

A possible solution might be to expand the type of information the courts collect for sentencing purposes. The Chaikens propose this course. The most helpful indicators of future high-rate serious criminality, such as extensive youth violence and multiple drug use, are matters that "could scarcely have gone unnoticed by schools" and other authorities.[26] They recommend the collection of school records and similar information for possible use in prediction of criminality.[27]

This approach might provide a richer data base for making the forecasts, but it brings its own problem—that of the trustworthiness of the information. If an individual is incarcerated on the basis of his supposed dangerousness, and if his dangerousness is decided on the basis of specified allegations about his history, he should be entitled to accurate and fair fact-finding about that history.* As one shifts from the traditional criminal record to information contained in school and welfare agency records, the problems of inaccuracy are aggravated. Notations in someone's school records that he has been violent or involved in drugs may have been based on shaky evidence, and not been open to challenge by the offender. I shudder to think that my liberty, or someone else's, could depend on the mass of untested stuff that goes routinely into school or welfare agency dossiers.

Another continuing problem will be that of overprediction. The rate of false positives depends chiefly on the "base expectancy rate"—that is, the prevalence in the sample of the characteristic to be predicted. For conventional prediction research, this offered some hope. If one were seeking merely to distinguish potential recidivists from nonrecidivists, one could select samples where the prevalence of recidivism was high. As the proportion of recidivists in the sample approaches 50 percent, the false-positive rate will begin to fall.[28]

This strategy, unhappily, is not available to selective incapacitation research. Since the entire point is to identify the small percentage of (say) robbers who will offend with unusual frequency, the characteristic to be predicted—being a frequent and serious offender—will *ex hypothesi* be of low prevalence in populations of

---

*This issue is usefully explored in Alan Dershowitz, "Indeterminate Confinement: Letting the Therapy Fit the Harm."

robbers. I am not optimistic that false-positive rates—if *accurately* reported*—will fall much below the high levels exhibited in the RAND studies. Selective incapacitation scales, if they can be made to work at all, will at best be crude instruments.

---

*Accurate reporting means adopting a definition of false positives that is consistent with the objective of the research. When that objective is the identification and segregation of high-rate serious offenders, then a false positive must be someone who is predicted to be a high-rate serious offender but who turns out not to be one (whether he proves to be a lesser recidivist or not to offend again at all). Some recent research—such as Greenwood's and a recent INSLAW (Brian Forst et al., "Targeting Federal Resources on Recidivists: An Empirical View")—artificially deflate the false-positive rate by ignoring this requirement.

CHAPTER 10

Impact on Crime Rates and Prison Populations

Traditional prediction studies made no special claims about being able to reduce the overall incidence of crime. Identifying the potential recidivist and imprisoning him safeguarded one from injury at his hands. Since other felons remained at large, however, his imprisonment did not necessarily reduce one's net risk of being victimized.

Selective incapacitation advocates, or some of them, now claim that their strategy can reduce that larger danger. Selective incapacitation, if applied in sentencing, supposedly can accomplish significant reductions in the incidence of serious crimes—without increasing the number of persons incarcerated. Greenwood, in particular, claims to have demonstrated that a selective incapacitation strategy could reduce the rate of robberies by as much as 15 percent, while simultaneously allowing a 5 percent reduction in prison populations.[1]* James Q. Wilson accepts Greenwood's estimates in his 1983 book and uses them as the basis of his own advocacy of predictive sentencing.[2] How sound are such claims?

Purported Effect on Serious Crime

Greenwood's model for projecting the impact on crime is borrowed from the "collective incapacitation" research done in the

*These figures represent Greenwood's estimates based on data for California (*Selective Incapacitation*, xix).

mid-1970s. The reader will recall this strategy from chapter 1. Prison sentences were to be imposed on defendants convicted of major felonies, and no attempt would be made to identify which individual felons were the high risks. By removing from circulation all persons convicted of such crimes for stated periods, this strategy supposedly would yield an incapacitative effect, preventing any such persons from offending again while they were confined. Wilson, then the leading advocate of the strategy, promised great crime-control gains, including a 20 percent reduction in robberies.[3]

Wilson derived his optimistic estimates from a projection technique developed by Reuel Shinnar.[4] Shinnar invented a new measure named Lambda (λ), which represents the average annual rate at which individual offenders commit offenses in the community. Given an appropriate estimate for Lambda, a simple formula can be derived for calculating the average fraction of time an offender spends on the street. This fraction, Shinnar showed, depends on the offense rate (λ); the average probability of being arrested, convicted, and incarcerated for a crime; and the average duration of confinement if incarcerated. If one knows the fraction of time offenders spend at liberty and has data on the number of the offenders now confined, one can readily estimate the total number of persons committing crimes. Next, one can calculate the resulting total number of crimes committed: multiply the number of persons committing crimes by the fraction of their time they spend on the street, and multiply that figure by Lambda, their average offense rate. A collective incapacitation strategy, if adopted, will alter one of the relevant variables: it could, for example, raise the likelihood of incarceration if convicted for given offenses to something approaching 100 percent. Given this change in policy, one can then recalculate the total crimes. The resulting decrease in the number of crimes, according to Shinnar, measures the preventive effect of the strategy.

In his calculations, Shinnar assumed a high average rate of offending.[5] With this high Lambda, his model suggested (not surprisingly) a large crime-reduction effect. However, when other researchers recalculated the effects using lower estimates for Lambda, the projected crime-reduction effects of the strategy shrank dramatically.[6] Little evidence was forthcoming to confirm higher or lower Lambda estimates.[7] As these difficulties became apparent, enthusiasm for collective incapacitation waned.

GREENWOOD'S PROJECTION MODEL: ALTERING THE
SHINNAR FORMULA TO FIT SELECTIVE INCAPACITATION

Shinnar's model was not forgotten, however. Greenwood resuscitated the Shinnar formula and revised it to fit selective incapacitation.[8] Greenwood's idea is to establish not one but *three*
Lambdas. The Lambdas would be the estimated average robbery
rates, respectively, of low-, medium-, and high-risk robbers. He asserts that these rates can be obtained from his data: one simply
uses the average self-reported annual robbery rates of the individuals falling into the three risk categories established by his predictive instrument. With these three Lambdas, Greenwood calculates
(in much the same way Shinnar did) the aggregate number of robberies contributed by each of the three groups under present sentencing policy. Next, he postulates how selective incapacitation
would alter that policy: that would involve, for high-rate offenders,
increasing the probability of imprisonment if convicted, or ex-
tending the duration of imprisonment, or both; and for low- and
medium-rate offenders, it would mean continuing present sentencing practices, or else shortening durations of confinement. Assuming these policy changes, Greenwood figures, for each risk group,
the effect on that group's total estimated crimes. The extent of the
reduction in estimated crime represents the crime-prevention impact of the new strategy. Greenwood's calculations suggest the
crime reduction could be substantially larger than that of a uniform policy for imprisoning convicted robbers.

DUBIOUS EVIDENCE ON INDIVIDUAL ROBBERY RATES:
EXTRAPOLATING FROM DATA ABOUT INCARCERATED
OFFENDERS

Greenwood's calculations depend on the soundness of his
method of estimating his principal measures—the Lambdas. The
three Lambdas purport to reflect the average individual robbery
rates of high-, medium-, and low-risk offenders. Supposedly, they
describe not only the former criminal activity of the incarcerated
robbers who were interviewed, but also the current activity of the
robbers at large in the community. It is because he supposedly
finds a very high Lambda for the robbers who are the bad risks
that he can claim them responsible for such a large proportion
of robberies.

In fact, Greenwood has no sound basis for his Lambda estimates. Given the research design, he only can study the purported robbery habits of incarcerated robbers—those who happen to be in prison or jail at the moment, and whose self-reports can be obtained. He reports that the probability of being incarcerated for a robbery is very low.* With a probability so low, Greenwood's sample of robbers—selected by virtue of its members' currently being incarcerated for robbery—may be a highly unrepresentative one. Perhaps only the more active robbers get caught, confined, and included in the sample. No data are available in the study to ascertain how much incarcerated offenders' self-reported robbery habits resemble the habits of robbers in the community.† Yet his calculations assume those self-reports *do* accurately portray the criminal activities of the robbers who are at large.

Greenwood's method is thus reminiscent of the researcher who makes "findings" about the drug habits of addicts in a community by studying the drug histories of a limited number of addicts residing in in-patient drug treatment centers. Such findings would likewise be of little or no value, because the addicts in treatment might be wholly unrepresentative of the general population of drug users.

Greenwood scarcely addresses this objection, except to make this comment: "Our sample has been criticized for including only

---

*In California, Greenwood (*Selective Incapacitation,* xvii, 108–113) reports, the probability of arrest and conviction for robbery is .03, and the present probability of incarceration if convicted is .86. This means that the probability of arrest, conviction and incarceration for a given robbery is a mere .0258—or less than 3 percent.

†A closer look at Greenwood's model for estimating crime-rate effects confirms the problem. The critical formula in Greenwood's calculations is, as we saw, that which allows one to calculate the fraction of time an offender typically spends on the street, based on the estimated Lambda and on the probability of incarceration given an offense and the duration of incarceration. That fraction is used to determine both the estimated number of persons offending and the incidence of offenses associated with a given sentencing policy. But one can estimate this fraction-of-time-free accurately only if one knows the true Lambda, that is, the actual average offense rate per robber. The data in the study cannot provide this; they can furnish only estimates of the average number of crimes per offender for *incarcerated* offenders whose self-reports can be obtained. The study can provide no data on the number of crimes per offender for those not confined when the research was done, and such numbers may be very different. If so, then Greenwood's estimates of the true Lambda for low-, medium-, and high-risk offenders may be seriously inaccurate when generalized to the whole population of robbers. To the extent those Lambda estimates are in error, the number of crimes committed by the target group of "high-rate" offenders may be substantially overestimated. Such overestimation will, in turn, distort the projections of the crime-prevention effects of a selective incapacitation strategy. (Readers interested in the mathematical specifics should consult Andrew von Hirsch and Don M. Gottfredson, "Selective Incapacitation. Some Queries about Research Design and Equity" 24–26, 46–48.)

incarcerated offenders. This criticism would perhaps be justified if there were evidence to suggest the existence of a significant group of offenders not subject to arrest and incarceration. There is no such evidence."[9] He is saying that his incarcerated-offender-based research design could be suspect only if one assumes there exist large numbers of high-frequency offenders who are never caught and punished. One can, however, challenge Greenwood's design without having to make this debatable supposition. If either of the following scenarios were true—and they are not the only possible ones—Greenwood's reliance on data taken from incarcerated offenders would lead to serious errors in his estimates. These scenarios do not require one to assume that there are many Dr. Moriartys of armed robbery at work, busily committing crimes and never being detected.

Scenario 1: Overestimating the Activity of High-Scoring Offenders. Among offenders who scored badly on his predictive index, Greenwood found startlingly high average annual robbery rates. This steep robbery rate may, however, have been an artifact of having considered only the incarcerated robbers. One can accumulate a score that puts one in the worst risk category in Greenwood's prediction index by being unemployed, being addicted with a history of addiction, having an early juvenile conviction, and having been confined as a juvenile.[10] Were it possible to examine the habits of *un*incarcerated offenders with these characteristics, it might have emerged that many such individuals never had high robbery rates or had since lost their criminal initiative. (In fact, it may be because they are committing fewer robberies that they are underrepresented in Greenwood's inmate sample.) Greenwood's research design, therefore, may have substantially overestimated the Lambda for robbers who fit his criteria for being a bad risk. This, in turn, would lead him to exaggerate the aggregate crimes committed by such persons and hence to overstate the incapacitative effect of confining this group.

Scenario 2: Underestimating the Impact of Occasional Criminals. Greenwood has assumed a uniform probability of arrest and conviction for a given robbery. In fact, he has derived that probability simply by dividing the number of robbery convictions by the number of robberies.[11] But it is easy to imagine a more complex scenario. The probability of arrest and conviction for an offense may vary considerably with the extent of the person's criminal history and other signs of "trouble," such as apparent drug addiction. It may be difficult or impossible to obtain any reliable estimate of that probability for occasional offenders with little previous contact with criminal justice agencies. Occasional offenders might be more numerous, and be responsible for a much larger proportion of aggregate robberies than Greenwood's calculations recognize. If this is the case, the crime-control effect of confining the robbers who do badly on his prediction index would be far more modest than claimed.

THE POTENTIAL SIZE OF THE DISTORTION

The distortion in Greenwood's estimates is substantial, because his extrapolations from the data are so large. Consider a possibly typical jurisdiction, X, where the average risk of being convicted and imprisoned for a robbery is assumed to be 2.5 percent.[12] Suppose one divides the inmates with robbery convictions in the manner that Greenwood did, into low, medium and high scorers on his prediction scale. Suppose the high scorers reported a fairly high average robbery rate, one well above the rates Greenwood reports for Texas,[13] but not quite so high as his California rates. Let us assume twenty robberies per year. Let us imagine, further, that these high scorers constitute one quarter of the population of imprisoned robbers.[14] Using these figures and Greenwood's method of calculation, one would extrapolate that there are nearly *twice* as many active high-rate robbers as those who can actually be identified as such in confinement[15]—and that members of this much larger group are each committing twenty robberies a year while at liberty. It is because Greenwood attributes the high robbery rate to so greatly enlarged a group that he can "derive" large crime reductions from a policy of selective incapacitation targeted on such offenders. What we have just seen, however, is that his estimates of both the size of this enlarged group and its average offense rate may be quite wrong. If so, his estimates of the benefits of selective incapacitation may be seriously in error as well.

CAN MORE CONSERVATIVE ESTIMATES BE MADE?

Can any inferences be made from Greenwood's self-report data? Much more caution would be necessary. On the basis of data about the robbery rates of incarcerated offenders, one might try to project the preventive effects of selective incapacitation policies, considering only *their* anticipated activities. Don Gottfredson and I calculated what the incapacitative effects of a selective incapacitation strategy would be using Greenwood's formula, but considering only the anticipated crimes upon release of those now incarcerated—and not, by extrapolation, an equivalent rate of criminality for unstudied offenders in the community. Using that approach, the estimated preventive impact would shrink by 50 percent.[16]

Even that conservative projected impact may well be overstated, however. The calculation ignores replacement effects. Removing a high-rate robber from circulation, it assumes, will eliminate a number of offenses exactly equal to his predicted number of robberies. This assumption is unrealistic. Albert Reiss has suggested, for example, that the bulk (over 70 percent) of robberies by younger offenders is committed in groups,[17] and Greenwood himself cites statistics suggesting a substantial incidence of robbery perpetrated by several offenders acting together.* Removal of one member from such a group is scarcely apt to terminate the group's activities. The group can recruit replacements or continue its robberies without a replacement, and in either event, little or no crime reduction will occur. (Reiss even raises the possibility of an increase in crime, if removal of a member causes the group to split into two nuclei that continue robbing separately.) Reiss's point about group robberies describes only one of a variety of replacement effects that could occur. Were allowance made for such possible effects, the crime-prevention payoff of selective incapacitation would be reduced even further. In sum, one ends with having scant reason for confidence in Greenwood's projections of crime reduction.†

Greenwood's response to such criticisms has been that even if his evidence does not fully support the conclusions about reduced crime rates, it is the only evidence now available.‡ I doubt, how-

---

*Greenwood's statistics (*Selective Incapacitation,* 109) indicate that the average number of offenders per robbery incident in California is 2.3. However, he ignores the implications of this fact and treats robbers in his calculations of preventive effect as though they are robbing alone.

†Shortly before this book went to press, further questions raised by other researchers have come to my attention. Dr. Christy Visher's reanalysis of the RAND data "The RAND Second Inmate Survey: A Reanalysis," commissioned for the ongoing National Academy of Sciences panel on criminal careers, found that the Greenwood study significantly overestimates the crime-reduction impact. Dr. Jacqueline Cohen, in recent not yet published work, has found that Greenwood's crime-reduction estimates would shrink substantially if realistic estimates were made of lengths of offenders' criminal careers.

‡Greenwood ("Response to Panelists," 73–74) thus asserts: "Looking back over the history of criminology, I would point out that we are not unique in using data on people who come in contact with the criminal justice system to make inferences about what criminals are like in general. If we exclude all the studies that

ever, that bad evidence supplies better support for a conclusion than no evidence at all. Were we so tolerant, other now discredited claims would be believed. It was always easy, for example, to give treatment programs the *appearance* of working: the doubts only arose when the research designs of such programs were scrutinized rigorously. Selective incapacitation should be given similar scrutiny. Unless there is good evidence that selective incapacitation reduces crime, one has no right to assume the strategy works.

COULD A BETTER RESEARCH DESIGN BE DEVELOPED?

Could estimates of preventive impact be made that are less defective than Greenwood's? Conceivably, one could pursue the "conservative" estimation method of which I have spoken. If the data are based on the activity of incarcerated offenders, then only the subsequent criminal activity of these offenders would be considered, not that of unstudied others in the community. However, this estimation method (as we have seen with Greenwood's data) will sharply reduce the projected incapacitative effect.

Is there any way of going beyond such conservative estimates—of making extrapolations about the activities of unincarcerated robbers in a manner less flawed than Greenwood's? One strategy might be to develop scenarios for the possible activities of the unincarcerated offenders and incorporate those into the calculation. This approach (known as a "sensitivity analysis") would be mathematically possible, but the results would vary with how favorable or unfavorable the scenarios were to the selective incapacitation advocates' thesis. On the basis of scenarios such as the two sketched earlier in this chapter, hardly any preventive impact would be added. In any event, we have no sound evidence favoring one scenario over another. Until such evidence becomes available, scenarios that impute the activities of unstudied robbers can only be speculative.

The other possibility would be to try to broaden the study of active robbers. Instead of examining only the criminal habits of incarcerated robbers, one could try to obtain samples that better reflect the criminal habits of robbers generally. That, however, is easier said than done. Any samples drawn from the criminal justice system (e.g., robbery arrestees, or robbery convicts) is likely to be biased in much the same way that Greenwood's sample of incarcerated robbers is biased. To the extent that committing more rob-

---

rely on arrest figures, or interviews with incarcerated offenders, we wouldn't have much knowledge about the behavior of serious criminals."

beries increases one's chances of arrest, the offense rates of those arrested for robbery may well be higher than, and hence misrepresent, the offense patterns of robbers generally.

Whatever technique is used, such estimates are hazardous. They require gauging the criminal activities not only of robbers now in hand but also of robbers in the bush—those active in the community and not under any form of official surveillance or control. The number of such persons can be surmised only by one or another fallible method. Still more fallible will be estimates of the frequency with which they commit robberies. The resulting projections of incapacitative effect will necessarily be speculative and need to be hedged by numerous caveats. Perhaps such estimates may still be useful for general criminological research. But one should be skeptical about their use to justify ambitious programs of depriving so-called high-risk offenders of their liberty for protracted periods.

Prison Overcrowding and Selective Incapacitation

Let us turn, then, to the issue of prison overcrowding. Selective incapacitation advocates assert that their strategy is uniquely useful for solving prison overcrowding.[18] Peter Greenwood has supplied calculations purporting to show how a predictive sentencing policy can conserve prison resources.[19] How sound are such assertions?

NEED FOR SELECTIVENESS

Selective incapacitation advocates begin with a true statement, indeed, a truism: to remain within the available prison resources, one must develop *some* policy of selection among convicted offenders. The unrestricted imprisonment of felons will simply overwhelm the prisons. It is therefore essential to supply a workable and systematically applied standard for deciding which felony cases are important enough to warrant the prison sanction and which are less important. One problem with many purported sentencing reforms to date is that they have failed to supply any such standard. California presents a case in point. The greatest deficiency of the California determinate-sentencing statute is that it furnishes no systematic standards for deciding whether or not a felon should be sent to prison; but merely regulates the duration of confinement *if* the judge exercises his discretion to imprison.[20] It is therefore not surprising that there has been an uncontrolled influx into California's already overcrowded state institutions.

To say one needs to be selective does not, however, decide the critical issue: the criterion for selection. One alternative criterion would be to rely principally on desert. Then, the people imprisoned would be those convicted of serious crimes, that is, crimes involving grave harm and a high degree of culpability. The alternative criterion would be one emphasizing prediction. Then, the main determinant for going to prison would be the gravity and frequency of the felon's expected future violations. It is far from obvious why the latter, predictive selection method is a superior way of conserving prison space than the former, desert-oriented one.

CHOOSING THE CRITERIA FOR SELECTION: THE MINNESOTA EXPERIENCE

An illuminating comparison between these criteria has already been made, in the construction of Minnesota's sentencing guidelines. That state's sentencing commission, as I mentioned in chapter 8, decided at the outset that its guidelines should take the availability of prison space into account. The commission then drew the in-out line on its sentencing grid. In determining the slope of the line, it compared two philosophies: a desert approach that would produce a relatively flat line, and an incapacitation approach that would produce a much steeper one. Ultimately, the commission decided to adopt a line that it characterized as a "modified" desert line, and that emphasized the gravity of the offense for most cases.[21] The basis of the commission's decision was, in part, a philosophical preference for a sentencing policy that stressed the blameworthiness of criminal conduct.

One can agree or disagree with the commission's decision on grounds of principle. But the commission's choice to adopt the flatter in-out line instead of a steeper one did not require increased prison space. The flatter line means that Minnesota imprisons a larger proportion of defendants convicted of serious crimes, but compensates by imprisoning fewer of those convicted of intermediate and lesser crimes.* Had the commission adopted instead the

---

*For the effect of the guidelines on sentencing practice, see Appendix 2.

steeper line reflecting a philosophy of individualized prediction* this would have reallocated the use of imprisonment. By focusing on the risk of future criminality, such a scheme would have allowed more selectivity in use of imprisonment among offenders convicted of the graver crimes. However, it would also have required the imprisonment of a larger proportion of offenders convicted of intermediate-level crimes where the length of their criminal record (or prediction scores) indicated they were bad risks. Either approach would have involved approximately the same aggregate prison resources.

Greenwood disregards this important point in his calculations of prison population impact. He takes his sample of convicted robbers and compares the impact of these two alternatives: (1) a policy of imprisoning or presumptively imprisoning all such robbers, and (2) a policy (which he identifies as predictive) of imprisoning only those robbers whom he identifies as high risks. It is scarcely surprising that the latter policy uses less prison space, because it imprisons only some, not all, of the convicted robbers. But this comparison is misleading. A predictive standard aimed at restraining potential high-risk offenders could not limit imprisonment to a selected subgroup of those convicted of such serious crimes as robbery. It would also have to imprison other dangerous persons— offenders who now stand convicted of intermediate crimes, but whose prior records suggest they may be dangerous. There may well be considerable numbers of such persons, and prison populations would soar once one began including them.

THE POLITICAL PRESSURES ARGUMENT

If a selective incapacitation rationale is not intrinsically the more parsimonious in its use of prisons, advocates of that rationale are left with a political argument—that a predictive approach is somehow less vulnerable to pressures to escalate punishments than other approaches. I find this argument unconvincing.

A desert model, we have seen, would limit the use of imprisonment principally to specified serious crimes. In Minnesota's and Washington's sentencing guidelines, this conception has been implemented, in part, as a policy that uses state imprisonment chiefly for crimes involving threatened violence such as robbery and worse

---

*For discussion of why a rationale of individualized prediction would call for a steep in-out line, see chap. 11.

offenses, and normally uses nonprison sanctions for not quite so serious offenses such as burglary (except where the offender's criminal record is lengthy).[22]

As a practical matter, can the line be held at this level? Given pervasive public fears of crime and the political benefits of taking tough anticrime postures, will there not be strong incentives for making the scheme more inclusive, for imprisoning large numbers of lesser offenders? Certainly, such pressures exist, and resisting them is no easy matter. The most useful safeguards may well be those which Minnesota and Washington both have utilized, to wit: Having the sentencing standards written by an independent rule-making body that is less vulnerable to law-and-order politics than the legislature, and tying the standard-setting process to the availability of prison resources.[23] Escalation in punishment levels have been more evident in states where these safeguards have been absent. In California, for example, the legislature sets durations of imprisonment and has given little consideration to the availability of prison space.[24] But even in jurisdictions such as Minnesota and Washington, demands for increased punishment will not be easily resisted. Only time will tell how well those states will be able to hold the line at present levels.

This problem of pressures to escalate would by no means be avoided, however, were one to make the dispositional line steeper —that is, were one to shift toward a selective incapacitation rationale for the system. Greenwood's calculations about prison space are made on the assumption that imprisonment is to be used chiefly to isolate those predicted to commit frequent robberies or other serious crimes in the future. This would mean that potential medium-rate robbers would be imprisoned only for short periods, or not at all. Such narrowly drawn incapacitative policies are hardly likely to satisfy law-and-order constituencies for long.

There is reason to suspect that an incapacitative approach is, if anything, more vulnerable to escalation than a desert-oriented system would be. The latter, at least, makes no promises to reduce crime. A system of predictive restraint, by contrast, promises to prevent crime by isolating dangerous people. Every time such a system misses (i.e., fails to imprison) offenders who subsequently rob or assault, pressures will increase to make the definition of dangerousness more inclusive. It should be recalled that selective incapacitation indices show a high false-negative rate. Greenwood's false-negative rate was about 16 percent (see chapter 9). So that one out of every six convicted robbers who are classified as medium or low risks will, in fact, commit frequent robberies on release. (The number of these false negatives thus may be nearly as great as the number of persons classified as high risks!)[25] As the high incidence of "misses" becomes known, demands will intensify to increase the numbers of offenders imprisoned or the duration of their imprisonment. A legislature or sentencing commission that opts for selective incapacitation is likely to face the difficulties that parole boards now face when they release prisoners who subsequently commit violent acts. They will be held responsible for failing to perform their self-proclaimed function of protecting the public from recidivists.

Selective incapacitation advocates thus have failed to establish that their predictive approach to sentencing is, in its impact on prison resources, a superior criterion for selection than an alternative criterion such as desert. On the contrary, by promising to protect the public from dangerous felons and yet overlooking substantial numbers of actually dangerous individuals, selective incapacitation is likely to prove particularly vulnerable to demands for increased use of imprisonment.*

---

*Another parallel comes to mind: the civil commitment to mental hospitals of persons acquitted on grounds of insanity. Because such persons are deemed incapable of choice, the only alternative basis for deciding commitments is the individual's dangerousness. Regardless of the definition of dangerousness adopted in such proceedings, calls are heard to make that definition more inclusive. Whereas the false positive has no opportunity to show he would not have caused the injury if released, the false negative remains at large, coming to public attention when he injures someone again. The public holds officials responsible for mistaken releases.

CHAPTER 11

Ethical Problems: The "No Conflict" Thesis

In the preceding two chapters, I have been speaking of the effectiveness of selective incapacitation. Let me turn, now, to its ethics.

During the first six decades of this century, few doubts were raised about the morality of using prediction in sentencing. The American positivist penal ethic, while giving rhetorical emphasis to rehabilitation, granted wide scope for prediction also. Doubts about the justice of predictive sentencing began to be voiced in earnest in the 1970s, as the traditional positivist doctrine began to lose its influence. One line of criticism concerned the tendency of forecasts of criminality to overpredict—the high rate of false positives. The more fundamental objection, one that could not be solved by increasing the accuracy of forecasts, was that of undeserved punishment: condemning people for choices not yet made (see chapter 1).

Some writers continued to espouse predictive sentencing,* and were prepared to brush these objections aside. Michael Sherman and Gordon Hawkins, in a 1981 book urging an incapacitative focus for sentencing, ridiculed the concern about false positives as a quest for "perfect justice" in an imperfect world.[1] A task force of the American Bar Association, in its 1979 report on criminal

---

*In chap. 1, I mentioned that support for predictive sentencing receded in the late 1970s. However, a neopositivist school did remain in existence, albeit with only modest influence. It sought to preserve the predictive (though not the rehabilitative) element in traditional America positivist doctrine. The American Bar Association's 1979 task force report on sentencing reflected this view. See Andrew von Hirsch, "Utilitarian Sentencing Resuscitated: The American Bar Association's Second Report on Criminal Sentencing."

sentencing,[2] argued that desert is no more than a marginal constraint barring gross disproportion in lenience and severity; within these broad limits, the task force argued, there could be no moral objection to reliance on prediction. The difficulty with such views is that they made predictive sentencing seem acceptable in utilitarian terms merely; those who wished to emphasize individual rights in criminal justice were not likely to be attracted.

The Prima Facie Moral Problems of Selective Incapacitation

Turning to currently proposed selective incapacitation strategies, the twin problems of overprediction and undeserved punishment seem very much present. The rate of false positives remains disturbingly high. In the Greenwood study, as I have noted, over half of those classified as high-risk offenders in fact show low or medium robbery rates (see chapter 9). The problem of undeserved punishment remains more formidable still. Selective incapacitation strategies potentially involve drastic infringment of the ordinal proportionality requirements of desert. We are not speaking of slight differences in the punishment of offenders convicted of similar crimes but of large ones. According to Greenwood's calculations, a selective incapacitation strategy could have a significant impact on robbery rates only if high-risk robbers are treated *much* more severely than lower-risk ones. These large differences in convicted robbers' sentences would depend on factors (such as those listed in Greenwood's prediction score)[3] that have little or no apparent bearing on the blameworthiness of the offender's criminal conduct.

Faced with these moral difficulties, some advocates of selective incapacitation opted for the tough line, of dismissing desert and similar moral constraints as unimportant.* Other proponents,

---

*Greenwood, in 1981 congressional testimony ("Statement before Subcommittee on Juvenile Justice," 106), made this memorable assertion:

> After reviewing the literature on prevention, rehabilitation, deterrence and incapacitation—the only four crime reduction mechanisms available to government—it is clear that only incapacitation theory provides reasonable grounds for determining the relative severity with which different convicted offenders should be sentenced. *The only other basis for distinguishing among offenders is deserved punishment or vengeance and here anyone's values are as good as anyone else's.* (Emphasis mine.)

however, have believed this course to be unwise. Disregard for the ethical issues, they felt, would limit the potential appeal of selective incapacitation. They have come forward with a variety of arguments suggesting that, contrary to appearances, it is fair to rely extensively on predictions of future criminality in sentencing decisions. Let me examine the main defenses that have been offered for the "justice" of selective incapacitation.

The "Sunlight" Argument

One defense that has been offered for selective incapacitation is that it brings prediction into the light of day. The sentencing system, the argument runs, long has relied and will continue to rely on forecasts of recidivism. An explicit, statistically based prediction scheme is preferable to the alternative of judicial decisions based on hunches about who is dangerous. A formalized selective incapacitation index, such as Greenwood's, is at least testable; the factors on which it relies are expressly specified; and its rate of error is knowable, and likely to be lower than the error rate of unverified predictive judgments.[4]

The argument strikes me as untenable. To say that selective incapacitation is better than prediction-by-hunch fails to show that it is good enough, or fair enough, to warrant use in decisions affecting the liberty of convicted persons. When all that sunlight is shed, what we chiefly observe is how flawed the prediction techniques are. With Greenwood's prediction scheme, I have noted the many problems already: its lack of predictive efficacy, when official data about defendants' criminal and social histories (rather than self-reports) are utilized; and the wide potential divergence in the punishment of high- and lower-risk robbers that is required in order to yield the promised crime-control benefits.[5] To say that such deficient methods are superior to univerified predictions says very little in their favor. If predictive sentencing is of such doubtful accuracy and fairness when formalized, it is not a sufficient justification to say that informal predictions are worse still.

The sunlight argument assumes that there is consensus on the propriety of predictive sentencing—and that the only choice is

Since then, however, even he has become more cautious, and concedes that desert might have some residual limiting role. For Greenwood's more recent views, see "Response to Panelists," 75.

the pragmatic one between predictive judgments informally made by individual judges versus systemwide predictive policies based on statistical studies. But no such consensus exists today. Sentencing standards and guidelines in several jurisdictions have attempted to restrict the use of prediction in sentencing and to rely principally (if not exclusively) on desert judgments.[6] Proponents of selective incapacitation such as Wilson and Greenwood have argued that imposing such restrictions is not the appropriate direction for reform; that predictions of future criminality should be emphasized rather than suppressed in formal sentencing standards.[7] They thus are aware that real disagreement exists today about the role of prediction in sentencing. Given such disagreement, it is misleading to say the sentencing system is bound to emphasize prediction anyway, and hence that problems of the accuracy and equity of predictive judgments need not be cause for concern.

The "No-Conflict" Argument: The Supposed Convergence of Selective Incapacitation and Desert Criteria

Another line of argument suggests that no real conflict exists between prediction and desert, if the concept of prediction is carefully analyzed. The dangerous offender may be punished more severely, according to this view, because his dangerousness makes him also deserving of more punishment. Professor Mark Moore has been the principal proponent of this position.[8]

The best single available predictor of future criminality, it long has been known, is the offender's criminal record.[9] Yet prior convictions may be germane as well to an offender's deserts. Although some desert theorists have argued that offenders' previous convictions should be disregarded, others (including myself) have maintained that prior criminality does have a legitimate role to play.[10] If the criminal history bears both on risk and on desert, then is not the conflict between these purposes more apparent than real? Mark Moore seizes upon this argument and makes it his central thesis. The criteria for prediction and for desert are or can be made to overlap or coincide. By focusing on the criminal record, one can both identify those who are bad risks and those who deserve to be punished more. In Moore's words:

The third line of defense for "selective incapacitation" is to shift our perspective and place the policy squarely in the context of "retributivist" or "justice" ideals. From this perspective, selective incapacitation is not a policy based on predictions of future misconduct, but is, instead, a policy designed to discriminate among criminal offenders according to their degree of "wickedness." We punish some offenders more harshly than others (given identical offenses) not because we "predict" that some offenders are more active than others, but because some offenders reveal themselves to be more determinedly criminal than others, and therefore more deserving of punishment. The willingness to commit serious offenses repeatedly merits punishment more than episodic offenses. In this view, enhanced punishment for habitual offenders is not based on predictions of future conduct but instead on retributivist ideas about how a person who has acted in certain ways in the past deserved punishment.[11]

Making prediction coincide with desert might, Moore admits, involve some loss of forecasting accuracy—because prediction factors unrelated to the defendant's prior criminal record have to be excluded.[12] Nevertheless, the overlap between desert and predictive criteria—the fact that both rest on prior criminality—means to Moore that one can pursue selective incapacitation without sacrificing equity.

In developing this thesis, one would have expected Moore to analyze the idea of desert in some detail. He does not do so and, in fact, examines virtually none of the desert literature.[13] Moore seems to view "retributivism" (as he calls it) as little more than a kind of popular moral theology. However, others (such as Gottfredson, Wilkins, and Hoffman in their influential book on parole and sentencing guidelines)[14] likewise have raised the question of the overlap of desert and predictive criteria. So we must ask: to what extent *do* those criteria overlap? My answer is, not much, for three important reasons.

WEIGHT GIVEN PRIOR CONVICTIONS

The first (and perhaps the most critical) distinction between desert and selective incapacitation concerns the weight given the prior criminal record. The recent desert literature explicitly addresses this issue of weight. I have argued that first offenders deserve to be penalized somewhat less severely than those previously convicted. Richard Singer and George Fletcher have, as I mentioned, taken the more uncompromising view: the person has been punished already for his prior convictions, and hence those convictions should not affect the punishment he now deserves at all. In other words, the prior criminal history should either receive secondary emphasis (my view) or none (theirs).

With prediction of individual risk, the focus shifts from the current offense to the previous convictions. Since one's aim is to select the high-risk individuals among those convicted of a specified crime, the current crime itself cannot be a very useful predictor. Traditional prediction indices did not rely much on the character of the current offense. Instead, they chiefly used factors related to the offender's previous criminal history, such as the number of previous arrests or convictions, number of previous incarcerations, or the presence or absence of parole revocations.[15]

The new selective incapacitation studies have continued this emphasis on previous offenses. The two RAND studies deal with the crime of robbery.[16] However, their robbery samples contain variations both in the degree of heinousness of offenders' current offenses, and in the extent and nature of their criminal records. Which of these two dimensions, the current offense or the prior history, do these studies emphasize? Plainly, the latter. Neither Greenwood's prediction score nor the Chaikens' use characteristics of the current robbery. In fact, the Chaikens explicitly state that information relating to the current crime—for example, the use of a weapon or injury to the victim—has little or no predictive value.[17] Both prediction indices rely heavily on the offender's previous offense history. In Greenwood's score, four of his seven predictive factors concern the criminal record.[18] Similarly, the factors that the Chaikens found to be most predictive of high robbery rates concerned the offender's history of violence as a juvenile.[19]

These differences between desert and selective incapacitation become strikingly apparent when illustrated on a sentencing grid. On a desert rationale, the gravity of the current crime would carry the preeminent weight (as was shown earlier in figure 7.3). The grid's in-out line would either be flat (reflecting the Fletcher-Singer position) or else slightly sloped (reflecting my position).

On a selective incapacitation rationale, by contrast, the in-out line would be much steeper. Where a prediction score is used as the horizontal axis, the predictive measure would by definition have to be emphasized. But even where the horizontal axis represents the criminal history, we have just seen how that history, rather than

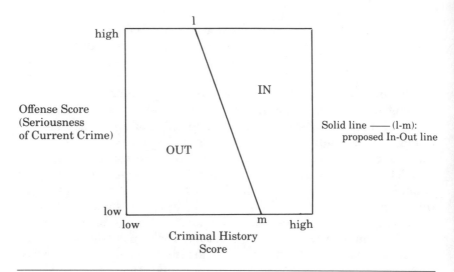

FIGURE 11.1. **In-Out Line in Selective Incapacitation Rationale**

the current offense, serves best to indicate individual risk. If the aim is to identify the high-risk offender, therefore, the horizontal dimension of the grid should influence sentences most, as shown in figure 11.1* The stark difference between the flat or gently sloped line of a desert model and the steeply sloped line of a selective incapacitation model demonstrates the implausibility of Moore's thesis that individual prediction coincides with desert.†

*The lower portion of the in-out line shown in figure 11.1 is only an approximation. Selective incapacitation involves prediction of serious recidivism, and the studies to date have focused on offenders convicted of serious or intermediate crimes. I am assuming here that similar factors concerning the criminal record could predict serious recidivism by those currently convicted of lesser crimes, to the extent such prediction is possible at all.

†Moore, at one point in his report (Mark Moore, Susan Estrich, and Daniel McGillis, *Dealing with Dangerous Offenders,* 139), tries to defend his position by as-

PRIOR CONVICTIONS VERSUS PRIOR ALLEGED CRIMES

A second distinction in the way desert and selective incapacitation use the previous criminal history concerns the treatment of past convictions versus past alleged crimes. The desert rationale for sentencing, as discussed in chapter 3, is a condemnation theory: it is based on the blaming implications of punishment. If an offender's deserts are to be affected at all by his prior criminal acts, they must be so only to the extent that those prior acts bear on the censure due the defendant.

Censuring someone through the criminal process surely should involve conviction. Not only does a conviction provide a more reliable indication of guilt than does an arrest or an indictment, but imposition of sentence following conviction is and should be the one formal mode of condemnation of the criminal process. Given this essential link between censure and adjudication, the degree of disapprobation now visited on the convicted defendant— if altered at all because of his earlier crimes—should be altered only if he has been duly and officially judged guilty of those prior crimes. On a condemnation theory of desert, it is difficult to imagine reliance on previous unadjudicated crimes. That is why desert theorists, to the extent they utilize prior criminal record, insist on taking only prior convictions into account.[20]

When developing a prediction index, the case is otherwise. One seeks criteria that best account for variations in the levels of offenders' criminal activity. To the extent that self-reports, arrests, or similar data provide a more complete statistical indication of the extent of criminal activity than do convictions, such evidence is more useful for predictive purposes. For current selective incapacitation research, this holds particularly. The research, as we saw, focuses on rates of criminal activity; its entire purpose is to distinguish high-rate offenders from offenders whose criminal activity is less intense. Because the likelihood of conviction for serious offenses is so low, information about frequency of conviction does not serve well to separate high-rate from low-rate felons. Selective incapacitation researchers have therefore been compelled to seek other ways of estimating felons' rates of offending. The RAND

---

serting that desert judgments in the criminal law are really judgments about the offender's "character"; and that his character is best revealed in the extent of his criminal history. He seems to be espousing a "whole life" theory of criminal desert, one that involves an evaluation not so much of the particular act before the court, but of the actor's entire career. I have spelled out the deficiencies of this view in chap. 7.

technique was to rely on the self-reports of incarcerated robbers (see chapter 9).

Mark Moore is explicit about the need to rely on more than convictions when developing a selective incapacitation index. In fact, he constructs a table comparing the potential crime-reduction effects of utilizing three types of indices: (1) a forecasting index using only prior convictions, (2) an index also using arrests and indictments, and (3) an index using all predictor variables, including employment and drug use. (The estimates are based on Greenwood's method of gauging the crime-reduction effect.) The table suggests substantial crime-reduction effects for indices (2) and (3)—namely, up to 12 to 15 percent reductions; but it shows only a minimal effect for (1), a selective-incapacitation index utilizing conviction records only.[21] What Moore overlooks is the devastating implications of this finding for his own argument. Predictive sentencing apparently can have the beneficial effects he promises only if it relies upon a criterion of prior criminality that a desert rationale cannot use—a criterion that sweeps in self-reports, arrests, or other nonadjudicative indications of past offending. He overlooks the point precisely because he has not considered the implications of the desert rationale as a condemnation theory.*

USE OF MORALLY IRRELEVANT FEATURES OF THE RECORD

A final distinction concerns what features of the prior criminal record are to be considered. To the extent that prior convictions

---

*Moore's insensitivity to this issue is illustrated by his argument that dangerous offenders deserve extra punishment for the many undetected crimes they "must have" committed. After stating that high-rate offenders commit more unpunished offenses than low-rate offenders, he asserts:

> To the extent that high rate offenders are treated more leniently (relative to their acts) than low-rate offenders, an important inequity is introduced into the system. One way of compensating for this inequity is to introduce a policy of selective incapacitation that would make the distribution of punishment fit the distribution of rates of offending much more closely than it would if we left the system to its natural operations. In this sense, then, the system would be fairer among offenders than it is now. (Moore, Estrich, and McGillis, *Dealing with Dangerous Offenders*, 145–146)

The argument is reminiscent of a person who argues that rapists deserve to suffer a trebling of the current rape penalty, because they supposedly get away with at least two rapes for every one for which they are convicted. No one who is aware that the desert rationale rests on notions of condemnation would seriously suggest that offenders deserve extra punishment for crimes for which they were never caught or convicted.

should affect offenders' deserts at all, the relevant dimension of the record would be the degree of blameworthiness of the previous conduct. That depends on how frequent, and possibly also on how serious, the prior conviction offenses were.[22] A predictive rationale, by contrast, permits one to treat the criminal record in a manner that has nothing to do with the degree of blameworthiness of the defendant's past choices. Morally irrelevant features of the prior offense may be considered, to the extent that these features help predict future crimes.

To see how heavily selective incapacitation strategies focus on aspects of the record having little relevance to blameworthiness, let us look again at Greenwood's predictive index.[23] Of Greenwood's seven factors, three do not measure the criminal record at all: they deal with the offender's drug involvement and employment history. Of the remaining four predictive factors, two concern the offender's age at first contact with the criminal justice system. These are "conviction before age of sixteen," and "served time in a juvenile facility." Consider two convicted robbers: one has a fairly lengthy record of serious crimes, but the convictions occurred while he was an adult; the other has a previous record of fewer serious crimes, but his criminal career began earlier—he was convicted and incarcerated as a juvenile. It is the latter offender who would fare worse on Greenwood's scale, although his record reflects the less reprehensible behavior. Youthfulness when first convicted or confined has long been known to be associated with recidivism.[24] If it has any bearing on an offender's desert, however, the fact that the crime was committed when the offender was very young should make him *less* culpable, not more.[25]

Greenwood's final two factors are "conviction of instant offense type," and "incarceration more than half the preceding two years." One might argue these have some bearing on the gravity of the criminal record, as they require a prior robbery conviction or some other recent conviction serious enough to impose at least a year's imprisonment. But the link is crude. The first of these two factors means that the sentence depends not on the gravity of the record but on the coincidence of past and present offense types. The robber convicted of a prior robbery meets the criterion; the robber with a *worse* record but one that does not hapen to involve robberies—say, the robber with a record of prior serious assaults— does not meet the criterion and hence potentially qualifies for the more lenient sentence. The second factor has comparable problems. The offender with a single recent robbery conviction may have served a larger proportion of the last two years in prison than an offender with a much more extensive record of crimes occurring somewhat less recently. Even after making allowances for "decay" of the criminal record,[26] the results hardly square with desert.

It would not be easy to cure such problems. These predictor items are designed as proxies for high self-reported rates of offending. The above items, or similar ones, happen to be correlated with that high robbery rate. Changing the items to correspond better with the gravity of the record could easily destory the correlation.

To summarize: a desert rationale utilizes the criminal record in a wholly different fashion than selective incapacitation would. (1) Desert calls for primary emphasis on the seriousness of the *current* crime, with only a secondary role (if any) given to the criminal record. Selective incapacitation, by contrast, rests almost entirely on the prior criminal history and on status factors such as employment and drug use.* (2) Desert relies on convictions, whereas selective incapacitation techniques need to utilize arrests or other nonadjudicative indicia of prior offending. (3) Desert requires the sentencer, to the extent that prior crimes are considered, to take into account only those features that bear on those crimes' blameworthiness, such as their number and seriousness; a selective incapacitation approach tends toward the use of other features of previous crimes that have no relevance to their reprehensibleness. Moore's thesis, that the criteria for selective incapacitation coincide or can be made to overlap closely with those for desert, is not sustainable.

---

*Some defenders of predictive sentencing, such as Barbara Underwood, have suggested it should be permissible not only to use criminal-record items, but also any other facts about the defendant's history concerning which he had a choice — so that only status factors such as age or race (and perhaps some constitutionally protected choices such as marital status) could be excluded. This would mean unemployment would be excluded as a factor — but drug use included. Included also might be voluntary actions that are not illegal, such as alcohol abuse. See Barbara Underwood, "Law and the Crystal Ball: Predicting Behavior with Statistical Inference and Individualized Judgment," 1436–1442; for a critique of Underwood's views, see von Hirsch, "Utilitarian Sentencing Resuscitated," 779–783.

This view, even more than Moore's, would make the sentence depend on matters concerning the offender's history that were not germane to the criminal character of his choices. The offender could suffer added punishment on account of past voluntary acts that were not crimes at all, and perhaps in no way reprehensible.

CHAPTER 12

Prediction within Broad Desert Limits?

With the failure of Moore's "no conflict" thesis, there is no escaping the proposition that desert and prediction of individual risk use different criteria and are in potential conflict. Can, then, a case for predictive sentencing be made on other than purely utilitarian grounds?

In his newest essay on the subject,[1] Norval Morris suggests it can.* Prediction, he asserts, is permissible within stated desert constraints. His proposals thus recognize the importance of desert, and acknowledge candidly the tension between retributive and utilitarian concerns. Morris's aim is to provide a synthesis—a mixed model embracing both prediction and desert. The question is whether the synthesis succeeds, and provides useful guidance to rulemakers.

Morris proposes two principles that should guide the use of forecasts of criminal conduct in sentencing. They are:

> 1. *Desert.* Punishment should not be imposed, nor the term of punishment extended, by virtue of a prediction of dangerousness, beyond that which would be justified as a deserved punishment independently of that prediction.
>
> 2. *Validation.* The base expectancy rate for the criminal predicted as dangerous must be shown by reliable evidence

---

*Norval Morris and Marc Miller, "Predictions of Dangerousness." Morris's present view represents a considerable change of position. In his 1974 book (*The Future of Imprisonment*, chap. 3), he opposed use of individual predictions in sentencing because of their high false-positive rates.

to be substantially higher than the base expectancy rate of another criminal, with a closely similar criminal record and convicted of a closely similar crime, but not predicted as unusually dangerous, before the greater dangerousness of the former may be relied upon to intensify or extend his punishment.[2]

The first proposition is intended to prevent disproportionately severe punishments. Traditional positivist sentencing schemes, with their high maximum penalties, permitted imposition of lengthy prison sentences on persons convicted of lesser felonies when those persons were deemed risks. (The Model Penal Code, for example, authorized prison sentences of up to ten years for supposedly dangerous offenders convicted of the *least* serious of the code's three degrees of felonies.)[3] Morris's proposition would rule out such harsh sentences, by barring reliance on prediction to raise sentences above the most that could plausibly be deemed deserved for the crime.

Prediction would be permissible below this upper desert limit, however. It could be used in the space between the manifestly too severe and the manifestly too lenient.[4] Morris's proposition thus reflects the position of his that I discussed in chapter 4, namely, that desert furnishes only the bounds on permissible punishment and does not govern decisions on relative severities within those limits. The ordinal requirements of desert are to be disregarded.* Offenders whose crimes are equally reprehensible could receive substantially unequal punishments if their degrees of dangerousness differ. In fact, offenders whose crimes were, comparatively, the less serious could receive severer punishments on predictive grounds.

I believe Morris is mistaken in thus downgrading the ordinal requirements of desert; that, given the censuring implications of punishment, it is unjust to give unequal punishments—and thereby unequal amounts of condemnation—to offenders whose

---

*In his 1982 book, Morris still speaks of the parity requirement—of treating equally blameworthy offenders equally—as a "guiding" if not determining principle (*Madness and the Criminal Law*, 198). This might give the ordinal proportionality requirements some significance, although it is not clear how much. In his more recent article on dangerousness, however, desert is treated purely as supplying limits (Morris and Miller, "Predictions of Dangerousness"). Parity is disregarded entirely.

conduct is equally reprehensible. Having spelled this objection out already in chapter 4, I need not reiterate it here.

Morris's proposed rejection of ordinal proportionality means that the only desert constraint left to him are the outer limits barring manifest disproportionality. How clearly has Morris delineated these bounds? Hardly at all. After stating that desert should be a "limiting" principle, Morris neither specifies the breadth of those limits nor suggests principles that would guide one in ascertaining them.

The failure to define the retributive constraints has worrisome implications for Morris's view of prediction. One simply does not know by how much a sentence may be increased—beyond that justified on other grounds—in reliance on forecasts of dangerousness. To say that prediction is permissible provided the sentence does not become excessive provides no guidance, if the criteria for excessiveness are left unspecified. Morris does say at one point that he wishes the desert limits to be meaningful ones, that he does not propose returning to the old positivist schemes which left unrestricted scope for predictive judgments subject only to statutory maximums designed for the worst conceivable case of the offense.[5] This, however, still leaves unexplained how much more restrictive the desert limits should be than that. Are narrow desert limits being urged that substantially restrict the scope of predictive judgments, or much wider limits that permit the sentence to be determined primarily on predictive grounds? Or are the limits somewhere in between? There is no way of telling.

To see how troublesome these ambiguities are, consider the following scenario. A sentencing commission is writing a hypothetical state's sentencing guidelines. The commission has agreed (or thought it has) upon Morris's principle of allowing the use of predictions within desert limits. A member of the commission, whom we shall call Commissioner A, comes forth with a scheme that he says takes both prediction and desert into account: his scheme emphasizes desert but makes allowance for "fine tuning" based on predictive considerations.[6] His proposal is shown by the dotted line (n-o) in figure 12.1. A's proposal is what sometimes has been called a "modified" desert model.[7] The basic structure of the scheme is shaped by the commensurate deserts principle, but prediction is given limited scope in the choice of penalties. Compared to the desert line, the proposed line has a modest clockwise twist: a few more matrix cells with low criminal history scores are

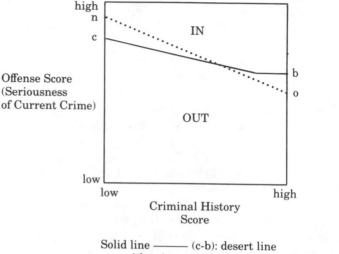

FIGURE 12.1. **Commissioner A's Proposed In-Out Line**

assigned nonprison dispositions, and a few more cells with high criminal histories qualify for prison terms.

Another commission member, Commissioner B, admires Wilson and Greenwood, and is a proponent of selective incapacitation. He objects to A's proposal, because it permits too small a differential in the punishment of low- and high-risk offenders. If prediction is given such a restricted role, he argues, the system will not be capable of yielding the large crime-prevention benefits that Wilson and Greenwood have projected (see chapter 10).

B comes forward with an alternative. The grid, instead of having a criminal history score, should have as its horizontal axis an explicit prediction score based on the newest selective incapacitation studies. This prediction score should carry the *primary*

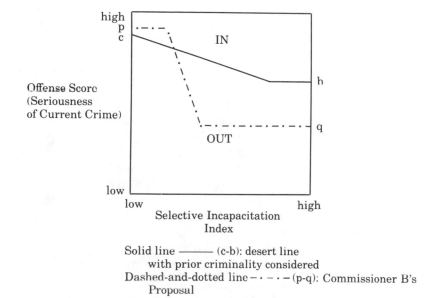

FIGURE 12.2. **Commissioner B's Proposed In-Out Line**

weight in the system. Desert should only prescribe the outer limits: very serious crimes should result in imprisonment, and minor
crimes should not, regardless of risk. His scheme, he asserts, could
be operationalized as the dashed-and-dotted line (p-q) in figure
12.2.* B's plan comes close to what I have elsewhere called a "neo-
positivist" scheme.[8] It relies mainly on prediction and only rules
out punishments that are plainly disproportionate. B could argue
that his scheme nevertheless meets Morris's requirements: although based heavily on prediction, it does not utterly trivialize
desert constraints in the manner that traditional positivist

---

*The desert line in this figure is only an approximation. With a prediction
score (rather than a criminal history score) as the horizontal axis, it is not clear that
this score should affect the slope of the desert line at all.

schemes did. B could point to passages in Morris's writings that seem to countenance, in the name of "parsimony,"* very substantial differences in the punishment of offenders convicted of similar crimes.[9]

The two approaches, A's and B's, are very different indeed. If Morris's theory is to be a useful guide to sentencing policy, it should provide some guidance as to which of two proposals is permissible or preferable, and why. Yet it is difficult to extract principles of choice from his stated views.† Both schemes seem to satisfy his requirements: both would permit use of prediction within desert limits, and neither would make desert either a determining principle or a purely marginal constraint. Yet their difference is crucial, since one scheme relies principally on desert and the other chiefly on prediction.

There is a further, practical difficulty. Suppose the commission accepts Commissioner B's preference for a steeply sloped line. And suppose it adopts, to match the philosophy expressed in that line, rather wide desert limits on durations of confinement: let us say the upper desert limit for robbery is agreed to be five years in prison, and the lower limit to be a year in jail,‡ in the absence of special aggravating circumstances. Once such a selective incapacitation scheme has been instituted, even its upper limits are likely

---

*My own critique of Morris's arguments about "parsimony" is developed in "Equality, 'Anisonomy' and Justice: An Analysis of *Madness and the Criminal Law*," 1105–07.

†The ambiguity is apparent in the one passage where Morris ("Predictions of Dangerousness,") discusses how his scheme might be operationalized. If a jurisdiction has adopted Minnesota-style guideline ranges, he asserts, prediction might be permitted within the upper and lower bounds of those ranges. This seems consistent with Commissioner A's proposal. Since Minnesota's grid relies, in most cases, chiefly on the gravity of the offense and since its ranges are narrow, the scope for prediction would be relatively modest.

If the jurisdiction has no guidelines, however, Morris suggests the following formula: "Presumably, the [statutory maximum] is . . . intended to apply to the "worst case—worst record" offender. We are not suggesting, in such a situation, that predictions of dangerousness justify increments of sentencing up to that maximum. The operating maximum in such a case must be what the judge would think "not undeserved" for such an offender as he has before him." Commissioner B could rely on this passage. The commission should set as its desert limits, he could argue, what a judge in the absence of guidelines could invoke: bounds that are not clearly excessive or insufficient in relation to the gravity of the offense. This could yield the wide desert limits, and extensive scope for prediction, that B's proposals embody.

‡Wide as these bounds seem, they would scarcely suffice for currently discussed selective incapacitation schemes. Greenwood's calculations of crime-preventive impact assume one-year jail terms for low- and medium-risk robbers, but terms of up to *eight* years for high-risk robbers. See Visher, "The RAND Second Inmate Survey."

to be tested. There may be strong incentives for locking up the allegedly most dangerous offenders for *very* long periods of time, and weakly-grounded upper constraints are likely to be ignored. If certain robbers are deemed to constitute long-term risks, and if the retributive ceiling on the permissible punishment for robbery is left so unclear in theory, the sentencing commission will have difficulty resisting demands that the dangerous robbers be confined so long as they are thought dangerous. The situation will be quite different from that obtaining were the ordinal requirements of desert taken seriously. A desert system calls for parity of treatment among convicted robbers—and few, if any systems have the resources to lock up the majority of robbers for a half a decade or more.

Morris's account, therefore, does not provide guidance on how wide should be the desert constraints within which individual predictions may operate. Could this problem be overcome? Could his assumptions be utilized to develop a more definite account? I am not certain of the answer, but a fuller delineation could encounter the following difficulty.

Of ordinal and cardinal desert requirements, the ordinal are considerably more definite. It is easier to judge whether comparative punishments comport with the seriousness ratings of crimes than to assess the conventions anchoring a penalty scale (see chapters 4 and 8). Yet it is precisely those more definite constraints of ordinality that Morris would downplay. I therefore fear that, if one pursues the logic of Morris's position, the result will be wide desert bounds. To draw the bounds more narrowly, one would have to begin relying on the parity and rank-ordering requirments of ordinal proportionality. A reasonably narrow band of permitted punishment for armed robbery cannot be derived, I suspect, solely from thinking of what plainly would be excessive for that crime. Reliance only on cardinal desert is likely to lead to a position such as Commissioner B's, where utilitarian concerns dominate and desert governs only the margins. Yet such a scheme strikes me as the most doubtful in its justice.

Morris's second proposition, dealing with validation, is likewise no strong safeguard. The offender who is treated as dangerous, he states, must fall within a class showing significantly higher offense rates than other offenders not so treated. But unless there were such a difference in rates, no statistical atttribution of risk can be made. Apparently, Morris's point is that the ostensibly dangerous offenders must show these higher rates of offending even after one has controlled for the seriousness of the current crime and the history of prior convictions. This, however, may well be a less stringent constraint than appears, given what has been said already about the limited predictive utility of convictions as opposed to arrests and other nonadjudicative indicia of risk (see chapter 11).

It is my conclusion that recent arguments about the supposed moral acceptability of selective incapacitation do not resolve but merely restate the familiar ethical dilemmas of predictive sentencing. Contrary to Mark Moore's thesis, the criteria for desert and for individual prediction do *not* coincide. Norval Morris's proposed formula leaves unresolved how much predictive restraint there is to be allowed within maximum and minimum bounds based on the gravity of the offense. The wider those maximum and minimum limits, the greater potential difference there may be among punishments of offenders whose blameworthiness is *ex hypothesi* similar. The narrower those limits, the less incapacitative payoff there is likely to be even under the most optimistic calculations. We know today what we long have known: predictive sentencing can be defended given sufficiently uncompromising utilitarian assumptions, but becomes increasingly difficult to defend as concerns about justice are taken seriously in sentencing policy.

Morris's discussion of dangerousness raises an important issue, however: that of synthesizing past and future, of combining desert and predictive elements in a sentencing scheme. If his formula does not succeed, are any alternative modes of synthesis possible?

A synthesis should provide *specific* guidance about the relative weight given desert and predictive elements. In providing that guidance, it should rule out schemes that rely chiefly on selective incapacitation and utilize desert as only a secondary constraint. Whatever the merits of Commissioner A's proposals, those of Commissioner B should be treated as unacceptable, because of the wide potential differences permitted in the punishment of offenders whose conduct is similar. Whether such a synthesis can be achieved, and whether it is desirable, will be the topic of the next part.

PART V

Synthesizing Past and Future

IF SELECTIVE INCAPACITATION is in potential conflict with desert, are there alternate crime-control techniques that are less so? Perhaps the problem is the *selectiveness* of selective incapacitation: picking and choosing defendants for different punishments, among those convicted of similar criminal acts. In chapter 13, I discuss a predictive strategy that is oriented to categories of criminal acts, and tries to avoid the picking and choosing.

Chapters 14 and 15 draw the book to a close. In the first of these, I deal with synthesizing past and future: with the feasibility and wisdom of trying simultaneously to punish proportionately and to enhance scale's crime control effects. In the second, I discuss more generally our aspirations to justice and to reducing crime.∎

CHAPTER 13

Categorial
Incapacitation

American prediction research has, by and large, focused on individual offenders. Various facts about the offender are recorded: age, prior criminal record, employment history, drug problems, and so forth. It is then statistically determined which of these factors are most strongly associated with the offender's criminal activity. This offender-oriented approach is evident not only in traditional prediction studies but also in today's selective incapacitation research.

We have seen the drawbacks already. Given the focus on offender characteristics, the studies yield a list of predictor items having little or no bearing on the blameworthiness of the offender's choices. When one looks for facts about offenders that happen to be associated with recidivism, one obtains just that—a list of predictive factors of no particular moral significance.

The source of the difficulty has, perhaps, been the purported value-free orientation of so much criminal justice research. Criminologists have been inclined to see themselves as scientists, seeking hard evidence about criminality. Values have been treated as peripheral to the research; as being, at most, limitations put on the application of the research once the facts were found. This outlook is manifest in current selective incapacitation studies. The job is seen as that of gauging offender dangerousness. The research design should accomplish this in the most direct possible way, by studying the characteristics of high-rate offenders. Desert constraints are value judgments (a phrase often used dismissively) that have no place in the social scientist's serious business of designing and carrying out the research. With values of proportionality not considered in the construction of the prediction technique, it should not be surprising when that technique conflicts with those values.

There is, however, an alternative: building the constraints of desert, or some of them, into the research design itself. The task of forecasting then changes: it is no longer just to find indicia of future criminality, but to find indicia that *are consistent with limitations dictated by values of desert*. When these limitations are taken seriously, they can change the prediction technique fundamentally. The emphasis may cease to be on individual offender characteristics.

Categorial Incapacitation:
The Cohen Study

Dr. Jacqueline Cohen of Carnegie-Mellon University has been pursuing this line of inquiry.[1] Her idea is to redesign prediction research so that it complies with a stated value, that of desert parity. She has investigated whether anything can be learned about prediction, while treating equally those offenders convicted of the same offenses.

The result of her inquiry is a different prediction strategy: categorial incapacitation. The focus no longer is on individual offender characteristics associated with recidivism but, rather, on *categories* of crimes. Conviction for some crimes may be predictive of an increased average likelihood of convicts' offending again. One tries to identify which crime categories are thus linked with higher recidivism rates.

There has long been some awareness of these links. It was known that convicted murderers seldom committed more acts of violence, and that convicted car thieves and writers of bad checks often stole more cars or wrote more bad checks. But not much systematic inquiry was undertaken until Dr. Cohen's work. She examines, moreover, not only the frequency of recidivism but its gravity: which crime categories are associated with high rates of *serious* recidivism.

Cohen's proposed strategy is distinct also from the "collective" incapacitation strategies that enjoyed a brief vogue in the mid-1970s, of which I spoke in chapter 1. These strategies involved imprisoning defendants convicted of common felonies in order to obtain an across-the-board incapacitative impact from so doing. Her approach is targeted at particular categories of crimes, rather than at felonies or major felonies in general. Its whole point is to identify which crime categories are associated with higher risk.

I shall not describe the design of the Cohen study in detail, as it is somewhat technical and is accessible for interested readers. The basic idea is not difficult, however. Dr. Cohen took a cohort of recently arrested offenders and classified them according to the type of crime for which they were last convicted: robbery, burglary, assault, or whatever. This made it possible to gauge recidivism rates associated with conviction for those various crimes. She tried to approximate that rate by measuring the number of rearrests since the last conviction, and the seriousness of the crimes allegedly involved. When these steps were taken for a cohort of adult offenders in Washington, D.C., Cohen found that conviction for the crime of robbery was associated with the highest rates of subsequent rearrests for serious crimes.

Cohen also considered the magnitude of the categorial incapacitation effects. To do so, she identified those members of her sample whose most recent conviction was for robbery, and estimated the number of rearrests, and number of crimes, that would have been averted had the offenders been incarcerated upon that conviction. She compared those results with the numbers of rearrests and crimes averted with respect to offenders whose most recent conviction was for crimes other than robbery. Using this technique, she found that a policy of imposing two-year prison terms on convicted robbers could have a larger preventive impact than imposing such terms on offenders convicted for other crimes. This policy, she finds, also would not call for large increases in prison populations.

Cohen is sanguine about categorial incapacitation. It can, she asserts, have significant preventive benefits, while observing the ethical constraints of desert. In a recent summary of her research, she asserts:

> This analysis indicates the potential for developing aggregate sentencing policies that achieve differential reductions in crime and are at the same time consistent with concerns for justice and equity in sentencing. Such policies avoid many of the ethical and empirical problems that accompany use of individual-level predictions. To begin with, the severity of the sentence must be commensurate with the seriousness of the offense. Offenders are then subjected to the sentence only on

the basis of the convicted offense and the prior criminal record. Moreover, the sentence is imposed uniformly within a category. No individual predictions of future criminality are employed, and thus the problem of false positives is avoided. Such sentences would immediately be acceptable from a modified just-deserts perspective. To accommodate a more restrictive view of just deserts that does not allow prior convictions to enter into the deserved punishment calculations, the aggregate policy could be reformulated to rely only on the convicted offense.[2]

This statement is somewhat confusing on the subject of the prior criminal record. Dr. Cohen's proposed incapacitation strategy does not use an offender's earlier record, but only his conviction offense.* The point is important because, as we saw in chapters 7 and 11, a heavy emphasis on the prior record is inconsistent with ordinal desert requirements; and one of the difficulties of selective incapacitation is its need to rely so much on the defendant's prior record.

Cohen claims that the problem of false positives is avoided, because individual predictions are not involved. In making this assertion, she does not deny that categorial incapacitation involves overprediction. When one attributes higher risk to conviction for robbery, the false positives are those persons who were so convicted but did not rob again. Cohen is, instead arguing the ethics of the question. Overprediction is objectionable, she is suggesting, when forecasts are used to impose different sentences on equally blameworthy offenders. The convicted robber who is the false positive is entitled to complain, if—on the basis of the mistaken forecast about his future behavior—he gets more punishment than other robbers not deemed dangerous. In categorial incapacitation, however, the robbers who are false positives will be treated no differently from other convicted robbers. (This issue of overprediction and its moral status is discussed further in Appendix 1.)

---

*Cohen takes prior criminal record into account in her research only in order to show that a policy of confining convicted robbers would have a greater preventive impact than the more selective policy of confining robbers having previous robbery records.

Her research design looks from the current arrest back to the offender's most recent conviction. The object, however, is to determine whether the current arrest crime would have been averted had the offender been confined when convicted. Were the research applied in sentencing policy, it would rely on the offender's current conviction offense only.

Does It Work?—Empirical Issues
in Categorial Incapacitation

Cohen admits her research is only a beginning. It is based on retrospective data and should be validated by follow-up studies of the members of her sample. It uses rearrests as the measure of recidivism and should be corroborated using reconvictions. Since her research is drawn from the somewhat unique area of Washington, D.C., it needs to be replicated in other jurisdictions.* But how much does her research establish, so far as it goes?

When speaking of individual prediction, we saw there were two senses in which a predictive sentencing policy might or might not "work." The first concerns whether convicted offenders who are high risks can be identified and isolated. Traditional prediction techniques long had, as we saw, a limited success in identifying offenders with higher than average recidivism rates, notwithstanding their tendency to misclassify many individuals (see chapter 9). The second, and stronger, sense of "working" concerns whether prediction methods, when applied in sentencing policy, are capable of reducing the aggregate incidence of serious crimes. There, the results are less encouraging. Notwithstanding Peter Greenwood's claims about the large crime-reduction potential, we have seen that there is little or no credible supporting evidence (see chapter 10).

A similar distinction needs to be observed for categorial incapacitation. For this prevention technique to work in the first, weaker sense means simply that it is possible to identify certain crime categories, conviction of which is associated with increased rates of serious recidivism. It is plausible that such "high-risk" crime categories exist, and that they could be identified. The research is, if anything, easier than for individual prediction: it is a matter of following the criminal careers of persons convicted of various types of crime. Dr. Cohen's work provides a preliminary indication that conviction for robbery *is* associated with an enhanced likelihood of subsequent criminality, in at least one jurisdiction. It would not be surprising if further research confirmed her findings.

For categorial incapacitation to work in the second, stronger sense means that its use in sentencing can reduce aggregate rates

---

*Dr. Cohen has recently been pursuing similar research on a Michigan sample.

of serious crime. For this to be true, it is not enough to show that conviction for (say) robbery is linked to higher than usual rates of future serious crimes. It is necessary also to show that such recidivism contributes significantly to the overall rate of such crimes; and that potential recidivists' criminal activity, if they are incarcerated, will not be replaced through new recruits. Cohen's calculations do not firmly establish this to be the case, nor does she make any such claim.*

However, success achieved in the first sense (even without reliable estimates of the impact on crime rates) has importance in its own right. If conviction for certain crimes indicates an increased risk of serious criminality, this might be reason itself for visiting such crimes with imprisonment—*if* that can be done in a manner consistent with desert principles.

A further question is the comparative effectiveness of categorial and selective incapacitation. In her report, Dr. Cohen states that categorial incapacitation has a somewhat smaller potential impact on crime, but the offsetting advantage of being fairer. She notes that her estimate of crime-reduction impact (about an 8 percent reduction in robberies) is about half of Greenwood's estimate for a selective incapacitation policy in California.[3] However, this comparison concedes too much. Much of the apparent superiority of selective incapacitation appears attributable to Greenwood's peculiarly optimistic methods of estimation (see chapter 10). Were comparable estimation methods applied, the possible impact of selective incapacitation—and thereby its apparent advantage over categorial incapacitation—would become smaller.

Is It Fair?—
Categorial Incapacitation and Desert

Let us turn, to the ethics of categorial incapacitation. In Dr. Cohen's example of robbery, the strategy seems attractive enough. This crime of threatened violence is serious and, prima facie, de-

---

*Her estimation methods, while more conservative than Greenwood's, involve an element of extrapolation. After obtaining data on the number of *rearrests* averted by confining robbers upon their most recent conviction, she makes an inference to the number of *crimes* averted—by assuming so many unreported crimes per arrest. Were one to eliminate this extrapolation, one could count as crimes averted only those leading to rearrest—or possibly, only to reconviction. The resulting crime-reduction impact from confining the convicted robbers would be considerably smaller.

serving of imprisonment. If two-year terms for robbery have a preventive effect, and if that effect can be achieved while treating equally culpable robbers equally, that is surely a good supporting reason for imposing such terms. With a different example, however, the results become less felicitous. Consider lesser crimes associated with high recidivism rates, such as auto theft. Suppose research were to show the recidivism was not only frequent but serious—that convicted auto thieves were, as a group, likely to graduate to worse crimes in the future. Should this warrant imposing the severe sanction of imprisonment on this less serious offense category?

This last example should remind us that categorial incapacitation addresses, by its definition, only one of the three requirements of commensurability: that of desert parity. The idea is that those convicted of the same type of crime should be punished equally. To satisfy desert principles, however, the two other requirements—of rank ordering and cardinal proportionality—also need to be met. In my auto theft example, they are not. To imprison car thieves because of the risk they pose, while not imprisoning those convicted of other crimes of greater seriousness, violates the rank-ordering requirement. And car theft may well not be serious enough in a cardinal sense to warrant the severe sanction of imprisonment, even if one were to visit similar penalties on other lesser felonies as well.

The fairness of categorial incapacitation depends, therefore, on how that tactic is used. Before invoking imprisonment for a given crime category on account of its incapacitative effects, it is necessary to consider whether *each* of the three requirements of desert are satisfied.

Parity. Because categorial incapacitation attempts to treat equally those convicted of the same offense, the parity requirement seems to be satisfied by definition. However, a little further inquiry is needed. Parity requires not only the equal punishment of equally reprehensible conduct, but the differential punishment of conduct of distinct blameworthiness (see chapter 4). If the statutory crime categories are excessively broad (as they are in some states, such as California)* then imposing a uniform penalty on

*California, for example, defines robbery to include a wide variety of forcible takings, regardless of the degree of force or threatened force used. See Andrew von Hirsch and Julia M. Mueller, "California's Determinate Sentencing Law: An Analysis of Its Structure," 274–276.

conduct of highly variable gravity violates the parity requirment. Such crime categories would need to be subcategorized for sentencing purposes. With reasonably compact categories, however, the parity requirement should normally be satisfied.*

Parity also requires equal treatment of separate crime categories having equal seriousness. Suppose crime categories X and Y have been assigned the same seriousness grade. If recidivism rates for category X offenders are greater than for category Y offenders, it violates parity to confine the former but not the latter. The high recidivism rates found by Cohen for robbers, therefore, would not justify punishing robbery any more severely than other crimes of corresponding gravity.

The risk category must also, let me reiterate, be defined by the current conviction offense—for example, by conviction of robbery. Were prior convictions permitted to enter the definition, one would shift from categorial to selective incapacitation. Suppose, for example, that the risk category is no longer defined simply as convicted robbers, but as convicted robbers having a previous record of robberies. To select this latter group would mean that the punishment of robbers would differ, depending whether their previous convictions were for robbery or for other, possibly no less reprehensible crimes.[4] And it would mean the strategy would lose the emphasis on the current conviction offense that ordinal desert requires.

Rank Ordering. Desert requires penalties to be graded in comparative severity to reflect the gravity of the conduct. Categorial incapacitation should not, therefore, be used to pull any offense out of its rank order. Suppose, for example, that the scale provides for nonprison sentences of varying degrees of onerousness for lesser and intermediate crimes; and that crime category Y has been so graded in seriousness. Suppose, however, that those convicted of crime Y were found to constitute a high risk. It still would be inappropriate to imprison those offenders, while retaining nonprison sentences for persons convicted of other offenses of comparable gravity.

---

*A further question concerns aggravation and mitigation. Even with compact categories, desert principles require that departures from the normally prescribed terms be permitted in cases involving aggravated or mitigated harm or culpability. As such departures would be exceptional, however, they should have little effect on the expected incapacitative impact.

Cardinal Proportionality. This requirement imposes, as we have seen, certain limits on the permissible anchoring points of a penalty scale—which must be observed even if crimes are penalized in the order of their comparative seriousness. Categorial incapacitation effects do not, for example, justify dropping the in-out line so as to imprison offenders convicted of crimes in the lower portion of the sentencing grid. As it happens, there also are strong pragmatic reasons—such as limitations in availability of prison space—militating against such sweeping imprisonment policies.

The preceding account has been a series of "don'ts"—admonitions about when categorial incapacitation would breach desert requirements. What is the remaining usefulness of the strategy? After all, one scarcely needs Dr. Cohen's evidence of categorial incapacitation effects in order to justify the imprisonment of those convicted for robbery. Is not such a violent offense serious enough to warrant imprisonment on desert grounds alone, regardless of the incapacitative consequences? What additional enlightenment does her evidence about the incapacitative effects offer?

To answer these questions, let us return to our hypothetical sentencing commission and its grid. The commission, let us suppose, is using a grid with a ten-point crime seriousness scale and has decided to draw a gently sloped in-out line, giving primary emphasis to the seriousness of the current offense as ordinal proportionality requires. On grounds of cardinal proportionality, it has decided to invoke imprisonment for the most serious crimes—say, crimes in seriousness-categories "8" and higher, including murder, rape, and aggravated assault. On similar grounds, it has ruled out imprisonment for the lesser felonies and for misdemeanors—say, crimes with seriousness scores of "5" and lower, including the common property crimes. The undecided question is what should be done with robberies (scoring "7" on the seriousness scale) and burglaries (scoring "6"). Some commissioners want to draw the line at robbery—so that robbers would be imprisoned, but burglars ordinarily would not (unless their records were lengthy enough to cross the slope of the in-out line). Other commissioners want to include burglars (or some types of burglars) as candidates for presumptive imprisonment. As a result, the commission would be choosing between two possible in-out lines—the dashed "robbers only" line (r-s), and the circle-dotted line (t-u) that imprisons both burglars and robbers—as shown in figure 13.1.

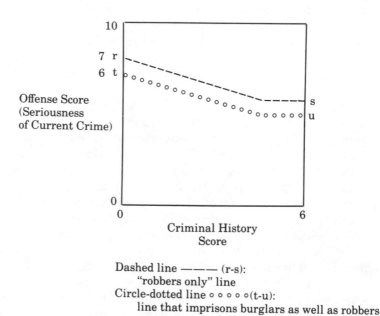

FIGURE 13.1. **Categorial Incapacitation and Fixing the In-Out Line**

The commission cannot resolve this choice by simply appeal-ing to desert principles. Parity provides no guidance, because ei-ther alternative treats equally reprehensible conduct with compa-rable severity. Rank ordering does not help, because either choice is ordered by rank. If the "robbers only" line is selected, then bur-glars would not be imprisoned, but robbers and those convicted of still worse crimes would be imprisoned for terms graded according to the comparative heinousness of those offenses. If the other line is selected, then burglary, robbery, and more heinous crimes would receive graduated prison terms. Cardinal proportionality is not precise enough to provide this guidance: it merely requires imprisonment for the worst crimes and rules it out for crimes less reprehensible than burglary.

In some jurisdictions, prison population constraints might help settle the issue, because confining the burglars would result in large increases in prison commitments (see chapter 8). It will not settle the issue, however, if the burglary caseload is comparatively small (as it is in the Federal judicial system), or if the funds are available to add more prison space.

At this point, evidence of categorial incapacitation effects might be helpful to the commission. Suppose the evidence confirmed Dr. Cohen's findings that convicted robbers had high rates of serious recidivism. Suppose the evidence also showed that burglars either recidivated at lower rates, or that their recidivist crimes tended to be less serious. Such evidence would be reason for preferring the higher, "robbers only" in-out line. Since the burglars constitute reduced risks, drawing the line at the robbers would be consistent with objectives of preventing serious crime and would also conserve prison resources. The choice is consistent with the constraints of ordinal and cardinal proportionality. Under such circumstances—and there may be others imaginable—data about categorial incapacitative effects might provide useful guidance without violating desert principles.

Let me emphasize how a categorial incapacitation strategy comporting with desert would differ from the individual prediction strategies to which I have objected. First, those convicted of equally reprehensible conduct would have to be treated similarly. Categorial incapacitation concentrates on offense categories, not on the selection of a subclass of dangerous persons within an offense category. The emphasis would be neither on the offender's prior record nor on status factors, as is the case with selective incapacitation. Second and equally important, the other requirements of desert need to be complied with: the requirements of rank ordering and cardinal proportionality. Thus it would not be permissible to give convicted car thieves substantial prison sentences, even if researchers were to find that these thieves were high risks. Categorial incapacitation effects might, however, help guide the sentencing commissioner's choice of where to set the elevation of the in-out line within the upper-middle portion of the grid.

CHAPTER 14

Strategies for Synthesis

In the preceding chapter, I described one possible method for introducing crime-prevention aims into sentencing policy, while still satisfying desert requirements. Are there any other possible strategies for synthesizing past and future? Is an attempt at synthesis desirable?

The Feasibility of Synthesis

Let me begin by describing, in more general terms than in the preceding chapter, how a rulemaker might introduce crime-control concerns into a fundamentally desert-oriented scheme. Imagine that the members of a commission have read the present book, and agree so wholeheartedly with its conclusions concerning proportionate punishments that they wish to implement them in the guidelines. (I ask the reader to indulge me in conjuring this happy state of affairs, for illustrative purposes.) However, the members also wish to have their penalty scale take crime-control objectives into account, to the full extent this can fairly be done. How can the commission approach this task? A two-stage process is called for, as follows.

STAGE ONE: CONSTRUCTION OF TENTATIVE GUIDELINES ACCORDING TO DESERT PRINCIPLES

The commission should treat desert as a starting point in constructing the penalty scale: it should first write tentative guidelines with desert principles exclusively in mind. Only after this first step is completed should the commission consider any possible modifications for the sake of crime-control ends. The reason for this two-stage procedure should be apparent. To achieve a synthesis, the commission needs to have the elements of that synthesis clearly delineated. If the commission tries from the outset simultaneously to inject the desert and crime-preventive components, only confusion will result.

To develop its initial, desert-based guidelines, the commission should: scale the seriousness of crimes (see chapter 6); determine the slope of the in-out line, making it comparatively flat to reflect desert principles (see chapter 7); and fix the scale's anchoring points by deciding on the elevation of the in-out line on the grid. In making this last decision, the commission would first delineate some rough upper and lower limits of cardinal proportionality, as described in chapter 8. Within these stated limits, it would then fix the elevation of the line, considering also the availability of prison space as discussed in that chapter. For the moment, the possible categorial incapacitation effects of locating the line somewhat higher or lower would not be considered. When these steps are done, and the grid cells are filled in with penalties of graduated duration, the first stage would be completed.

STAGE TWO: ADJUSTMENTS FOR PREVENTIVE ENDS

In the second stage, the commission's task would be to consider adjustments in the initial guidelines for crime-preventive ends. Those adjustments, however, would need to be done in a manner that preserves the orientation of the system to proportionate, deserved punishments. There are two possible strategies.

One is the strategy of inclusion. The anchoring points on the penalty scale would be reset so as to reflect non-selective crime-control aims, such as categorial incapacitation or (were data available) general deterrence. How that might be done with respect to categorial incapacitation has been described already (chapter 13). The in-out line would be examined, to determine the extent to which it provides prison sentences for those felony categories associated with high rates of serious recidivism. The elevation of the line might then be adjusted to enhance that incapacitation effect. The adjustment should not be so large as to infringe on limits established by cardinal proportionality, however. And any change should not disturb the comparative ordering of punishments developed by the commission in its first stage. The flattish slope of the in-out line should also be preserved, as should the relationships of the penalties in the grid cells.

An alternative possible strategy would be one of limited deviation. The restraints of desert parity would be relaxed to some degree, in order to reflect selective crime-control aims—notably, individual prediction. Variations in the punishment of equally deserving offenders would be permitted on predictive grounds, but the amount of those variations would be strictly limited. Major departures from the requirements of ordinal proportionality would thus continue to be barred as unjust. The model would represent a compromise between desert and selective crime control, but one strongly emphasizing commensurability.

In earlier writing, I have termed this second approach a "modified desert model,"[1] but the term has since been so variously used as to cease to be illuminating.[2] Its theory is to permit use of the existing (albeit very imperfect) capacity to predict individual dangerousness within a system that remains primarily a commensurable one. While modest differences in the punishment of equally blameworthy offenders involves some sacrifice of equity, that sacrifice is not a great one so long as those differences are restricted. The system remains fair, assertedly, because desert continues to have the preeminent role in deciding comparative severity of punishment.

This last approach is different from Norval Morris's theory of prediction within broad desert limits, which I criticize in chapter 12. It requires the rule-making body first to identify what penalties would strictly be deserved, before proceeding with any modifications. This should compel an awareness of how large the departures for predictive purposes are. If the commission initially must draw a relatively flat in-out line to reflect ordinal desert requirements, the extent of deviation from desert will become plainly apparent if the commission starts tilting the line toward the vertical for predictive purposes. In the illustrations in chapter 12, Commissioner A's proposed tilt (figure 12.1) seems a modest deviation, but Commissioner B's (figure 12.2) is surely more than that. Imprecise as the notion of a "modest" deviation is, it should be possible to perceive when prediction rather than desert begins to become the primary determining factor in the grid.* My objection to Morris's

---

*Indeed, as one begins to depart from the initial desert-based scheme, the extent of that departure can be described mathematically. Richard Sparks ("The

theory was that it provided no such guidance. Since that theory does not recognize ordinal proportionality at all, it cannot start with prima facie equal and rank-ordered sanctions but must instead rely on tenuous outer bounds of manifest *dis*proportionality. The theory thus failed, as we saw, to provide guidance as to the comparative weight given the desert and predictive elements.

What are the relative merits of the inclusion and limited deviation strategies? The second strategy, of limited deviation, has the temporary advantage of being capable of implementation today. Since a technology of individual prediction (notwithstanding its limitations) has long been in existence, that technology could be put into immediate use by the commission in its second-stage work of reviewing and possibly modifying the initial guidelines. The first strategy—inclusion—would require some further research, since categorial incapacitation is only beginning to receive serious study.

Nevertheless, the limited deviation strategy seems to me to be much the less desirable of the two approaches. Its drawback in principle is that it necessarily infringes on desert parity; differences on grounds of risk are permitted in the punishments of those whose conduct is equally reprehensible. True, these differences are meant to be modest ones, in order to lessen the sacrifice of equity; but sacrifice it nevertheless is. Requiring only modest deviations will, in turn, restrict the preventive impact: a scheme that offers only slight differences in the punishment of high- and low-risk offenders cannot hope to offer much added public protection.

Still more worrisome is the vulnerability of the scheme to erosion. In practice, it may prove quite difficult to permit only small deviations from desert parity, while holding the line at larger deviations. The operation is like inviting the hungry Doberman to share in the family picnic, but only one bite. Given public fears of the dangerous criminal, the notion of individual risk, once introduced into the guidelines, will be hard to contain. How can the commission publicly justify only a modest increase in the sentence of dangerous criminals, when its own guidelines classify those persons as high risks and when larger increases might seem better to protect the public?

The inclusion strategy strikes me as theoretically and practically more sound. In principle, it involves no deviation from desert

---

Structure of the Oregon Parole Guidelines") has developed a method of identifying the comparative effects on guidelines of the grid's vertical and horizontal axes. His method provides a formula for comparing "row effects" with "column effects."

parity. With the requisite empirical knowledge, it would be possible to consider categorial incapacitation effects in fixing the scale's anchoring points, while simultaneously assuring that penalties are graded to reflect the gravity of crimes and that equally serious crimes are punished equally. The approach could also be less vulnerable in practice. One would not be trying to gauge offenders' dangerousness and yet narrowly restricting the amount of added punishment for offenders who are the high risks. Individual dangerousness would not be part of the guidelines at all, and the incapacitative element would be recast in a nonselective manner. Benefits of crime prevention would be welcomed without restrictions on their magnitude, as long as comparative severities continued to be based on the gravity of the criminal conduct, and as long as the adjustments in the anchoring points of the scale did not cause the scale to violate the limits of cardinal proportionality.

The superiority of the inclusion strategy suggests a shift in the focus of crime-control research. A higher priority should be placed on examining the preventive effects of sanctions that do not call for individualization of punishment. Research on categorial incapacitation needs to be pursued, and even general deterrence merits some new scrutiny.* Criminologists would be wise to relinquish their current preoccupation with selective incapacitation.

In pursuing the inclusion strategy, the rulemaker's caution should increase with the proposed extent of intervention. The sufferings of those imprisoned are inescapable, and will multiply with greater use of imprisonment. The benefits in terms of crimes prevented are contingent on the accuracy of researchers' projections. This warrants particular skepticism about proposals to increase aggregate use of imprisonment beyond that contemplated in the first-stage guidelines.

Let me illustrate. Assume that the first stage of writing the sentencing guidelines produces the dashed in-out line (r-s) shown in figure 13.1—whereby only robbers and those convicted of worse crimes would ordinarily be imprisoned. Suppose research in the jurisdiction were to find a categorial incapacitation effect associated with imprisonment for the less heinous crime of residential burglary. Suppose the commission were to respond by including burglars as candidates for imprisonment—thereby lowering the in-out line to the circle-dotted level (t-u) shown in figure 13.1. This drop

---

*In *Doing Justice* (93–94), I offered some speculations on how deterrence might conceivably be used to anchor a penalty scale, but data is now lacking. See chap. 8, above.

in the elevation of the line would mean that not only burglars but also those convicted of crimes of comparable seriousness would be imprisoned—even though no special risk is found associated with those latter crimes. To maintain proportionality, offenses higher on the seriousness scale may also have to have their prison terms increased. Making imprisonment more comprehensive on categorial incapacitation grounds is thus a very blunt instrument, indeed: its effects extend well beyond the particular offense categories found to involve risk. The sweeping quality of such a measure is reason for hesitancy in invoking it.

The Hazards of Synthesis

Le us next consider the desirability of attempting a synthesis. Once the first-stage desert-based guidelines have been written, *should* the commission proceed to the second stage of possibly changing them for preventive purposes?

My question may seem strange. Surely, we want both to punish past crimes fairly and prevent future crimes. If there are ways of achieving commensurability and enhancing crime prevention, is it not obvious we should seek to do so? Perhaps, but we should pause to reflect on the hazards.

The preventive benefits may be elusive. While having a sentencing system undoubtedly is necessary to prevent crime, tinkering with that system will not necessarily prevent crime much better. The desert-based penalty scale of the first stage may well have collateral incapacitative effects, because it prescribes imprisonment for the more serious crimes. But gauging those effects reliably will not be easy, given what has been said already about the problems of measuring incapacitative impact. Still more difficult will it be to gauge, with precision, how much the preventive yield can be improved by adjusting the scales' anchoring points in the second stage of writing the guidelines. We cannot (as I shall elaborate in the next chapter) expect to achieve a great deal of added prevention through changes in sentencing policy.

The preemptiveness of crime-control aspirations is a further matter for concern. Introducing incapacitation (even through the preferable inclusion strategy) gives the sentencing guidelines an explicit crime-control mission. By giving the guidelines that mission, the commission asks that its work be judged in crime-control terms. If the crime rate subsequently does not diminish (as it might well not), the commission will appear to have failed by its own definition of purpose; the guidelines will not have "worked" to prevent crime. In the rough-and-tumble of criminal justice politics, explanations for that failure may receive scant hearing, and the search may go on for alternative strategies that disregard the constraints of proportionality. The danger of seeking to synthesize past and future—even if that synthesis were theoretically possible in the manner I have suggested—is that the concern with preventing future crimes can too easily eclipse the concern for a fair and proportionate punishment of past crime.[3]

Should the commission, then, proceed to the second stage of seeking to synthesize preventive concerns into the guidelines? That depends, in part, on the level of empirical knowledge. Until more is known about categorial incapacitation effects, for example, I would think it would be premature to attempt the inclusion strategy of which I have spoken. It should depend also on the commission's capacities and the atmosphere in which it operates. Is the commission, once embarked on a discussion of preventive effects, capable of observing the limitations described in this and the preceding chapter? Or is it likely to become preoccupied with prevention at the expense of proportionality? Were I a member of a sentencing commission, therefore, my willingness to embark on the second stage would depend on my perception of the commission's sense of balance and self-restraint in dealing with preventive concerns; and on my perception of the environment within which the commission must eventually present and defend its standards, once it had written them.

CHAPTER 15

Concluding Observations

The Need for Principled Argument

This book should make clear the need for a principled resolution of the question of past or future crimes. The value of a desert conception must be decided by addressing the notions of justice that underlie it; the value of incapacitation schemes, determined by addressing their ethical and empirical issues. There are no shortcuts. No simple "practical" arguments exist that can successfully avoid these fundamentals.

The question of deservedness or dangerousness cannot be settled by pointing to "experience" with a rationale's use in a particular jurisdiction. A decade ago, critics attacked the positivist penal ethic by citing the evils of its application in California's old indeterminate-sentencing law.[1] Now, some critics of desert theory try the reverse: to refute the desert ethic by citing problems with its supposed implementation in California's present determinate-sentencing scheme.[2] Such arguments overlook the complexities of carrying out *any* sentencing rationale in a given place. Desert is not bad because of the deficiencies of California's present law,[3] any more than it is good because Minnesota or Washington used the idea more competently in their guidelines.[4] Perhaps, the latter states might have done better than California in carrying out *any* sentencing theory, whether emphasizing desert or prediction. Perhaps California's problems, and Minnesota's and Washington's comparative successes, are due to other factors—such as the competence of the drafters of the standards, the sense of responsibility of the rule-making body, and the extent of political polarization on crime issues.[5]

A given rationale for sentencing can be implemented with greater or less constraints on discretion. In the United States, advocates both of desert and of selective incapacitation have tended to support detailed, numerical guidelines for sentencing. The issue of desert and prediction cannot depend, however, on one's degree of optimism or pessimism about the workability of detailed sentencing guidelines. As the use of guidelines has spread in the United States, so has the debate over their utility. How can one be assured of a reasonably competent rule-making body, capable and willing to devote the necessary thought, time, and care to fashioning the guidelines? How can that rule-making body resist political pressures to inflate the prescribed penalties to unrealistic levels? How can such standards effectively control discretion, as long as prosecutors retain wide charging powers? I doubt there are uniform answers to such questions.[6] Political demands to escalate punishments will be stronger in some states than others. Prosecutors in some places may be willing to utilize the standards to help guide their charging and plea-bargaining decisions; prosecutors elsewhere may prefer to ignore or manipulate them. Much depends on the character of criminal justice in the place, and the manner in which the rules are written and enforced. But such problems, to the extent they exist, will affect the implementation of guidelines whether those emphasize desert or prediction. Numerical guidelines based on a selective incapacitation rationale can as much be frustrated through sentence bargaining as desert-based guidelines can. Desert or selective incapacitation are not *about* controlling discretion. Either conception calls for constraints on discretion, in greater or less detail, if it is to be applied consistently. What these theories help explain is not how detailed the standards for sentencing should be, but what their substantive content ought to be: what features of the offender or his offense chiefly should determine the penalty.

A desert or predictive rationale can be implemented with greater or less economy in the use of severe punishments. A desert scheme, as we saw in chapter 8, offers some leeway in fixing a scale's anchoring points, and hence in its aggregate use of imprisonment. A selective incapacitation rationale contains comparable leeway, about how probable and how harmful the predicted future criminal conduct must be before warranting use of imprisonment.[7] We should therefore be skeptical of claims that one or the other rationale is preferable because it is intrinsically more "parsimonious" in its use of imprisonment.[8] It is conceivable that the aggregate use of imprisonment might to *some* extent be affected by the choice of sentencing rationale. I argued earlier that selective incapacitation has an escalatory potential: as those misclassified as good risks commit new crimes, the scheme will face increasing demands to make definitions of dangerousness more inclusive (see chapter 10). But such influences will not be easy to trace. A jurisdiction's traditions in punishment, its politics, and its public's degree of fear of crime and criminals probably will affect leniency or severity more than any choice of sentencing theory.

My Account of Desert

I have argued that a fair conception of sentencing should emphasize desert. A desert theory, however, is too easily misunderstood, by advocates as well as by critics. The theory, it has variously been said, relies on outré philosophical ideas of merited punishments; claims that all questions about quanta of sentences can be answered by reference to what is deserved; and excludes all consideration of crime-prevention effects. This book should make clear that *none* of these characterizations are accurate.

The account of desert offered in this book does not presuppose arcane notions of "righting" the moral imbalance wrought by criminal misconduct. In *Doing Justice*, I did at one point speak of punishment as restoring a correct allocation of the "benefits" and "burdens" of wrongdoing.[9] I am now convinced such explanations are unenlightening. Desert in punishment can rest on a much simpler idea, used in everyday discourse: the idea of censure (see chapters 3 and 5). Punishment connotes censure. Penalties should comport with the seriousness of crimes, so that the reprobation visited on the offender through his penalty fairly reflects the blameworthiness of his conduct.

Desert cannot answer, and should not be claimed to answer, all questions about punishment. To understand what answers it can supply, the questions need be framed with care. Any reasonably sophisticated penal theory, as H. L. A. Hart pointed out long ago,[10] supplies different principles for dealing with problems at different levels. I have distinguished three major levels, and offered principles for dealing with each. These are:

Ordinal penalty gradations. This issue concerns the comparative severity of punishments for offenders convicted of similar or different crimes. Desert should be controlling, here: the gradation of gravity of criminal conduct should determine the ordering of penalties (see chapters 4, 6, and 7).

The magnitude and anchoring points of a penalty scale. This deals with the absolute or cardinal dimensions of a scale: how severe the most severe penalty should be; how lenient the mildest; where the dividing line should be drawn between the system's most onerous type of sanction (i.e., imprisonment) and other penalties. The concept of censure, I have suggested, can provide constraints on inflation or deflation of the scale as a whole, but not unique solutions. To the extent that it leaves leeway, other considerations become relevant: the availability of resources, and also crime-prevention effects—provided these are the type that do not infringe on ordinal proportionality (see chapters 4, 8, and 13).

The existence of the criminal sanction. This concerns the justification for the very existence of legal punishment. I have argued that desert is a necessary but not sufficient justification for the criminal sanction. The case for having a system of punishments rests both on crime prevention and on censure. Prevention explains why the state should impose material deprivations on offenders. Reprobation for wrongdoing justifies why those deprivations should be visited in the condemnatory fashion that characterizes punishment. These two ideas of prevention and reprobation are not reducible into one another (see chapter 5).

Keeping these questions separate will help resolve many of the current perplexities of sentencing theory. Thus: (1) Is desert determining or merely limiting? That depends on which of the foregoing questions is being asked. In deciding comparative punishments, desert should be determining. But in anchoring the penalty scale, it can provide no unique answers—but only the bounds for how much penalties can be increased or decreased pro rata (see chapter 4). (2) Why can't desert tell us exactly how much punishment is deserved? The leeway that desert allows for deciding cardinal magnitudes explains why we cannot perceive a single right or fitting penalty for a given crime (see chapters 4 and 8). Whether x is the appropriate penalty for crime Q depends on how the scale has been anchored and what punishments are prescribed for other crimes. When the anchoring points of a penalty scale have been fixed, however, the more restrictive requirements of ordinal proportionality explain why it is wrong to rely on utilitarian grounds to decide comparative punishments. (3) Does a desert theory permit or preclude consideration of crime-prevention aims in deciding sentences? That depends on which aims and what their criteria are. Specifically, it depends whether they violate parity by selecting individuals for enhanced punishment from among those convicted of a given crime, or breach ordinal proportionality by ordering penalties on a basis other than the seriousness of the conduct. Selective incapacitation necessarily involves such infringement (see chapters 11 and 12); categorical incapacitation may not, if used in this manner I discussed (chapters 13 and 14).

This book will not appeal to those who want a single, simple formula. Desert enthusiasts will be disappointed, if they want a complete rejection of all preventive concerns. Crime-prevention enthusiasts will likewise be disappointed, if they want broad authority to pursue preventive aims. I have distilled the idea of penal desert into more specific requirements of ordinal and cardinal proportionality. The acceptability of crime-prevention strategies depends on the extent to which they square with those requirements.

Justice and Crime Prevention

The selection of a rationale for sentencing depends, ultimately, on underlying assumptions about justice and crime control. My arguments have concentrated on the moral connotations of punishment: the role of criminal sanctions in censuring reprehensible conduct. Basing punishments on the gravity of crimes recognizes offenders as *persons*—as individuals capable of choice, responsible for their actions, and punishable according to their degree of fault. This conception is consistent with—in fact, an outgrowth of—longstanding traditions of taking choice and culpability seriously in the substantive criminal law, in concepts of criminal intent and excuses.[11]

Selective incapacitation, as now advocated by Wilson, Greenwood, and others, reflects a very different outlook. It sees sentencing policy as a device for the control of undesirables. It downplays the condemnatory features of punishment and reflects little concern for offenders as autonomous persons, whose liability should depend on their choices. It goes without saying that the differences between those approaches reflect deeper philosophical divergences concerning individual rights and the maintenance of public order in the commonwealth.

What more is to be said about these differences? I must confess my impatience with attempts to treat justice as anything but central to sentencing policy. If sentencing is not a proper matter for emphasizing notions of equity, I cannot imagine anything that is. Sentencing affects our most fundamental interests in liberty and reputation. It involves the possibility of drastic deprivations of freedom, under circumstances involving severe moral stigma. Given the stakes for those punished, I cannot see the justification for ignoring such concerns or assigning them only secondary importance.

What of the interest in crime prevention? Even if justice requires proportionate sentences, is it the only value of importance? Might it not be legitimate to sacrifice fairness concerns in order to promote other values—particularly that of protecting citizens against criminal victimization?

In certain situations, we seem prepared to sacrifice justice to utility. Medical quarantine, of which I have spoken earlier, is a case in point. The person quarantined does not deserve to lose his liberty at all, and is being confined to protect others from disease. If such measures can be justified at all, they are so by their exceptional character: by the magnitude of the threat from epidemic disease; the intervention's apparent effectiveness and absence of explicit moral stigma; and by the limited scope of its permissible use.

One kind of policy should be rejected out of hand, however. It is that which involves drastic sacrifices of equity, to be imposed in routine fashion, in order to achieve limited and ill-verified preventive gains. A sentencing policy that relies heavily on selective incapacitation would be objectionable on this ground. Consider Greenwood's suggestion of imposing prison terms in excess of five years on "high-risk" robbers, and of one year on other robbers—in order to yield a supposed 15 percent reduction in the robbery rate. The proposal involves a very serious sacrifice of fairness, given the size of the punishment differential imposed on persons involved in similarly reprehensible conduct. Yet the claimed crime-control benefits are not of great magnitude on their face—and are highly dubious and contingent, when the evidentiary problems are considered (see chapters 9 and 10). I do not think we should have any difficulty rejecting proposals that are both so unjust and so doubtfully workable.

The pursuit of crime prevention in sentencing should be restrained by a healthy skepticism about how much prevention can be achieved and by an effort to shape preventive strategies so as to be consistent with the requirements of desert. What is so troublesome about the current enthusiasm for selective incapacitation is that it observes neither restraint.

A sensible view of crime control should begin with the hypothesis that sentencing policy can, at best, have limited impact on crime rates. Insofar as anything is known about the determinants of crime, levels of criminality seem influenced chiefly by demography and by economic and social factors—the age, class, income, and opportunity structure of the society; and the strength and pervasiveness of informal social controls over individual behavior. These are not matters that can be altered by the state's criminal justice policies in general, or by its sentencing policies in particular. If changes in sentencing measures can enhance crime prevention at all, the impact is likely to be marginal compared to those larger influences.

A sensible view of crime prevention should also bear the possibility of failure in mind. Past research about rehabilitation, deterrence, and collective incapacitation showed a depressing cycle of optimistic projections, followed by those projections' deflation under more careful scrutiny (see chapter 1). We see the same cycle in selective incapacitation research today: first, a breakthrough proclaimed in prediction techniques; next, increasing doubts, as the research is given closer examination. As foreign as caution and skepticism have been to American criminal justice research, they are virtues. Favorable outcomes in a study or series of studies show at most that a given strategy *might* have some preventive value, which further inquiry may fail to confirm. We should be prepared for the eventuality of failure, and sentencing policy should take the eventuality into account.

Such a "failure model," as David Rothman has called it,[12] could influence the choice among preventive strategies. If failure is seen as a possibility, one must reflect upon how acceptable the proposed sentencing policy would be if the promised crime-prevention effects do *not* materialize. Consider the two incapacitative techniques discussed herein: selective and categorial incapacitation. Selective incapacitation makes use of features of offenders' criminal records and social histories that have little bearing on the blameworthiness of their conduct. The conflict with ordinal proportionality is manifest. Such a strategy, if relied upon extensively in sentencing, would be morally unattractive enough if it succeeds in its crime-prevention aims, and more repulsive still if it fails. Categorial incapacitation—to the extent it is used in a manner consistent with ordinal and cardinal proportionality requirements, as discussed in chapters 13 and 14—could be less troublesome. Were the strategy able to reduce crime to some extent, so much the better; but even were it unsuccessful, the sentencing system would still reflect the blameworthiness of criminal conduct.

Let us, finally, beware of miracle cures. Sentencing systems might be made somewhat more equitable through careful observance of the principles of proportionality of which I have spoken. Even here, "somewhat" is the operative word, given the difficulty of implementing desert principles in law and in daily sentencing practice. It may also be worthwhile to continue to study the collateral crime-prevention effects of sentencing policy—paying particular attention to those preventive strategies designed with proportionality constraints in mind. But the crime problem cannot be solved through sentencing methods, however ingenious—at least, not through methods that would be acceptable in a free society. We should disbelieve those who promise it can.

The Question of False Positives

When critics of positivism started questioning predictive sentencing in the early 1970s, they had two arguments: one that concerned overprediction, and the other, desert. Prediction of recidivism yielded an unacceptably high incidence of false positives. It also punished persons for wrongful choices not yet made. The two arguments, it was thought, fitted nicely together, and prediction restraint was obnoxious for both reasons. I took this stand myself in a 1972 article on the subject.[1]

The attraction of the false-positives argument—the reason it seemed a useful supplement to the desert contention—is that it was less intellectually ambitious. To sustain the desert claim, one needed to justify a theory of punishment oriented to the past; to explain why it was wrong in principle to sentence on consequentialist grounds. The false-positive argument required no such philosophical underpinnings. One could, it seemed, simply hoist the prediction advocate with his own petard: even if the confinement of those who would recidivate were assumed justified, most of those predicted to be recidivists would *not* in fact return to crime. The unfairness arose from visiting predictive restraint on actually harmless persons.

Sometimes, prediction advocates responded by denying the existence of the false-positive problem. A prediction of dangerousness, it was said, is a statement of present condition, not a claim about future results.[2] To say A is dangerous is to say he is now able and possibly inclined to injure someone; and that claim is not falsified by the fact that he does not inflict the harm. The analogy sometimes cited is to unexploded bombs. After World War II, these were found at various sites in England and Germany, and had to be defused. There were few injuries—hence the rate of false positives was high. Yet no one could say that therefore the bombs were not dangerous.

The critics of prediction, however, had a ready reply. We can say bombs are dangerous because we can identify what makes them so—fuses, explosives, and so on. "Dangerous" individuals do not provide us with such convenient indica. The recidivist has not a perceptibly different makeup from the nonrecidivist, and predicting dangerousness is almost exclusively a matter of following up offenders' subsequent conduct. Hence it *is* important how often the predicted conduct does actually occur. Moreover, bombs are not thought of as individuals with rights; the destruction of a bombshell that would not have exploded is not something that should trouble us. Offenders, by contrast, are persons with rights, and when confined they surely suffer. If that suffering is justified by reference to the injury they would have visited on others, it becomes a matter of legitimate concern whether the person would have committed the predicted misdeed. The bomb analogy fails.

Critics of predictive sentencing could be comfortable with the false-positive argument, moreover, because overprediction seemed so tenacious. Earlier prediction studies showed rates of up to eight false positives for every one true.[3] Later prediction indices did somewhat better, but they still tended to show overprediction rates of 60 percent or more: there were about two false positives for every true.[4] The state of the predictive art seemed such that the false-positive objection could not be overcome. Critics had a simple, empirically based reason for resisting individual prediction in sentencing.

Further reflection has brought out, however, that matters are not quite so simple. The two arguments, about false positives and desert, turn out to be in considerable conflict with one another. Pursuit of the desert line may lead to different conclusions than pursuit of the overprediction line, and vice versa.

The false-positive argument does not in principle question the appropriateness of predictive sentencing. The issue becomes only one of accuracy: were one able to reduce the number of false positives, selective incapacitation would become unobjectionable. The argument does not address the prediction criteria—with sufficient accuracy, it would not matter whether those criteria relied on the current crimes, past crimes, or social factors; and whether or not they observed parity among offenders convicted for similar crimes.

Desert works differently. The acceptability of any given set of sentencing standards depends on whether and to what extent they meet the cardinal and ordinal proportionality requirements. Standards that violate these requirements would be objectionable, even if they happened to be highly accurate indicia of recidivism. Standards that comply with these requirements are acceptable, regardless of whether or not they also predict future misconduct and of how accurately they do so. That is why I have been more critical of selective incapacitation than of categorial. The latter, as discussed in chapters 13 and 14, might conceivably be squared with desert requirements, whereas selective incapacitation necessarily infringes on parity and rank ordering (see chapter 11).

Concentrating on the false-positive issue, with its emphasis on accuracy, therefore could have troublesome implications. To minimize the number of false positives, one needs a predictive device that is quite discriminating—that is, which accounts for a substantial percentage of variability in offender behavior. To achieve that degree of sensitivity, one probably needs a highly selective prediction device: one that uses a combination of items about the offender's criminal and social past. Of the two prediction strategies discussed in this book, an individual-prediction scheme would probably have a lower incidence of false positives than would a categorial incapacitation scheme. Use of only the current conviction offense would make the prediction less sensitive. Consequently, a preoccupation with false positives could lead one to prefer those prediction schemes that are most sensitive and selective—and hence potentially most in breach of the parity requirements of desert. This is the direction I wish to avoid. It is preferable, I think, to sacrifice the predictive accuracy of sentencing criteria, if by doing so one can better satisfy desert requirements.

Some desert theorists might disagree with me on categorial incapacitation and claim that *any* use of preventive concerns violates the spirit of a desert rationale. Their objection, however, would focus on my distillation of the idea of desert into cardinal and ordinal proportionality requirements. Something, they might argue, has been lost through this distillation: a "real" desert theory should be concerned exclusively with past crimes, and not permit consideration of future crimes in sentencing policy. This objection, however, is not concerned with the accuracy of predictions. Such theorists would no more allow predictions with low false-positive rates to affect the penalty, than predictions with high false-positive rates—or, for that matter, than they would permit use of general deterrence considerations, which do not relate to offender's own conduct at all. The debate between these more heroic desert theorists and myself relates, instead, to the criteria for desert.

One truth remains, however, from the old arguments: the most blatantly objectionable schemes are those which both violate desert and have high false-positive rates. Individual prediction schemes that pick and choose particular offenders deemed dangerous from among those convicted of a given crime, and that do so with much over prediction, cannot be sustained by any concept of fairness. Selective incapacitation in its present state, as exemplified by the Greenwood prediction index, should therefore fall, for it combines a high rate of false positives with total disregard of the parity requirements (see chapters 9 and 11). The complications of which I have just spoken will arise later, as one tries to develop prediction schemes that either are more accurate or are better designed in order to meet desert requirements.

A Note on Minnesota's Sentencing Guidelines

Throughout this book, I refer with approval to Minnesota's sentencing guidelines (see chapters 2, 8, 10, and 15). I speak, in particular, of two innovations the Minnesota Sentencing Commission developed when writing its original guidelines. First, the commission determined the character of the guidelines by making an *explicit* choice of sentencing philosophy. To decide the slope of the in-out line on the grid, the commission compared the effects of a desert and an incapacitative rationale, respectively. The commission then opted for a desert rationale in modified form—and attempted to reflect that choice by writing guidelines that would utilize imprisonment chiefly for those convicted of serious crimes. Second, the commission took the capacity of the state's prison system into account in deciding the aggregate amount of imprisonment the guidelines prescribe. The commission sought thereby to reduce the risk that the guidelines would inflate the overall severity of the sentencing system. The use of prison capacities also has some theoretical implications that I explore in chapter 8.

In the initial year that the guidelines went into effect, both these strategies seemed to bear fruit. Reflective of the desert emphasis chosen by the commission, there was a striking shift in patterns of prison commitments. A much higher percentage of first offenders convicted of serious crimes were being imprisoned; and a much lower percentage of lesser offenders with prior convictions were going to prison. Moreover, prison populations were remaining reasonably stable, as the commission had intended.[1]

The guidelines as originally written had, however, some structural anomalies. Principal among these was the slope of the in-out line on the right-hand portion of the grid, for offenders with lengthy criminal records. On the basis of the commission's purported modified desert rationale, the line should have sloped moderately downward—so that most such offenders would not be imprisoned unless their current offense was fairly serious. The commission decided, however, to be quite severe with such offenders, and to prescribe imprisonment for most cells in the grid's right-hand portion. The data available to the commission suggested that there would be few offenders with high criminal history scores, so that the impact of imprisoning such offenders would be small. Taking a tough line with the minority of multiple recidivists seemed to increase the potential political acceptability of the guidelines. Another potential problem concerned the standards for departure from the guidelines. The aggravating or mitigating factors listed in the guidelines mostly concerned the harm or culpability of offenders' criminal conduct—and thus comported with a desert rationale. However, the list of factors was nonexclusive, thus permitting the courts to introduce other, less consistent factors.[2]

Both of these deficiencies have come back to haunt the commission. Prosecutors have been "building up" records of lesser felons by obtaining, multiple convictions—thus pushing such cases toward the right-hand portion of the grid where imprisonment is prescribed for most grid cells. The courts have begun to consider "amenability" or "unamenability" to probation as grounds for departure from the guidelines' presumptive penalties, although this factor appears to be predictive rather than desert-based in its rationale. As a result, an increasing number of offenders convicted of violent crimes are beginning to receive probation; and an increasing number of felons convicted of routine property crimes are being imprisoned.[3]

Both problems are remediable. By flattening the in-out line more in the right-hand portion of the grid, or by changing the method of computing the criminal history, the commission could reduce the rate of prison commitments for lesser felons with long records. By tightening the guidelines' definitions of aggravating and mitigating circumstances, the commission could restrict departures from the guidelines on the basis of supposed amenability or unamenability to probation or similar predictive grounds. Such changes, however, would require the commission to resume its original role—fashioning the guidelines according to a stated, consistent sentencing rationale. The composition of the commission has substantially changed since the writing of the original guidelines, and the present membership has shown a reduced willingness to deal with such issues of principle. Instead, the commission has recently been willing to make changes in the guidelines only where necessary to prevent prison populations from rising above the prisons' capacity.

Whether the Minnesota guidelines live up to their original promise depends upon whether the commission—as presently constituted, or with newly appointed members at some future date—will be prepared once again to examine the guidelines' rationale and make appropriate amendments. No guidelines will be perfect when first written. Success depends on a commission's willingness to continue the process of making principled choices.

Notes

Chapter 1

1. See, for example, Francis A. Allen, *The Decline of the Rehabilitative Ideal: Penal Policy and Social Purpose.*

2. See Francis A. Allen, *The Borderland of Criminal Justice,* 25–41.

3. David J. Rothman, *Conscience and Convenience: The Asylum and Its Alternatives in Progressive America,* 379–421.

4. The most well-known study is Douglas Lipton, Robert Martinson, and Judith Wilks, *The Effectiveness of Correctional Treatment: A Survey of Treatment Evaluation Studies.* For a bibliography of other studies, see Hyman Gross and Andrew von Hirsch, eds., *Sentencing,* 186.

5. For further readings, see Gross and von Hirsch, *Sentencing,* 42–147.

6. Allen, *Decline of the Rehabilitative Ideal,* 11–20.

7. Rothman, *Conscience and Convenience,* 71–72.

8. National Council on Crime and Delinquency, Advisory Council of Judges, "Model Sentencing Act."

9. American Law Institute, *Model Penal Code,* § 7.01(1)(a).

10. See, for example, Stanley E. Grupp, ed., *The Positive School of Criminology: Three Lectures by Enrico Ferri,* 102–103.

11. See Don M. Gottfredson, "Assessment and Prediction Methods in Crime and Delinquency."

12. Don Gottfredson discussed the high incidence of false positives in his 1967 essay, "Assessment and Prediction Methods." Perhaps the first extensive analysis of the ethical problems raised by false positives in sentencing was my 1972 article, "Prediction of Criminal Conduct and Preventive Confinement of Convicted Persons."

13. von Hirsch, "Prediction of Criminal Conduct"; John Monahan, *Predicting Violent Behavior: An Assessment of Clinical Techniques.* For

further readings and bibliography, see Gross and von Hirsch, eds., *Sentencing*, 148–186.

14. James Q. Wilson, *Thinking about Crime*, chaps. 8 and 10.

15. Ernest van den Haag, *Punishing Criminals: Concerning a Very Old and Painful Question*; Ernest van den Haag, "Punishment as a Device for Controlling the Crime Rate."

16. Richard Posner, *Economic Analysis of Law*, 163–173.

17. The first systematic recent statement of this economic perspective was by Gary S. Becker ("Crime and Punishment: An Economic Approach").

18. Richard Posner writes: "The function of the criminal law, viewed from an economic standpoint, is to impose additional costs on unlawful conduct where the conventional damages remedy alone would be insufficient to limit that conduct to the efficient level" (*Economic Analysis of Law*, 163).

19. Johannes Andenaes, "The Morality of Deterrence."

20. Jeremy Bentham, *An Introduction to the Principles of Morals and Legislation*, 156–279.

21. Posner, *Economic Analysis of Law*, 163–173.

22. Wilson, *Thinking about Crime*, chaps. 8 and 10.

23. Wilson's estimates are based on a model developed in Reuel Shinnar and Shlomo Shinnar, "The Effects of Criminal Justice on the Control of Crime: A Quantitative Approach."

24. Wilson, *Thinking about Crime*, 200.

25. John Rawls, *A Theory of Justice*, 333–391; Bernard Williams, "A Critique of Utilitarianism"; Nicholas Rescher, *Distributive Justice: A Constructive Critique of the Utilitarian Theory of Distribution*, 25–46.

26. For bibliography, see Gross and von Hirsch, eds., *Sentencing*, 300.

27. Herbert Morris, "Persons and Punishment."

28. American Friends Service Committee, *Struggle for Justice*.

29. See, for example, Twentieth Century Fund, Task Force on Criminal Sentencing, *Fair and Certain Punishment*; David Fogel, *We Are the Living Proof*. For a Scandanavian report of similar import, see the National Swedish Council for Crime Prevention, *A New Penal System: Ideas and Proposals*.

30. John Kleinig, *Punishment and Desert*.

31. See, for example, Richard G. Singer, *Just Deserts: Sentencing Based on Equality and Desert*; David A. J. Richards, "Rights, Utility, and Crime." For further bibliography, Gross and von Hirsch, eds., *Sentencing*, 300. For a recent application of the desert model to issues of probation, see Patrick McAnany, Doug Thomson, and David Fogel, eds., *Probation and Justice: A Reconsideration of Mission*.

32. Andrew von Hirsch, *Doing Justice: The Choice of Punishments*, chaps. 8, 13, 14, 16.

33. Ibid., 125–126.
34. Ibid., chap. 16.
35. Singer, *Just Deserts,* 42–48.
36. For a survey of the influence of the desert rationale on sentencing guidelines and standards in this country, see Andrew von Hirsch and Kathleen J. Hanrahan, "Determinate Penalty Systems in America: An Overview."
37. *Oregon Parole Reform Act* § 2(2). For a description of Oregon's scheme, see Ira Blalock, "Justice and Parole: The Oregon Experience."
38. See *Minnesota Sentencing Guidelines and Commentary*; Minnesota Sentencing Guidelines Commission, *Report to the Legislature*. For an analysis of the structure and rationale of the guidelines, see Andrew von Hirsch, "Constructing Guidelines for Sentencing: The Critical Choices for the Minnesota Sentencing Guidelines Commission."
39. *Washington Sentencing Guidelines.*
40. von Hirsch, *Doing Justice,* 64–65; Alan H. Goldman, "Beyond the Deterrence Theory: Comments on van den Haag's 'Punishment as a Device for Controlling the Crime Rate.'"
41. See, for example, James Q. Wilson, "Thinking about 'Thinking about Crime.'"
42. See, for example, Stephen S. Brier and Stephen E. Fienberg, "Recent Econometric Modelling of Crime and Punishment: Support for the Deterrence Hypothesis?"
43. Jacqueline Cohen, "The Incapacitative Effect of Imprisonment."
44. The panel's report is set forth in Alfred Blumstein, Jacqueline Cohen, and Daniel Nagin, eds., *Deterrence and Incapacitation: Estimating the Effects of Criminal Sanctions on Crime Rates,* 3–90.
45. Peter W. Greenwood, *Selective Incapacitation.*
46. Ibid.
47. He reports quite low false-positive rates (Greenwood, *Selective Incapacitation,* 60).
48. Ibid., xix.
49. Ibid.
50. Jan Chaiken and Marcia Chaiken, *Varieties of Criminal Behavior.*
51. James Q. Wilson, *Thinking about Crime,* rev. ed., chap. 8.
52. Mark Moore, Susan Estrich, Daniel McGillis and William Spelman, *Dangerous Offenders: The Elusive Target of Justice.* See also Kenneth Feinberg, "Selective Incapacitation and the Effort to Improve the Fairness of Existing Sentencing Practices"; Harvard Law Review Student Note, "Selective Incapacitation: Reducing Crime through Prediction of Recidivism."
53. Wilson, *Thinking about Crime,* rev. ed., 256.

Chapter 2

1. Andrew von Hirsch, "Commensurability and Crime Prevention: Evaluating Formal Sentencing Structures and Their Rationale," 244–245.

2. See, for example, James Q. Wilson, *Thinking about Crime,* rev. ed., 256.

3. For readings and bibliography, see Hyman Gross and Andrew von Hirsch, eds., *Sentencing,* 303–335.

4. For readings and bibliography on the choice of standard-setter, see ibid., 337–369.

5. Andrew von Hirsch and Kathleen J. Hanrahan, "Determinate Penalty Systems in America: An Overview," 299–303.

6. The judicial guidelines developed in New Jersey and Massachusetts had this deficiency, for example. Richard F. Sparks et al., *Stumbling toward Justice: Some Overlooked Research and Policy Questions about Statewide Sentencing Guidelines.* Whether all historically based judicial guidelines thus fail to address policy issues has been a matter of argument. See, for example Michael R. Gottfredson and Don M. Gottfredson, "Guidelines for Incarceration Decisions: A Partisan Review."

7. The best parole guidelines, in terms of sophistication in drafting and care in application, have been Oregon's and the federal system's. See von Hirsch and Hanrahan, "Determinate Penalty Systems," 309–312.

8. Marvin E. Frankel, *Criminal Sentences: Law without Order,* 118–123. See also Michael H. Tonry, "The Sentencing Commission in Sentencing Reform."

9. von Hirsch and Hanrahan, "Determinate Penalty Systems," 292–294.

10. *Minnesota Sentencing Guidelines and Commentary.*

11. Minnesota Sentencing Guidelines Commission, *Report to the Legislature,* 8–10.

12. *Washington Sentencing Guidelines.*

13. *Pennsylvania Sentencing Guidelines.* For a history of the vicissitudes of the development of the guidelines, see Susan E. Martin, "Interests and Politics in Sentencing Reform: The Development of Sentencing Guidelines in Minnesota and Pennsylvania."

14. New York's sentencing commission, established in 1983, was developing its guidelines as of the time of this writing—but its prospects for success do not seem bright. The federal sentencing commission was established by legislation enacted in October 1984, and its members had not yet been appointed when this book went to press.

15. *Minnesota Sentencing Guidelines,* § II.B. For discussion of the Minnesota criminal history score, see Andrew von Hirsch, "Constructing Guidelines for Sentencing: The Critical Choices for the Minnesota Sentencing Guidelines Commission," 200–202.

16. The Minnesota guidelines have a nonexclusive list of aggravating and mitigating circumstances, set forth in *Minnesota Sentencing*

Guidelines, § II.D., and analyzed in von Hirsch, "Constructing Guidelines for Sentencing," 205–207.

17. *Minnesota Sentencing Guidelines,* § IV.

18. von Hirsch, "Constructing Guidelines for Sentencing," 181–191.

19. See Andrew von Hirsch, *Doing Justice: The Choice of Punishments,* chap. 13.

20. In *Doing Justice,* 107–109, 137–139, I took the latter approach.

21. *Minnesota Sentencing Guidelines,* § II.C.; von Hirsch, "Constructing Guidelines for Sentencing," 207–208.

22. For contrasting views, see excerpts and bibliography in Gross and von Hirsch, eds., *Sentencing,* 303–351.

23. Some broad assertions about their failure are found, for example, in Francis T. Cullen and Karen E. Gilbert, *Reaffirming Rehabilitation.*

24. For a preliminary survey of some of the successes and failures, see von Hirsch and Hanrahan, "Determinate Penalty Systems."

25. *Finnish Criminal Code,* chap. 6, § 1, Further sections of that chapter define mitigating and aggravating circumstances. The text was translated for this author by Matti Joutsen.

26. The committee (Fängelsestraffkommittèn) is drafting chapters on sentencing principles for the Swedish Criminal Code. A working group of the committee has developed a draft that makes sentences depend chiefly on the "penal value" of the crime, and the penal value depend on the harm and culpability of the criminal conduct.

Chapter 3

1. Cesare Beccaria, *Of Crimes and Punishments,* chap. 23.

2. Jeremy Bentham, *An Introduction to the Principles of Morals and Legislation,* chap. 14.

3. Beccaria, *Of Crimes and Punishments,* chap. 23; Bentham, *Principles of Morals and Legislation,* 168.

4. Ernest van den Haag, "Punishment as a Device for Controlling the Crime Rate," 711–720. For an illuminating critique, see Alan H. Goldman, "Beyond Deterrence Theory: Comments on van den Haag's 'Punishment as a Device for Controlling the Crime Rate.'"

5. Chapter 1; see also the report of the Panel on Research on Deterrent and Incapacitative Effects, in Alfred Blumstein, Jacquelin Cohen, and Daniel Nagin, eds., *Deterrence and Incapacitation: Estimating the Effects of Criminal Sanctions on Crime Rates* 19–63.

6. See, for example, his advocacy of sentences in excess of what is proportionately deserved where needed to incapacitate offenders constituting high risks of recidivism (Ernest van den Haag, "Punitive Sentences," 131–134).

7. Johannes Andenaes, "General Prevention: Illusion or Reality?" 7–8.

8. Claus Roxin, "Zur jüngsten Diskussion über Schuld, Prävention und Verantwortlichkeit im Strafrecht," 304–307. For a similar Scandinavian perspective, see Patrik Törnudd, "Deterrence Research and the Needs for Legislative Planning."

9. Johannes Andenaes, "The Moral or Educational Influence of Criminal Law."

10. Nils Christie, "Die Versteckte Botschaft des Neo-Klassizismus."

11. For a more complete definition, see John Kleinig, *Punishment and Desert,* chap. 3, See also, Joel Feinberg, "Justice and Personal Desert."

12. Richard Wasserstrom, "Punishment." See also, Joel Feinberg, "The Expressive Function of Punishment."

13. Such a requital account of the commensurate-deserts principle is set forth, for example, in Alan H. Goldman, "The Paradox of Punishment." The difficulties of such theories are discussed at the end of chapter 5.

14. Christie, "Die Versteckte Botschaft."

15. That, indeed, is Christie's eventual solution. Nils Christie, *Limits to Pain,* chap. 9–11. The problems of this view are discussed in chap. 5.

Chapter 4

1. Norval Morris, *Madness and the Criminal Law,* chap. 5. For earlier statements of Morris's view, see his 1974 book, *The Future of Imprisonment,* chap. 3, and his essay, "Punishment, Desert, and Rehabilitation."

2. In his 1974 book, Morris (*Future of Imprisonment,* chap. 3) opposed relying on predictions in sentencing, on account of the high rate of false positives. However, he has now changed his position; see Norval Morris and Marc Miller, "Predictions of Dangerousness."

3. Morris, *Madness and the Criminal Law,* 199.

4. Ibid., 198.

5. Ibid., 187–196.

6. Morris, *Madness and the Criminal Law,* 202. In the quoted passage, he is responding to my own criticisms of his views, set forth in my "Utilitarian Sentencing Resuscitated: The American Bar Association's Second Report on Criminal Sentencing," 783–789.

7. This would be analogous to Barbara Wooton's view, expressed in her *Crime and the Criminal Law.* For a critique of her position, see H. L. A. Hart, "Punishment and the Elimination of Responsibility."

8. Morris, *Madness and the Criminal Law,* 204–205.

9. Andrew von Hirsch, "Utilitarian Sentencing Resuscitated," 788.

10. Morris, *Madness and the Criminal Law,* 204–205.

Chapter 5

1. Nils Christie, *Limits to Pain,* chaps. 10, 11.

2. Christie suggests that the response might be comparable to the

expression of sorrow that takes place at funerals. Ibid., 98–103. I think the funeral analysis is misplaced, for reasons set forth in Andrew von Hirsch, book review of *Limits to Pain,* by Nils Christie.

3. This point is elaborated in Andrew von Hirsch, *Doing Justice: The Choice of Punishments,* chap. 5, See also the discussion of deterrence in chap. 1, above.

4. His account is sketched in Klaus Mäkelä, "Om straffens verkningar." The author has provided me with an unpublished English summary.

5. H. L. A. Hart, "Prolegomenon to the Principles of Punishment."

6. See Joel Feinberg, "The Expressive Function of Punishment," 101–104.

7. See, for example, von Hirsch, *Doing Justice,* chap. 5.

8. The influence of Kant's notion of treating persons as ends on modern moral theory is sketched by David Richards in the first chapter of his recent book on decriminalization, *Sex, Drugs, Death, and the Law,* 7–20. See also D. D. Raphael, *Moral Philosophy.*

9. John Rawls, *A Theory of Justice*; Alan Gewirth, *Reason and Morality*; John Taurek, "Should the Numbers Count?"

10. H. L. A. Hart, "Punishment and the Elimination of Responsibility."

11. von Hirsch, *Doing Justice,* 47–48.

12. Herbert Morris, "Persons and Punishment."

13. Jeffrie G. Murphy, "Kant's Theory of Criminal Punishment."

14. von Hirsch, *Doing Justice,* 47–48.

15. Hugo Adam Bedau, "Retribution and the Theory of Punishment," 617. Murphy himself has pointed out this difficulty in his "Marxism and Retribution."

16. Richard Burgh, "Do the Guilty Deserve Punishment?" See also, J. L. Mackie, "Morality and the Retributive Emotions."

17. See D. J. Galligan, "The Return to Retribution in Penal Theory," 158–159.

18. von Hirsch, *Doing Justice,* 52–55.

Chapter 6

1. One of the few recent works that discusses the rationale of gauging seriousness is Andrew Ashworth's *Sentencing and Penal Policy,* chap. 4.

2. *Minnesota Sentencing Guidelines,* § V; *Washington Sentencing Guidelines,* § 3; *Pennsylvania Sentencing Guidelines,* § III. For discussion of the Minnesota seriousness rankings, see Andrew von Hirsch, "Constructing Guidelines for Sentencing: The Critical Choices for the Minnesota Sentencing Guidelines Commission," 192–199.

3. *Pennsylvania Sentencing Guidelines* (proposed 1980).

4. Burglary, for example, was subcategorized according to whether

or not the inhabitant was present and other factors. *Pennsylvania Sentencing Guidelines* (proposed 1980) § III.

5. See Susan E. Martin, "Interests and Politics in Sentencing Reform: The Development of Sentencing Guidelines in Minnesota and Pennsylvania," 61–99.

6. The guidelines' current seriousness rankings have a marked similarity to the proposed 1980 rankings.

7. Andrew von Hirsch *Doing Justice; The Choice of Punishments*, chap. 9.

8. Ibid.; see also, Andrew von Hirsch, "Desert and White-Collar Criminality: A Response to Dr. Braithwaite," especially 1168–1169.

9. Marvin Wolfgang, "Seriousness of Crime and a Policy of Juvenile Justice."

10. Thorsten Sellin and Marvin Wolfgang, *The Measurement of Delinquency*.

11. The leading English study is by Richard F. Sparks, Hazel Genn, and David Dodd, *Surveying Victims: A Study of the Measurement of Criminal Victimization*; see chap. 7. A summary of various studies is provided by Stanley Turner in his introduction to the 1978 reprint edition of Sellin and Wolfgang, *The Measurement of Delinquency,* x–xxi.

12. The study, done under the auspices of the Center for Studies in Criminology and Criminal Law of the University of Pennsylvania, will shortly be published by the Bureau of Criminal Statistics of the National Institute of Justice.

13. Sparks developed this view in an unpublished lecture at a colloquium on punishment and desert held under the auspices of the Rutgers University School of Criminal Justice, at Sterling Forest Conference Center, Tuxedo, N.Y., 19–21 November 1978.

14. Ibid.

15. For a useful summary of recent victimization studies, see Richard F. Sparks, "Surveys of Victimization—An Optimistic Assessment."

16. See, for example, Dworkin, "Liberalism"; John Rawls, *A Theory of Justice*.

17. Joel Feinberg, *Harm to Others,* 37–45, 185–214. In an earlier draft of this chapter I used my own analogous, but less well articulated, notion of a "priority interest." I am grateful to John Kleinig for pointing out to me how Feinberg's definition of welfare interests is more illuminating.

18. John Kleinig, "Crime and the Concept of Harm."

19. Nicholas Rescher, *Welfare: The Social issue in Philosophical Perspective*.

20. Feinberg, *Harm to Others,* 37–38.

21. Ibid., 42.

22. Ibid., 206–207.

23. Ibid., 37, 57–58.

24. Ibid., 207.

25. Ibid.

26. For useful analysis, see George Fletcher, *Rethinking Criminal Law*.

27. American Law Institute, *Model Penal Code*, § 2.02.

28. Ibid., § 211.1(2).

29. Even Pennsylvania's elaborate offense classification system does not make these distinctions.

30. Michael H. Tonry, "Criminal Law: The Missing Element in Sentencing Reform." Professor Nils Jareborg has recently developed a proposed reclassification of property crimes in the Swedish Penal Law. Swedish Ministry of Justice, *Översyn av lagstiftninger om Förmögenhetsbrott utom gäldenärsbrott*.

31. Ibid., 638.

32. American Law Institute, *Model Penal Code*, § 2.09, 3.02. For a critique of the *Model Penal Code's* definitions, see Fletcher, *Rethinking Criminal Law*, chap. 10.

33. For discussion of provocation in the law of homicide, see Fletcher. *Rethinking Criminal Law*, 242–250.

34. von Hirsch, *Doing Justice*, 80.

35. *Minnesota Sentencing Guidelines*, §§ II.D.2d(1), (2).

36. The half-madness issue is discussed in Norval Morris, *Madness and the Criminal Law*, chap. 4, and in my "Equality, 'Anisonomy' and Justice: An Analysis of *Madness and the Criminal Law*."

37. *Minnesota Sentencing Guidelines*, § II.D.2a(3).

38. *Washington Sentencing Guidelines*, § 10.

39. This chapter, n. 2.

40. For discussion of this and other problems of the California sentencing law, see Andrew von Hirsch and Julia M. Mueller, "California's Determinate Sentencing Law: An Analysis of Its Structure," 282–286, and passim.

41. See Andrew von Hirsch and Kathleen J. Hanrahan, "Determinate Penalty Systems in America: An Overview," 299.

42. This chapter, n. 2.

43. von Hirsch, "Constructing Guidelines for Sentencing," 197–199.

44. In doing so, the commission might examine the rankings proposed in Richard G. Singer, *Just Deserts: Sentencing Based on Equality and Desert*, 40–41.

Chapter 7

1. See Don M. Gottfredson, "Assessment and Prediction Methods in Crime and Delinquency."

2. Andrew von Hirsch, *Doing Justice: The Choice of Punishments*, chap. 9.

3. George Fletcher, *Rethinking Criminal Law,* 460–466.

4. Richard G. Singer, *Just Deserts: Sentencing Based on Equality and Desert,* chap. 5.

5. von Hirsch, *Doing Justice,* 85.

6. See, for example, American Law institute, *Model Penal Code,* § 2.04.

7. George Fletcher, "The Recidivist Premium," 57.

8. Andrew von Hirsch, "Desert and Previous Convictions in Sentencing."

9. Singer, *Just Deserts,* 67, n. 2; Fletcher, "The Recidivist Premium." Fletcher, at one point (58–59) concedes that a discount for first offenders might be justified, but states that a premium for recidivists cannot be—and he goes on to assert that sentencing practice involves the latter.

10. James Thurber, *The Thirteen Clocks,* 20–21.

11. von Hirsch, "Desert and Previous Convictions," 613–615. 622–623.

12. For further discussion of anchoring points, see chap. 8.

Chapter 8

1. See chap. 4.

2. Andrew von Hirsch, *Doing Justice: The Choice of Punishments,* 92–94.

3. See chap. 1; see also the report of the Panel on Research on Deterrent and Incapacitative Effects, in Alfred Blumstein, Jacqueline Cohen, and Daniel Nagin, eds. *Deterrence and Incapacitation: Estimating the Effects of Criminal Sanctions on Crime Rates,* 19–63.

4. Andrew von Hirsch, "Constructing Guidelines for Sentencing: The Critical Choices for the Minnesota Sentencing Guidelines Commission," 175–180.

5. Ibid., 177–178.

6. Ibid., 179.

7. See, Andrew von Hirsch, "Commensurability and Crime Prevention: Evaluating Formal Sentencing Structures and Their Rationale," 219–226. See also, Alfred Blumstein, "Sentencing Reforms: Impacts and Implications," 132.

8. von Hirsch, *Doing Justice,* 5.

Chapter 9

1. S. B. Warner, "Factors Determining Parole from the Massachusetts Reformatory"; Hornell Hart, "Predicting Parole Success."

2. Sheldon Glueck and Eleanor Glueck, *500 Criminal Careers,* For a

description of subsequent prediction studies during the next two and a half decades, see Hermann Mannheim and Leslie Wilkins, *Prediction Methods in Relation to Borstal Training*; F. H. Simon, *Prediction in Criminology*.

3. Don M. Gottfredson, "The Practical Application of Research."

4. Don M. Gottfredson, Leslie T. Wilkins, and Peter B. Hoffman, *Guidelines for Parole and Sentencing: A Policy Control Method,* chaps. 1–4.

5. For a discussion of prediction techniques, see Don M. Gottfredson, "Assessment and Prediction Methods in Crime and Deliquency."

6. Ibid.

7. The coefficient of determination, which is the square of the correlation coefficient, measures the amount of variability "accounted for" by a predictor item or scale. Often it is not reported. But it can be estimated from the data; for traditional prediction studies, the coefficient varies from about 15 to 30 percent. These correlations are substantial in relation to much of social science; but they must be considered quite modest if the aim is to use them in criminal justice decisions involving the liberty of individual offenders. For a discussion of the California Base Expectancy Score see Michael R. Gottfredson and Don M. Gottfredson, *Decisionmaking in Criminal Justice: Toward the Rational Exercise of Discretion,* 257–279. For an analysis based on United States Parole Commission data, see Stephen Gottfredson and Don M. Gottfredson, *Screening for Risks: A Comparison of Methods*.

8. For an analysis of error rates, based on the California Base Expectancy Score, see David F. Greenberg, *Mathematical Criminology,* 222–229.

9. For fuller discussion of the false-positives problem and its implications in sentencing, see Andrew von Hirsch, "Prediction of Criminal Conduct and Preventive Confinement of Convicted Persons," 730–744.

10. John Monahan, *Predicting Violent Behavior: An Assessment of Clinical Techniques,* 73–80, 101–104.

11. von Hirsch, "Prediction of Criminal Conduct," 735; Greenberg, *Mathematical Criminology,* 222–229.

12. See chap. 1.

13. Peter W. Greenwood, *Selective Incapacitation*.

14. Marcia R. Chaiken and Jan M. Chaiken, *Varieties of Criminal Behavior*.

15. Greenwood, *Selective Incapacitation,* xiii.

16. Chaiken and Chaiken, *Varieties of Criminal Behavior,* 86–88.

17. Ibid., 113.

18. These calculations are made in Andrew von Hirsch and Don M. Gottfredson, "Selective Incapacitation: Some Queries about Research Design and Equity," 20–21.

19. Greenwood, *Selective Incapacitation,* 59–60.

20. This false-positive rate is calculated in von Hirsch and Gottfredson, "Selective Incapacitation," 21–22. For further discussion, see John

Blackmore and Jane Welsh, "Selective Incapacitation: Sentencing According to Risk," 516–517.

21. This false-positive rate is calculated in von Hirsch and Gottfredson, "Selective Incapacitation," 44.

22. Chaiken and Chaiken, *Varieties of Criminal Behavior,* 180.

23. Jan M. Chaiken and Marcia R. Chaiken, "Deficiencies in Official Records for Identifying Serious Offenders."

24. Marcia R. Chaiken and Jan M. Chaiken, "Offender Types and Public Policy," 211–213.

25. Ibid., 212–217.

26. Ibid., 217.

27. Ibid.

28. See Paul Meehl and Albert Rosen, "Antecedent Probability and the Efficiency of Psychometric Signs, Patterns and Cutting Scores."

Chapter 10

1. Peter W. Greenwood, *Selective Incapacitation.*

2. James Q. Wilson, *Thinking about Crime,* rev. ed., chap. 8.

3. See chap. 1.

4. See, for example, Reuel Shinnar and Shlomo Shinnar, "The Effects of the Criminal Justice System on the Control of Crime: A Quantitative Approach."

5. Ibid. at 605–608.

6. These other studies are summarized and discussed in Jacqueline Cohen, "The Incapacitative Effect of Imprisonment."

7. Ibid. See also the report of Panel on Research on Deterrent and Incapacitative Effects, in Alfred Blumstein, Jacqueline Cohen, and Daniel Nagin, eds., *Deterrence and Incapacitation: Estimating the Effects of Criminal Sanctions on Crime Rates,* 64–75.

8. Greenwood, *Selective Incapacitation,* 70–87.

9. Ibid., 89.

10. Ibid., 50. Greenwood's seven predictive factors are listed in the footnote on pp. 109–10 of the preceding chapter.

11. Greenwood, *Selective Incapacitation,* 109.

12. This is approximately the same probability as Greenwood uses for his California calculations. (ibid., 77).

13. According to Greenwood's study (ibid., 58), the average robbery rate for high-scoring robbers is 31 in California, 20 and 7, respectively, in Michigan and Texas. The assumed rate of 20 robberies a year thus coincides with Greenwood's figures for Michigan.

14. This corresponds to Greenwood's initial definition of high-scoring robbers as those having robbery rates in the upper quartile (ibid., 49).

15. For calculations, see Andrew von Hirsch and Don M. Gottfred-

son, "Selective Incapacitation: Some Queries about Research Design and Equity." 28, 49–50.

16. The calculations are set forth in ibid., 29, 48–50.

17. Albert J. Reiss, Jr., "Understanding Changes in Crime Rates."

18. Wilson, *Thinking about Crime*, rev. ed., 158–159.

19. Greenwood, *Selective Incapacitation*, 75–85.

20. For fuller analysis of the California law, see Andrew von Hirsch and Julia M. Mueller, "The California Determinate Sentencing Law: An Analysis of Its Structure."

21. For a fuller analysis, see Andrew von Hirsch, "Constructing Guidelines for Sentencing: The Critical Choices for the Minnesota Sentencing Guidelines Commission," 181–191.

22. *Minnesota Sentencing Guidelines,* § IV; *Washington Sentencing Guidelines,* § 2.

23. Both states have sentencing commissions, and both commissions considered the possible impact on prison populations in drafting the guidelines.

24. von Hirsch and Mueller, "The California Determinate Sentencing Law," 269–274.

25. Greenwood's initial definitions assumed one-fourth of his sample would be classified as high risks.

Chapter 11

1. Michael Sherman and Gordon Hawkins, *Imprisonment in America: Choosing the Future,* 106. For a critique of this book, see my review of Allen, *The Decline of the Rehabilitative Ideal,* and of Sherman and Hawkins's book.

2. American Bar Association, Task Force on Sentencing Alternatives and Procedures, *Sentencing Alternatives and Procedures,* 2d ed. For a critique of this report, see my "Utilitarian Sentencing Resuscitated: The American Bar Association's Second Report on Criminal Sentencing."

3. See chap. 9.

4. Kenneth Feinberg, "Selective Incapacitation and the Effort to Improve the Fairness of Existing Sentencing Practices"; Harvard Law Review Student Note, "Selective Incapacitation: Reducing Crime Through Prediction of Recidivism."

5. See chaps. 9 and 10.

6. Andrew von Hirsch and Kathleen J. Hanrahan, "Determinate Penalty Systems in America: An Overview." See also the discussion of the Minnesota and Washington guidelines in chap. 1.

7. James Q. Wilson, *Thinking about Crime,* rev. ed., chap. 8; Peter W. Greenwood, "Controlling the Crime Rate through Imprisonment," 264–269.

8. Mark Moore, Susan Estrich, and Daniel McGillis, *Dealing with Dangerous Offenders.* This report has just been published under a some-

what different title. Moore, Estrich, McGillis, and Spelman, *Dangerous Offenders: The Elusive Target of Justice.*

9. Don M. Gottfredson, "Assessment and Prediction Methods in Crime and Delinquency"; Don M. Gottfredson, Leslie T. Wilkins, and Peter B. Hoffman, *Guidelines for Parole and Sentencing: A Policy Control Method,* chap. 3.

10. See chap. 7.

11. Moore, Estrich, and McGillis, *Dealing with Dangerous Offenders,* 114–115.

12. Ibid., 115–116.

13. His only citation (Ibid., 171) is to an article of mine, "Desert and Previous Convictions in Sentencing" which, he asserts, supports his position. However, that article does *not* support his contention. It explicitly argues that a prior criminal record must receive much less weight on a desert rationale than it could receive on a predictive one.

14. Gottfredson, Wilkins, and Hoffman, *Guidelines for Parole and Sentencing,* 149.

15. This is true, for example, of the predictive index that is used as the horizontal axis in the United States Parole Commission's guidelines. For a description of that index and its genesis see ibid., chap. 3.

16. The Greenwood study (*Selective Incapacitation*) looks only at robbers. The Chaiken study deals also with other types of offenders, but concentrates on robbery (Jan M. Chaiken and Marcia R. Chaiken, *Varieties of Criminal Behavior*).

17. Chaiken and Chaiken, *Varieties of Criminal Behavior,* 108.

18. Greenwood, *Selective Incapacitation,* 50.

19. Chaiken and Chaiken, *Varieties of Criminal Behavior,* 101–112.

20. For fuller discussion, see von Hirsch, "Desert and Previous Convictions," 607–613.

21. Moore, Estrich, and McGillis, *Dealing with Dangerous Offenders,* 145–146.

22. See chap. 7.

23. The index is set forth in the footnote on pp. 109–110, above.

24. Gottfredson, Wilkins, and Hoffman, *Guidelines for Parole and Sentencing,* chap. 3.

25. See, for example, Twentieth Century Fund, Task Force on Sentencing Policy Toward Young Offenders, *Confronting Youth Crime,* 7.

26. von Hirsch, "Desert and Previous Convictions," 617.

Chapter 12

1. Norval Morris and Marc Miller, "Predictions of Dangerousness." For a shorter version of this article, see Norval Morris, "On 'Dangerousness' in the Judicial Process."

2. Morris and Miller, "Predictions of Dangerousness."

3. American Law Institute, *Model Penal Code* § 6.07(3).

4. In "Predictions of Dangerousness," Morris and Miller do not discuss a lower desert limit. Morris mentions it, however, in his 1982 book, *Madness and the Criminal Law,* chap. 5.

5. Morris, *Madness and the Criminal Law,* 202–204.

6. Ibid., 199.

7. Andrew von Hirsch, "Desert and Previous Convictions," 628–629.

8. Ibid., 626–628.

9. See, for example, Morris's suggested treatment of tax offenders in *Madness and the Criminal Law,* 189–192.

Chapter 13

1. Dr. Cohen's research is summarized in Jacqueline Cohen, "Incapacitation as a Strategy for Crime Control: Possibilities and Pitfalls," 56–77.

2. Ibid., 73.

3. Ibid., 73–74.

4. See my criticism in chap. 11 of the factor "prior conviction for instant offense type" in Greenwood's prediction scale.

Chapter 14

1. Andrew von Hirsch and Kathleen J. Hanrahan, *The Question of Parole: Retention, Reform, or Abolition?,* 18–19; Andrew von Hirsch, "Desert and Previous Convictions in Sentencing," 628–629.

2. John Monahan ("The Case for Prediction in the Modified Desert Model for Criminal Sentencing"), for example, suggests a "modified desert" model that, in fact, resembles Norval Morris' limiting retributivism. Monahan contends that crimes cannot be graded in seriousness with any specificity. He asserts that desert is capable only of supplying the limits within which sentences should be decided on utilitarian grounds. Those limits, he suggests, might be broad or narrow, depending on the consensus within the sentencing commission about how much punishment is deserved.

3. See Andrew von Hirsch, "Constructing Guidelines for Sentencing: The Critical Choices for the Minnesota Sentencing Guidelines Commission," 187–189.

Chapter 15

1. American Friends Service Committee, *Struggle for Justice.*

2. See, for example, Francis T. Cullen and Karen Gilbert, *Reaffirm-*

ing Rehabilitation; see also, Leonard Orland, "From Vengeance to Vengeance: Sentencing Reform and the Demise of Rehabilitation."

3. For an analysis of the California law, see Andrew von Hirsch and Julia M. Mueller, "California's Determinate Sentencing Law: An Analysis of Its Structure."

4. For an analysis of the Minnesota guidelines, see Andrew von Hirsch, "Constructing Guidelines for Sentencing: The Critical Choices for the Minnesota Sentencing Guidelines Commission."

5. For fuller discussion, see Andrew von Hirsch and Kathleen J. Hanrahan, "Determinate Penalty Systems in America: An Overview."

6. See, Hyman Gross and Andrew von Hirsch, eds., *Sentencing*, 304–369.

7. Alan M. Dershowitz, "Indeterminate Confinement: Letting the Therapy Fit the Harm."

8. A crude version of the parsimony argument appears in the American Bar Association's 1979 report on sentencing. After defining parsimony in crime-control terms, the report concludes (not surprisingly, given that definition) that predictive restraint is more "parsimonious" than desert (*Sentencing Alternatives and Procedures*, 16–18). For a critique of this argument, see Andrew von Hirsch, "Utilitarian Sentencing Resuscitated: The American Bar Association's Second Report on Criminal Sentencing," 776–779.

Norval Morris, in his latest book, uses a more sophisticated but nevertheless analogous argument. His definition of "parsimony" has a strong utilitarian flavor, that seems to countenance substantial increases in severity for some offenders, if counterbalanced by modest decreases in severity for a larger number of other offenders (*Madness and the Criminal Law*, chap. 5). For a critique of that argument, see Andrew von Hirsch, "Equality, 'Anisonomy,' and Justice: An Analysis of *Madness and the Criminal Law*," 1105–1107.

9. Andrew von Hirsch, *Doing Justice: The Choice of Punishments*, chap. 6.

10. H. L. A. Hart, "Prolegomenon to the Principles of Punishment."

11. American Law Institute, *Model Penal Code*, art. 2. For an attempt to defend and reinforce the culpability elements in the substantive criminal law, see George Fletcher, *Rethinking Criminal Law*.

12. David Rothman, "Doing Time: Days, Months, and Years in the Criminal Justice System."

Appendix 1

1. Andrew von Hirsch, "Prediction of Criminal Conduct and Preventive Confinement of Convicted Persons."

2. Norval Morris and Marc Miller, "Predictions of Dangerousness."

A decade ago, however, Morris took the opposite view, rejecting predictive sentencing because of the high false-positive rates. (*Future of Imprisonment*, chap. 3.)

3. von Hirsch, "Prediction of Criminal Conduct," 735–737.

4. See chap. 9.

Appendix 2

1. See, Minnesota Sentencing Guidelines Commission, *The Impact of the Minnesota Sentencing Guidelines: Three Year Evaluation.*

2. For fuller discussion, see Andrew von Hirsch, "Constructing Guidelines for Sentencing: The Critical Choices for the Minnesota Sentencing Guidelines Commission."

3. See, Kay A. Knapp, "What Sentencing Reform in Minnesota Has and Has Not Accomplished."

Bibliography

Allen, Francis A. *The Borderland of Criminal Justice.* Chicago: University of Chicago Press, 1964.

————.*The Decline of the Rehabilitative Ideal: Penal Policy and Social Purpose.* New Haven: Yale University Press, 1981.

American Bar Association. Task Force on Sentencing Alternatives and Procedures. *Sentencing Alternatives and Procedures.* 2d ed. Washington, D.C.: American Bar Association, 1979.

American Friends Service Committee. *Struggle for Justice.* New York: Hill and Wang, 1971.

American Law Institute. *Model Penal Code.* Philadelphia: American Law Institute, 1962.

Andenaes, Johannes. "General Prevention: Illusion or Reality." In *Punishment and Deterrence,* by Johannes Andenaes, 3–33, Ann Arbor: University of Michigan Press, 1974.

————."The Moral or Educational Influence of Criminal Law." In *Punishment and Deterrence,* by Johannes Andenaes, 110-128. Ann Arbor: University of Michigan Press, 1974.

————."The Morality of Deterrence." In *Punishment and Deterrence,* by Johannes Andenaes, 129–151. Ann Arbor: University of Michigan Press, 1974.

Ashworth, Andrew. *Sentencing and Penal Policy.* London: Weidenfeld and Nicholson, 1983.

Beccaria, Cesare. *Of Crimes and Punishment.* Translated by Henry Paolucci. Indianapolis: Bobbs-Merrill, 1963.

Becker, Gary S. "Crime and Punishment: An Economic Approach." *Journal of Political Economy* 76 (1968): 169–217.

Bedau, Hugo Adam. "Classification-Based Sentencing: Some Conceptual and Ethical Problems." *New England Journal on Criminal and Civil Confinement* 10 (1984): 1–26.

————."Retribution and the Theory of Punishment." *Journal of Philosophy* 75 (1978): 601–620.

Bentham, Jeremy. *An Introduction to the Principles of Morals and Legislation*. Edited by J. H. Burns and H. L. A. Hart. London: Methuen, 1982.

Blackmore, John, and Jane Welsh. "Selective Incapacitation: Sentencing According to Risk." *Crime and Delinquency* 29 (1983): 504–528.

Blalock, Ira. "Justice and Parole: The Oregon Experience." In *Justice as Fairness: Perspectives on the Justice Model*, edited by David Fogel and Joe Hudson, 100–117. Cincinnati: Anderson Publishing, 1981.

Blumstein, Alfred. "Sentencing Reforms: Impacts and Implications." *Judicature* 68 (1984): 129–139.

Blumstein, Alfred, Jacqueline Cohen, Susan Martin, and Michael Tonry, eds. *Research on Sentencing: The Search for Reform*. Washington, D.C.: National Academy Press, 1983.

Blumstein, Alfred, Jacqueline Cohen, and Daniel Nagin, eds. *Deterrence and Incapacitation: Estimating the Effects of Criminal Sanctions on Crime Rates*. Washington, D.C.: National Academy of Sciences, 1978.

Brier, Stephen S., and Stephen E. Fienberg. "Recent Econometric Modelling of Crime and Punishment: Support for the Deterrence Hypothesis?" In *Indicators of Crime and Criminal Justice: Quantitative Studies*, edited by Stephen E. Fienberg and Albert J. Reiss, Jr., 82–97. Washington, D.C.: U.S. Government Printing Office, 1980.

Burgh, Richard, "Do the Guilty Deserve Punishment?" *Journal of Philosophy* 79 (1982): 193–210.

Card, Claudia. "On Mercy." *Philosophical Review* 81 (1972): 182–207.

Cedarblom, J. B., and William Blizek, eds. *Justice and Punishment*. Cambridge, Mass.: Ballinger Publishing, 1977.

Chaiken, Jan M., and Marcia R. Chaiken. "Deficiencies in Official Records for Identifying Serious Offenders." Presentation at Conference of American Society of Criminology, Denver. November 1983. Unpublished.

———.*Varieties of Criminal Behavior*. Santa Monica, Calif.: RAND Corporation, 1982.

Chaiken, Marcia R., and Jan M. Chaiken, "Offender Types and Public Policy." *Crime and Delinquency* 30 (1984): 195–226.

Christie, Nils. "Die Versteckte Botschaft des Neo-Klassizismus." *Kriminologisches Journal* 15, no. 1 (1983): 14–33.

———.*Limits to Pain*. Oslo: Universitetsforlaget, 1981.

Coffee, John C., Jr. "The Repressed Issues of Sentencing: Accountability, Predictability, and Equality in the Era of the Sentencing Commission." *Georgetown Law Journal* 66 (1977–1978): 975–1107.

Cohen, Jacqueline. "Incapacitation as a Strategy for Crime Control: Possibilities and Pitfalls." In *Crime and Justice: An Annual Review of Research*, edited by Michael H. Tonry and Norval Morris, vol. 5, 1–84. Chicago: University of Chicago Press, 1983.

————."The Incapacitative Effect of Imprisonment." In *Deterrence and Incapacitation: Estimating the Effects of Criminal Sanction on Crime Rate*, edited by Alfred Blumstein, Jacqueline Cohen, and Daniel Nagin, 187–243. Washington, D.C.: National Academy of Sciences, 1978.

Cullen, Francis T., and Karen E. Gilbert. *Reaffirming Rehabilitation.* Cincinnati: Anderson Publishing, 1982

Dershowitz, Alan M. "Indeterminate Confinement: Letting the Therapy Fit the Harm." *University of Pennsylvania Law Review* 123 (1974): 297–339.

————."The Law of Dangerousness: Some Fictions about Predictions." *Journal of Legal Education* 23 (1970): 24–47.

Dworkin, Ronald. "Liberalism." In *Public and Private Morality*, edited by Stuart Hampshire, 113–143. Cambridge: Cambridge University Press, 1978.

————.*Taking Rights Seriously.* Cambridge, Mass.: Harvard University Press, 1977.

Feinberg, Joel. "The Expressive Function of Punishment." In *Doing and Deserving: Essays in the Theory of Responsibility,* by Joel Feinberg, 95–118. Princeton: Princeton University Press, 1970.

————.*Harm to Others.* New York: Oxford University Press, 1984.

————."Justice and Personal Desert." In *Doing and Deserving: Essays in the Theory of Responsibility,* by Joel Feinberg, 55–87. Princeton: Princeton University Press, 1970.

Feinberg, Kenneth R. "Selective Incapacitation and the Effort to Improve the Fairness of Existing Sentencing Practices." *New York University Review of Law and Social Change* 12 (1983–1984): 53–69.

Fletcher, George. "The Recidivist Premium." *Criminal Justice Ethics* 1, no. 2 (1982): 54–59.

————.*Rethinking Criminal Law.* Boston: Little, Brown, 1978.

Floud, Jean, and Warren Young. *Dangerousness and Criminal Justice.* London: Heinemann, 1981.

Fogel, David. *We Are the Living Proof. . .* Cincinnati: W. H. Anderson, 1975.

Forst, Brian. "Selective Incapacitation: An Idea Whose Time Has Come?" *Federal Probation* 47, no. 3 (1983): 19–23.

Forst, Brian, William Rhodes, James Dimm, Arthur Gelman, and Barbara Mullin. "Targeting Federal Resources on Recidivists: An Empirical View." *Federal Probation* 47, no. 2 (1983): 10–23.

Forst, Martin L., ed. *Sentencing Reform: Experiments in Reducing Disparity.* Beverly Hills: Sage Publications, 1982.

Frankel, Marvin E. *Criminal Sentences: Law without Order.* New York: Hill and Wang, 1972.

Galligan, D. J. "The Return to Retribution in Penal Theory." In *Crime, Proof and Punishment: Essays in Memory of Sir Rupert Cross*, edited by C. F. H. Tepper, 144–171. London: Butterworths, 1981.

Gardner, Martin. "The Renaissance of Retribution—An Examination of *Doing Justice.*" *Wisconsin Law Review* (1976): 781–815.

Gewirth, Alan. *Reason and Morality.* Chicago: University of Chicago Press, 1978.

Glueck, Sheldon, and Eleanor Glueck. *500 Criminal Careers.* New York: Alfred A. Knopf, 1934.

Goldman, Alan H. "Beyond the Deterrence Theory: Comments on van den Haag's 'Punishment as a Device for Controlling the Crime Rate.'" *Rutgers Law Review* 33 (1981): 721–729.

———."The Paradox of Punishment." *Philosophy and Public Affairs* 9 (1979): 42–58.

Gottfredson, Don M. "Assessment and Prediction Methods in Crime and Delinquency." In *Task Force Report: Juvenile Delinquency and Youth Crime,* President's Commission for Law Enforcement and Administration of Justice, 171–187. Washington, D.C.: U.S. Government Printing Office, 1967.

———."The Practical Application of Research." *Canadian Journal of Corrections* 5 (1963): 212–28.

Gottfredson, Don M., Leslie T. Wilkins, and Peter B. Hoffman. *Guidelines for Parole and Sentencing: A Policy Control Method.* Lexington, Mass.: D. C. Heath, 1978.

Gottfredson, Michael R., and Don M. Gottfredson. *Decisionmaking in Criminal Justice: Toward Rational Exercise of Discretion.* Cambridge, Mass.: Ballinger Publishing, 1980.

———."Guidelines for Incarceration Decisions: A Partisan Review." *University of Illinois Law Review* (1984): 291–317.

Gottfredson, Stephen, and Don M. Gottfredson. *Screening for Risk: A Comparison of Methods.* Washington, D.C.: National Institute of Corrections, 1979.

Greenberg, David F. *Mathematical Criminology.* New Brunswick: Rutgers University Press, 1979.

———."The Incapacitative Effect of Imprisonment: Some Estimates." *Law and Society Review* 9 (1975): 541–580.

Greenwood, Peter W. "Controlling the Crime Rate through Imprisonment." In *Crime and Public Policy,* edited by James Q. Wilson, 251–269. San Francisco Institute for Contemporary Studies, 1983.

———."Response to Panelists." *New York Review of Law and Social Change* 12 (1983–1984): 71–76.

———.*Selective Incapacitation.* Santa Monica, Calif.: RAND Corporation, 1982.

———."Statement before Subcommittee on Juvenile Justice." In *Hearings on S. 1688 etc.* held before the Subcommittee on Juvenile Justice, Committee on the Judiciary, U.S. Senate, 97th Congress, 1st Session, 97–108. Washington, D.C.: U.S. Government Printing Office, 1981.

Gross, Hyman. *A Theory of Criminal Justice*. New York: Oxford University Press, 1979.

Gross, Hyman, and Andrew von Hirsch, eds. *Sentencing*. New York: Oxford University Press, 1981.

Grupp, Stanley E., ed. *The Positive School of Criminology: Three Lectures by Enrico Ferri*. Pittsburgh: University of Pittsburgh Press, 1968.

Hampshire, Stuart. "Dispositions." In *Freedom of Mind and Other Essays*, by Stuart Hampshire, 34–41. Princeton: Princeton University Press, 1971.

Hampton, Jean. "The Moral Education Theory of Punishment." *Philosophy and Public Affairs* 13 (1984): 208–238.

Harris, M. Kay. "Disquisition on the Need for a New Model of Criminal Sanctioning Systems." *West Virginia Law Review* 77 (1975): 263–326.

Hart, H. L. A. "Prolegomenon to the Principles of Punishment." In *Punishment and Responsibility*, by H. L. A. Hart, 1–27. New York: Oxford University Press, 1968.

———."Punishment and the Elimination of Responsibility." In *Punishment and Responsibility*, by H. L. A. Hart, 158–185. New York: Oxford University Press, 1968.

Hart, Henry M., Jr. "The Aims of the Criminal Law." *Law and Contemporary Problems* 23 (1958): 401–441.

Hart, Hornell. "Predicting Parole Success." *Journal of Criminal Law and Criminology* 14 (1923): 405–413.

Harvard Law Review Student Note. "Selective Incapacitation: Reducing Crime through Prediction of Recidivism." *Harvard Law Review* 96 (1982): 511–533.

Hassemer, Winfried. *Einführung in die Grundlagen des Strafrechts*. Munich: C. H. Beck Verlag, 1981.

Heckscher, Sten, Annika Snare, Hannu Takala, and Jörn Westergaard, eds. *Straff och rättfärdighet. ny nordisk debatt*. Stockholm: Norstedts, 1980.

Hinton, John W., ed. *Dangerousness: Problems of Assessment and Prediction*. London: George Allen and Unwin, 1983.

Honderich, Ted. "On Justifying Protective Punishment." *British Journal of Criminology* 22 (1982): 268–275.

———.*Punishment: The Supposed Justifications*. Rev. ed., Harmondsworth: Penguin, 1984.

Jacobs, James B. "The Politics of Prison Expansion." *New York University Review of Law and Social Change* 12 (1983–1984): 209–241.

Kant, Immanuel. *Groundwork of the Metaphysic of Morals*. Translated by H. J. Paton. New York: Harper and Row, 1964.

Kleinig, John. "Crime and the Concept of Harm." *American Philosophical Quarterly* 15 (1978): 27–36.

————.*Paternalism.* Totowa, N.J.: Rowman and Allenheld, 1984.

————.*Punishment and Desert.* The Hague: Martinus Nijhoff, 1973.

Knapp, Kay. "What Sentencing Reform in Minnesota Has and Has Not Accomplished." *Judicature* 68 (1984): 181–189.

Lackner, Karl, ed. *Strafgesetzbuch mit Erlaüterungen.* Munich: C. H. Beck Verlag, 1980.

Lipton, Douglas, Robert Martinson, and Judith Wilks. *The Effectiveness of Correctional Treatment: A Survey of Treatment Evaluation Studies.* New York: Praeger Publishers, 1975.

MacCormick, Neil. *Legal Right and Social Democracy: Essays in Legal and Political Philosophy.* Oxford: Clarendon Press, 1982.

Mackie, J. L. "Morality and the Retributive Emotions." *Criminal Justice Ethics* 1, no. 1 (1982): 3–10.

Mäkelä, Klaus. "Om straffens verkningar." *Jurisprudentia* 6 (1975): 237–280.

Mannheim, Hermann, and Leslie T. Wilkins. *Prediction Methods in Relation to Borstal Training.* London: Her Majesty's Stationery Office, 1955.

Martin, Susan E. "Interests and Politics in Sentencing Reform: The Development of Sentencing Guidelines in Minnesota and Pennsylvania." *Villanova Law Review* 29 (1984): 21–113.

McAnany, Patrick, Doug Thomson, and David Fogel, eds. *Probation and Justice: A Reconsideration of Mission.* Cambridge, Mass.: Oelgeschlager, Gunn, and Hine, 1984.

Meehl, Paul, and Albert Rosen. "Antecedent Probability and the Efficiency of Psychometric Signs, Patterns and Cutting Scores." *Psychological Bulletin* 52 (1955): 194–216.

Messinger, Sheldon L., and Phillip Johnson. "California's Determinate Sentence Law: History and Issues." In *Determinate Sentencing: Reform or Regression?* National Institute of Law Enforcement and Criminal Justice, 13–57. Washington, D.C.: U.S. Government Printing Office, 1978.

Miethe, Terance D. "Types of Consensus in Public Evaluations of Crime: An Illustration of Strategies for Measuring 'Consensus'." *Journal of Criminal Law and Criminology* 75 (1985): 459–473.

Minnesota Sentencing Guidelines and Commentary. Revised August 1, 1984, St. Paul: Minnesota Sentencing Guidelines Commission.

Minnesota Sentencing Guidelines Commission. *The Impact of the Minnesota Sentencing Guidelines: Three Year Evaluation.* St. Paul: Minnesota Sentencing Guidelines Commission, 1984.

————.*Preliminary Report on the Development and Impact of the Minnesota Sentencing Guidelines.* St. Paul: Minnesota Sentencing Guidelines Commission, 1982.

————.*Report to the Legislature.* St. Paul: Minnesota Sentencing Guidelines Commission, 1980.

Moberly, Walter. *The Ethics of Punishment.* Hamden, Conn.: Archon Books, 1968.

Monahan, John. "The Case for Prediction in the Modified Desert Model for Criminal Sentencing." *International Journal of Law and Psychology* 5 (1982): 103–113.

―――.*Predicting Violent Behavior: An Assessment of Clinical Techniques.* Beverly Hills: Sage Publications, 1981.

Moore, Mark, Susan Estrich, and Daniel McGillis. *Dealing with Dangerous Offenders.* Cambridge, Mass.: Kennedy School of Government, 1983. Unpublished manuscript.

Moore, Mark, Susan Estrich, Daniel McGillis, and William Spelman. *Dangerous Offenders: The Elusive Target of Justice.* Cambridge, Mass.: Harvard University Press, 1985.

Morris, Herbert. "A Paternalistic Theory of Punishment." *American Philosophical Quarterly* 18 (1981): 263–271.

―――."Persons and Punishment." *Monist* 52 (1968): 475–501. Reprinted in *Sentencing,* edited by Hyman Gross and Andrew von Hirsch, 93–109. New York: Oxford University Press, 1981.

Morris, Norval. *The Future of Imprisonment.* Chicago: University of Chicago Press, 1974.

―――.*Madness and the Criminal Law.* Chicago: University of Chicago Press, 1982.

―――."On 'Dangerousness' in the Judicial Process." *Record of the Association of the Bar of the City of New York* 39 (1984): 102–128.

―――."Punishment, Desert, and Rehabilitation." Reprinted in *Sentencing,* edited by Hyman Gross and Andrew von Hirsch, 256–271. New York: Oxford University Press, 1981.

Morris, Norval, and Marc Miller. "Predictions of Dangerousness." In *Crime and Justice: An Annual Review of Research,* edited by Michael Tonry and Norval Morris, Vol. 6. Chicago: University of Chicago Press, 1985.

Murphy, Jeffrie G. "Cruel and Unusual Punishments." In *Retribution, Justice, and Therapy,* by Jeffrie G. Murphy, 223–249. Dordrecht: D. Riedel Publishing, 1979.

―――."Kant's Theory of Criminal Punishment." In *Retribution, Justice, and Therapy,* by Jeffrie G. Murphy, 82–92. Dordrecht: D. Riedel Publishing, 1979.

―――."Marxism and Retribution." *In Retribution, Justice, and Therapy,* by Jeffrie G. Murphy, 93–115. Dordrecht: D. Riedel Publishing, 1979.

National Council on Crime and Delinquency, Advisory Council of Judges. "Model Sentencing Act." *Crime and Delinquency* 9 (1963): 337–369.

National Swedish Council for Crime Prevention. *A New Penal System: Ideas and Proposals.* Stockholm: National Swedish Council for Crime Prevention, 1978.

Newman, Graeme. *Just and Painful: A Case for the Corporal Punishment of Criminals.* New York: Macmillan, 1983.

Nozick, Robert. *Philosophical Explanations.* Cambridge, Mass.: Harvard University Press, 1981.

Oregon Parole Reform Act. Oregon Session Laws of 1977, chap. 372.

Orland, Leonard. "From Vengeance to Vengeance: Sentencing Reform and the Demise of Rehabilitation." *Hofstra Law Review* 7 (1978): 29–56.

Palmer, Ted. "Treatment and the Role of Classification: A Review of the Basics." *Crime and Delinquency* 30 (1984): 245–267.

Pennsylvania Sentencing Guidelines (Proposed 1980). *Pennsylvania Bulletin* 10 (1980): 4181–4196.

Pennsylvania Sentencing Guidelines. Pennsylvania Consolidated Statutes, title 204, §§ 303.1–303.9 (1983).

Pincoffs, Edmund. *The Rationale of Legal Punishment.* New York: Humanities Press, 1966.

Posner, Richard A. *Economic Analysis of Law.* 2d ed. Boston: Little, Brown, 1977.

Raphael, D. D. *Moral Philosophy.* Oxford: Oxford University Press, 1981.

Rawls, John. *A Theory of Justice.* Cambridge, Mass.: Harvard University Press, 1971.

Reiss, Albert, J., Jr. "Understanding Changes in Crime Rates." In *Indicators of Crime and Criminal Justice: Quantitative Studies,* edited by Stephen E. Fienberg and Albert J. Reiss, Jr., 11–17. Washington, D.C.: U.S. Government Printing Office, 1980.

Rescher, Nicholas. *Distributive Justice: A Constructive Critique of the Utilitarian Theory of Distribution.* Indianapolis: Bobbs-Merrill, 1966.

———.*Introduction to Value Theory.* Englewood Cliffs: Prentice-Hall, 1969.

———.*Welfare: The Social Issue in Philosophical Perspective.* Pittsburgh: University of Pittsburgh Press, 1972.

Richards, David A. J. "Rights, Utility, and Crime." In *Crime and Justice: An Annual Review of Research,* edited by Michael H. Tonry and Norval Morris, vol. 3, 247–294. Chicago: University of Chicago Press, 1981.

———.*Sex, Drugs, Death, and the Law: An Essay on Human Rights and Overcriminalization.* Totowa, N.J.: Rowman and Littlefield, 1982.

Rosen, Albert. "Detection of Suicidal Patients: An Example of Some Limitations in the Prediction of Infrequent Events." *Journal of Consulting Psychology* 18 (1954): 397–403.

Ross, Alf. *On Guilt, Responsibility and Punishment.* Berkeley and Los Angeles: University of California Press, 1975.

Rothman, David J. *Conscience and Convenience: The Asylum and Its Alternatives in Progressive America.* Boston: Little, Brown, 1980.

———."Doing Time: Days, Months and Years in the Criminal Justice System." In *Sentencing,* edited by Hyman Gross and Andrew von Hirsch, 374–385. New York: Oxford University Press, 1981.

Roxin, Claus. "Zur jüngsten Diskussion über Schuld, Prävention und Verantwortlichkeit im Strafrecht." In *Festschrift für Paul Bockelmann,* edited by Arthur Kaufmann, Günter Bemmann, Detlev Krauss, and Klaus Volk, 279–309. Munich: C. H. Beck Verlag, 1979.

Scheid, Don E. "Kant's Retributivism." *Ethics* 93 (1983): 262–282.

———."*Theories of Legal Punishment.*" Ph.D. diss., New York University, 1977.

Schoeman, Ferdinand D. "On Incapacitating the Dangerous." *American Philosophical Quarterly* 16 (1979): 27–35. Reprinted in *Sentencing,* edited by Hyman Gross and Andrew von Hirsch, 175–185. New York: Oxford University Press, 1981.

Sechrest, Lee, Susan O. White, and Elizabeth D. Brown, eds. *The Rehabilitation of Criminal Offenders: Problems and Prospects.* Washington, D.C.: National Academy of Sciences, 1979.

Sellin, Thorsten, and Marvin E. Wolfgang. *The Measurement of Delinquency.* Reprint ed. Montclair, N.J.: Patterson Smith, 1978.

Sherman, Michael, and Gordon Hawkins. *Imprisonment in America: Choosing the Future.* Chicago: University of Chicago Press, 1981.

Shinnar, Reuel, and Shlomo Shinnar. "The Effects of Criminal Justice on the Control of Crime: A Quantitative Approach." *Law and Society Review* 9 (1975): 581–611.

Shover, Neal. "The Later Stages of Ordinary Property Offender Careers." *Social Problems* 31 (1983): 208–218.

Simon, F. H. *Prediction Methods in Criminology.* London: Her Majesty's Stationery Office, 1971.

Singer, Richard G. *Just Deserts: Sentencing Based on Equality and Desert.* Cambridge, Mass.: Ballinger Publishing, 1979.

Sparks, Richard F. "The Structure of the Oregon Parole Guidelines." School of Criminal Justice, Rutgers University, Newark, N.J., 1982. Unpublished paper.

———."Surveys of Victimization—An Optimistic Assessment." In *Crime and Justice: An Annual Review of Research,* edited by Michael H. Tonry and Norval Morris, vol. 3, 1–60. Chicago: University of Chicago Press, 1981.

Sparks, Richard F., Hazel Genn, and David Dodd. *Surveying Victims: A Study of the Measurement of Criminal Victimization,* Chichester: John Wiley and Sons, 1977.

Sparks, Richard F., Bridget Stecher, Jay Albanese, Peggy Shelly, and Donald Barry. *Stumbling toward Justice: Some Overlooked Research and Policy Questions about Statewide Sentencing Guidelines.* School of Criminal Justice, Rutgers University, Newark, 1982. Unpublished report.

Strawson, P. F. "Freedom and Resentment." In *Freedom and Resentment and Other Essays,* by P. F. Strawson, 1–25. London: Methuen, 1974.

Swedish Ministry of Justice, *Oversyn av lagstiftningen om förmö-*

genhetsbrott utom gäldenärsbrott. Stockholm: Stadens Offentliga Utredningar, 1983: 50.

Taurek, John. "Should the Numbers Count?" *Philosophy and Public Affairs* 6 (1977): 293–316.

Thurber, James. *The Thirteen Clocks.* New York: Simon and Schuster, 1950.

Tonry, Michael H. "Criminal Law: The Missing Element in Sentencing Reform." *Vanderbilt Law Review* 35 (1982): 607–641.

———. "The Sentencing Commission in Sentencing Reform." *Hofstra Law Review* 7 (1979): 315–353.

Törnudd, Patrik. "Deterrence Research and the Needs for Legislative Planning." In *General Deterrence,* National Swedish Council for Crime Prevention, 326–343. Stockholm: Brottsförebyggande rådet, 1975.

Twentieth Century Fund. Task Force on Criminal Sentencing. *Fair and Certain Punishment.* New York: McGraw-Hill, 1976.

———.Task Force on Sentencing Policy toward Young Offenders. *Confronting Youth Crime.* New York: Holmes and Meier, 1978.

Underwood, Barbara. "Law and the Crystal Ball: Predicting Behavior with Statistical Inference and Individualized Judgment." *Yale Law Journal* 88 (1979): 1408–1448.

Visher, Christy A. "The RAND Second Inmate Survey: A Reanalysis." Washington: National Academy of Sciences, July 1984. Unpublished draft.

van den Haag, Ernest. *Punishing Criminals: Concerning a Very Old and Painful Question.* New York: Basic Books, 1975.

———."Punishment as a Device for Controlling the Crime Rate." *Rutgers Law Review* 33 (1981): 706–720.

———."Punitive Sentences." *Hofstra Law Review* 7 (1978): 123–138.

———."Thinking About Crime Again." *Commentary* 76, no. 6 (1983): 73–77.

von Hirsch, Andrew. "Commensurability and Crime Prevention: Evaluating Formal Sentencing Structures and Their Rationale." *Journal of Law and Criminology* 74 (1983): 209–248.

———."Constructing Guidelines for Sentencing: The Critical Choices for the Minnesota Sentencing Guidelines Commission." *Hamline Law Review* 5 (1982): 164–215.

———."Desert and Previous Convictions in Sentencing." *Minnesota Law Review* 65 (1981): 591–634.

———."Desert and White-Collar Criminality: A Response to Dr. Braithwaite." *Journal of Criminal Law and Criminology* 73 (1982): 1164–1175.

———.*Doing Justice: The Choice of Punishments.* Report of the Committee for the Study of Incarceration. New York: Hill and Wang, 1976.

———."Equality, 'Anisonomy' and Justice: An Analysis of *Madness and the Criminal Law.*" *Michigan Law Review* 82 (1984): 1093–1112.

————."The Ethics of Selective Incapacitation: Observations on the Contemporary Debate." *Crime and Delinquency*, 30 (1984): 175–194.

————."Giving Criminals Their Just Deserts." *Civil Liberties Review* 3 (1976): 23–35.

————."'Neoclassicism,' Proportionality, and the Rationale for Punishment: Thoughts on the Scandinavian Debate." *Crime and Delinquency* 29 (1983): 52–70.

————."The New Indiana Sentencing Code: Is It Indeterminate Sentencing?" In *An Anatomy of Criminal Justice: A Systems Overview,* edited by Cleon Foust and D. R. Webster, 143–156. Lexington, Mass.: D. C. Heath, 1980.

————."Prediction of Criminal Conduct and Preventive Confinement of Convicted Persons." *Buffalo Law Review* 21 (1972): 717–758.

————."Recent Trends in American Criminal Sentencing Theory." *Maryland Law Review* 42 (1983): 6–36.

————.Review of *The Decline of the Rehabilitative Ideal,* by Francis Allen, and *Imprisonment in America,* by Michael Sherman and Gordon Hawkins. *Pennsylvania Law Review* 131 (1983): 819–834.

————.Review of *Limits to Pain,* by Nils Christie. *Crime and Delinquency* 28 (1982): 315–318.

————."Utilitarian Sentencing Resuscitated: The American Bar Association's Second Report on Criminal Sentencing." *Rutgers Law Review* 33 (1981): 772–789.

von Hirsch, Andrew, and Don M. Gottfredson. "Selective Incapacitation: Some Queries about Research Design and Equity." *New York University Review of Law and Social Change* 12 (1983–1984): 11–51.

von Hirsch, Andrew, and Julia M. Mueller. "California's Determinate Sentencing Law: An Analysis of Its Structure." *New England Journal on Criminal and Civil Confinement* 10 (1984): 253–300.

von Hirsch, Andrew, and Kathleen J. Hanrahan. "Determinate Penalty Systems in America: An Overview." *Crime and Delinquency* 27 (1981): 289–316.

————.*The Question of Parole: Retention, Reform or Abolition?* Cambridge, Mass.: Ballinger Publishing, 1979.

Warner, S. B. "Factors Determining Parole from the Massachusetts Reformatory." *Journal of Criminal Law and Criminology* 14 (1923): 172–207.

Washington Sentencing Guidelines. Revised Code of Washington § 9.94A.

Wasik, Martin. "Excuses at the Sentencing Stage." *Criminal Law Review* (1983): 450–465.

Wasserstrom, Richard. "The Obligation to Obey the Law." In *Philosophy and Social Issues: Five Studies,* by Richard Wasserstrom, 83–111. Notre Dame: University of Notre Dame Press, 1980.

————."Punishment." In *Philosophy and Social Issues: Five Studies,* by Richard Wasserstrom, 112–151. Notre Dame: University of Notre Dame Press, 1980.

Williams, Bernard. "A Critique of Utilitarianism." In *Utilitarianism: For and Against,* by J. J. C. Smart and Bernard Williams, 75–150. Cambridge: Cambridge University Press, 1973.

Wilson, James Q. *Thinking about Crime.* New York: Basic Books, 1975.

———.*Thinking about Crime.* Rev. ed. New York: Basic Books, 1983

———."Thinking about 'Thinking about Crime,'" *Society.* March-April 1977, 10–20.

Wolfgang, Marvin E. "Seriousness of Crime and a Policy of Juvenile Justice." In *Delinquency, Crime, and Society,* edited by James Short, Jr., 267–286. Chicago: University of Chicago Press, 1976.

Wooton, Barbara. *Crime and the Criminal Law.* London: Sweet and Maxwell, 1963.

Zimring, Franklin E. "Making the Punishment Fit the Crime: A Consumer's Guide to Sentencing Reform." *Hastings Center Report* 6, no. 6 (1976): 13–17. Reprinted in *Sentencing,* edited by Hyman Gross and Andrew von Hirsch, 327–335. New York: Oxford University Press, 1981.

———."Sentencing Reform in the States: Lessons from the 1970s." In *Reform and Punishment: Essays on Criminal Sentencing,* edited by Michael Tonry and Franklin Zimring. Chicago: University of Chicago Press, 1983.

Index

Abolition of punishment, 47–48, 60
Accumulative interests, 70–71
Aggravating circumstances, 73, 81, 156n, 181, 186n.16
Allen, Francis, 4
American Bar Association, 128n
Anchoring points. See Penalty scale
Andenaes, Johannes, 7, 33
Assassination, Jewish law and, 79n
Assault, 69

Beccaria, Cesare, 31–32
Bedau, Hugo Adam, 39n, 58
Benefits-and-burdens theory, 57–60
Bentham, Jeremy, 31–32
Blameworthiness, 2, 35, 152; insanity defense and, 73; parity and, 140n; penal sanction and, 81; punishment and, 135
Blumstein, Alfred, 13, 112n
Brown, Elizabeth D., 4n
Burglary, 43, 64, 65, 189n.4; categorial incapacitation and, 158, 159; seriousness of crimes, rating for, 69, 76n

California, 154, 155, 167, 191n.40, 193n.7, 193n.8, 194n.12, 198n.3; determinate sentencing and, 123–124; Greenwood's data and, 118n, 120; prison space and sentencing in, 126; RAND study and, 108

Cardinal magnitudes (of punishment), 39, 43–46, 92–94, 171, 177; anchoring of penalty scale and, 92–94, 100, 101; categorial incapacitation and, 155, 157–159; desert and first offender versus recidivist and, 90; desert and prediction and, 145; desert and proportionality and, 43–46
Car theft, 66
Categorial incapacitation, 95, 161, 163, 174, 177; cardinal proportionality and, 155, 157–159; Cohen study of, 150–152; empirical issues in, 153–154; ethics of, 154–159; parity and, 155–156; rank-ordering and, 156, 158. See also Incapacitation; Prediction
Censure, 50–51, 52, 53, 82, 170; criminal process and, 135; moral arguments and, 57; repetition and, 84, 87; routine crimes and, 93
Chaiken, Jan, 14, 107, 109, 110, 111, 112, 113, 133
Chaiken, Marcia, 14, 107, 109, 110, 111, 112, 113, 133
Christie, Nils, 34, 36, 47
Civil disobedience, 73n
Cohen, Jacqueline, 121n; categorial incapacitation and, 150–152, 153, 154, 156, 157, 159
Collective incapacitation, 13, 15,

Collective incapacitation (*cont.*) 115–116, 150. *See also* Incapacitation; Prediction

Commensurate deserts, principle of, 31–37

Committee for the Study of Incarceration, 10

Condemnatory implications of punishment, 34-37, 47, 50, 52, 53, 56, 81, 82, 84, 135, 140. *See also* Punishment

"Constructing Guidelines for Sentencing: The Critical Choices for the Minnesota Sentencing Guidelines Commission" (von Hirsch), 21, 180

Convictions (previous). *See* Criminal record (previous convictions)

Corporal punishment, 25n

Crime control: desert-oriented scheme and, 160–166; justice and crime prevention and, 172–173; penalty scale and, 94–95; selective incapacitation and, 148; "sunlight" argument and, 130

Crime prevention, 170; desert-oriented scheme and, 161–165; features of punishment and, 52, 59; justice and, 171–174; reprobation and, 48–51; treating persons as ends and, 54–57

Crime reduction, 129n; selective incapacitation and, 115–123

Crimes: censure and routine, 93; Cohen's study and categories of, 150–151; debate over past or future, 2, 167–169; desert principle and past, 30; deterrence model and, 13, 32; focus on categories of, 150; punishment and criminal law and, 80; social system and, 58. *See also* Seriousness (of crime)

Criminal fault, behavior and motives and, 71–74

Criminal intent, 55

Criminal law, 55, 56, 57, 171; "character" of offender and, 135n; criminal career and, 81, 85; habitual offender laws and, 91n; punishment for particular crime and, 80

Criminal record (previous convictions), 77–91, 132–134; alleged crimes versus, 135-136; alteration of seriousness of present act and, 78–80; categorial incapacitation and, 152, 159; criminal career and, 80–81, 109n; issue of, 77–78; previous standards of behavior and, 81–85; selective incapacitation and, 132–134; sentencing grid and prior, 85–88; use of morally irrelevant features of, 136–138

"Cruel and Unusual Punishments" (Murphy), 26n

Cullen, Francis T., 4n

Culpability, 171; prior convictions and, 78, 79, 82; seriousness of crimes and, 64, 69, 71-74

Dangerousness, 17, 104, 125, 127n, 136n, 145, 146, 163, 167, 175, 176

Dealing with Dangerous Offenders (Moore, Estrich, McGillis), 196n.11

Death penalty, 26n

Dershowitz, Alan, 113

Desert (deserved punishment): anchoring of penalty scale and, 43–46, 92–94, 100; cardinal magnitudes (as limiting principle), 43–46; categorial incapacitation and, 149, 150, 154–159; condemnatory implications of punishment and, 34–37; convergence of criteria with selective incapacitation and, 131–138; crime prevention and, 49; criminal career and, 80, 81n, 83; as determining principle, 38, 39, 40–43; deterrence and principle of, 31–32; German Penal Code and, 27n; imprisonment and, 25–26; inhibition-reinforcement and principle of, 33–34; as limiting principle, 38–39, 43–46; Minnesota sentencing guidelines and, 179; "modified" model of, 162; ordinal magnitudes (as determining principle) and, 40–43; past and future crimes debate and, 2; prediction within limits of, 139–146; prior criminality and, 77–91; selective incapacitation and, 16, 128–138; sentencing grid and prior convictions and, 85–88; seriousness of crimes and, 63; study analysis and, 16, 17; synthesis with crime control and, 160–166. *See also* Punishment

Deterrence, 17n; analysis of theory of, 7–9; Beccaria and Bentham's argument and, 31–32; crime control and, 95; decline of model of, 13; sentencing and, 8–9, 12, 13

District of Columbia, 151, 153

Dodd, David, 190n.11

Doing Justice: The Choice of Punishments (von Hirsch), 10, 11, 17, 26n, 30, 34n, 95; benefits-and-burdens argument and, 57–58, 59–60; previous convictions and, 77, 78

Drug use, 56

Dworkin, Ronald, 73n

Estrich, Susan, 134n, 185n.52

Ethical issues: categorial incapacitation and, 154–159; selective incapacitation and, 128–129; treating persons as ends and, 54. *See also* Moral *entries*

Extenuating circumstances, 73, 81

False negatives, 107, 111

False positives, 6–7, 110–111, 113–114, 175–178; categorial incapacitation study (Cohen) and, 152; desert and, 11; prediction and analysis of, 175–178; selective incapacitation and, 107, 110, 111, 113, 114, 126–127

Feinberg, Joel, 52n, 67–69, 70, 190n.17

Felony classes (preexisting statutory), 75

Ferri, Enrico, 5

Finnish Criminal Code, 27, 28, 187n.25

First offenders, 78, 79, 80–85, 86, 88–90

Fletcher, George, 77, 79, 80, 88, 133, 192n.9

Forecasting techniques. *See* Prediction

Frankel, Marvin E., 20

Fraud, 74

"Freedom and Resentment" (Strawson), 51n

Friends Service Committee, 10

Garofalo, Raffaele, 5

General deterrence. *See* Deterrence

Genn, Hazel, 190n.11

German Penal Code, 27n, 73n

Gilbert, Karen, 4n

Glueck, Eleanor, 105

Glueck, Sheldon, 105

Gottfredson, Don, 21n, 105n, 120, 132, 183n.11

Grading criteria (school grades), 35n, 49, 67

Greenberg, David, 14

Greenwood, Peter, 14, 107, 108n, 109, 110, 111, 112, 115, 117–122, 123, 125, 126, 129, 130, 131, 133, 137, 142, 144n, 153, 154, 171, 178, 194n.12, 194n.13, 194n.14

Guilt, eliminating term of, 42

Habitual offender. *See* Criminal record (previous convictions)

Hampshire, Stuart, 83n

Hampton, Jean, 59n

Harm: desert and, 11–12; prior convictions and, 79; punishment justification and, 55; seriousness of crimes and, 64, 65, 66–71, 75

Harm to Others (Feinberg), 67

Hart, H. L. A., 48, 55, 105, 169

Hassemer, Winfried, 27n

Hawkins, Gordon, 96n, 128

Hoffman, Peter B., 21n, 132

Homicide, 72

Ignorance of the law, 79n

The Impact of the Minnesota Sentencing Guidelines: Three Year Evaluation (Minnesota

Impact Minn. Sent. Guidelines
(*cont.*)
  Sentencing Guidelines Commission), 199n.1
Imprisonment: defined, 26; elements
  of punishment and, 52; ordinal
  magnitudes of punishment and,
  40; sentencing grid and, 24–26
Incapacitation, 165; imprisonment
  and, 24–25; value of schemes of,
  167. *See also* Categorial incapacitation; Collective incapacitation; Prediction; Selective
  incapacitation
Inclusion strategy (synthesis analysis), 161–165
Individual rights and interests,
  treating persons as ends and,
  54-57
Inhibition-reinforcement argument:
  desert and, 33–34; reprobation
  and crime prevention and, 48–51,
  52
Innocence, eliminating concept of,
  42
In-out line. *See* Sentencing grid, the
  "in-out" line
Insanity defense, 73, 127n

Jacobs, James, 99n
Jareborg, Nils, 191n.30
Judicial guidelines, 20, 186n.6
Judiciary, sentencing and, 20
Justice: crime prevention and,
  171–174
Juvenile justice system, 42, 52, 137

Kant, Immanuel, 54n, 57n
Kleinig, John, 10, 56n, 67, 190n.17
Knapp, Kay A., 24n, 199n.3
Knowing behavior, 71

Lackner, Karl, 27n
Lambda (average individual offense
  rate), 116, 117, 118n; overestima-
  tion of, 119
Legislatures, sentencing and, 20
Limited-modification strategy (syn-
  thesis analysis), 162–165
Limiting retributivism, 38. *See also*
  Retributivism

MacCormick, Neil, 56
McGillis, Daniel, 134n, 185n.52
Madness issue (half-madness), 73
Mäkelä, Klaus, 48, 49, 50
Mental hospitals, commitment to,
  127n
Michigan, 108, 194n.13
Miethe, Terance D., 65
"Milieu therapy," 4
Miller, Marc, 139n
Minnesota, 11, 72, 144n, 167,
  186n.10, 186n.15, 186n.16,
  198n.4; political pressure and,
  125, 126; prison capacity and, 95,
  98; selective incapacitation and,
  124–125; sentencing commission
  in, 21, 22, 23, 26, 63–64, 74, 75;
  sentencing commission analysis
  and, 179–181; seriousness of
  crimes and, 189n.2
Mitigating circumstances, 73, 81,
  156n, 181, 186n.16
Model Penal Code, 5, 140; gravity of
  conduct and, 71-72
Model Sentencing Act, 5
Monahan, John, 106, 197n.2
Moore, Mark, 15, 131–132, 134,
  136, 138n, 139, 146, 185n.52
Moral inhibitions: connection between punishment and, 33–34;
  disapprobation and, 51; victimizing acts and, 50
Moral judgments, 9–10; censure
  and, 57; past acts and, 82; seriousness of crimes and, 74
Moral neutrality, punishment and,
  52, 53
Moral problems: of punishment,
  171, 174; of selective incapacitation, 129–130; of use of irrelevant
  features of prior record, 136–138
Moral stigma, 42
Moral theory, Kant and, 54n
Morris, Herbert, 9, 57; paternalistic
  theory of punishment and, 59n
Morris, Norval, 38–39, 41, 42, 45,
  139–146, 191n.36, 197n.2, 198n.8;
  desert as only limiting, and
  38–45; prediction within desert
  limits and, 139-146, 162

Motivation, 73
Mueller, Julia M., 155n, 190n.40
Murphy, Jeffrie G., 26n, 57

National Academy of Sciences, 112n
National Council on Crime and Delinquency, 5
National Crime Survey, gravity of
offenses and, 65
Negligent behavior, 71
"No-conflict" argument (supposed
convergence of selective incapacitation and desert criteria),
131–138
Nozick, Robert, 59n

Offender characteristics, 149, 150
Offense score (sentencing grid), 22
Ordinal magnitudes (of punishment), 40–43, 163, 174, 177; anchoring of penalty scale and, 100;
desert and prediction and, 145;
desert and proportionality and,
40–43; von Hirsch on desert and,
170, 171

Panel on Research on Criminal Ca-
reers, 112n
Parity, 40, 45, 163; categorial inca-
pacitation and desert and,
150-152; Morris and, 140n, 145
Parole agents, 5
Parole boards, sentencing and, 20
Paroling guidelines, 22, 186n.7; California Base Expectancy Score
and, 105
Parsimony argument, 144, 169,
198n.8
Penal resources, penalty scale anchoring and, 95–100
Penal system abolition, 60
Penalties. *See also* Death penalty;
Penalty scale
Penal treatment ethic, decline of,
3–7
Penalty scale: anchoring of, 43, 44,
45, 92, 100–101; cardinal proportionality and anchoring of, 92–94;
crime control and anchoring of,
94–95, 161; deterrence and, 32;
discounting for first offense and,

85, 86, 88–91, 192n.9; ordinal
magnitudes of punishment and,
40; penal resources and anchoring, 95–100; von Hirsch on
desert and, 170–171
Pennsylvania, 186n.13; sentencing
commission in, 21, 63–64, 74, 75,
76
Personal assaults, harm and,
66–67, 68
Persons and Punishment (Morris),
9–10
Physical integrity, harm and,
66–67
Politics, 58, 168; prison capacity and
anchoring points and, 99; selective incapacitation and, 125–127
Positivism: decline of penal treatment ethic and, 3–7; deterrence
theory and, 8; neo-positivist
scheme and prediction and desert
and, 143–144; sentencing and, 20
Posner, Richard, 7, 9
Praiseworthiness, 35
Prediction, broad desert limits and,
139–146; crime control and, 95;
desert and, 11, 131–138; deterrence model and, 13; ethical problems connected with, 128–129;
false positives and, 106, 175–178;
first offender's plea and, 132–134;
German Penal Code and, 27n;
overprediction and, 128, 129, 152;
past or future crimes debate and,
2; penal treatment ethic debate
and, 5–7, 168; previous standards
of behavior and, 84; risk measurement and, 15; "sunlight" argument and sentencing and,
130–131; traditional method of,
105–107. *See also* Categorial
incapacitation; Selective
incapacitation
Prevention. *See* Crime prevention
Previous convictions. *See* Criminal
record (previous convictions)
Prison capacity: Minnesota's
sentencing commission and, 95,
179–180; sentencing and, 95–100
Prison overcrowding: categorial in-

Prison overcrowding (*cont.*)
capacitation and, 159; selective
incapacitation and, 123–127
Probation, 107, 184n.31
Probation agents, 5
Property: harm and, 66–67, 68
Proportionality: anchoring penalty
scale and cardinal, 92–94;
categorial incapacitation and cardinal, 157, 159; condemnation-
based justification of, 36–37; desert as determining principle (ordinal magnitudes) and, 38, 39,
40-43; desert as limiting principle
(cardinal magnitudes) and,
38–39, 43–46; desert principle
and, 38–39; deterrence argument
and, 32; inhibition-reinforcement
argument and, 33–34; past and
future crimes debate and, 2;
prison resources and cardinal, 96
Prostitution, decriminalization of,
56n
Punishment: abolition of, 47–48;
benefits-and-burdens argument
and, 57–60; condemnatory implications of, 34–37, 47, 50, 52, 53,
56, 81, 82, 84, 135, 140, 179-181;
consistency of, 49; corporal 25n;
crime prevention justification for,
54; criminal record and, 77–91;
culpability component of seriousness and, 64, 69, 71–74; debate
over past and future crimes and,
2, 167–169; desert and condemnatory implications of, 34–37;
desert philosophy and, 10, 11, 12;
deterrence and, 8, 31–32; disproportionate, 42–43; first offenders
and, 88–90; habitual offenders
and, 91; hard treatment element
in, 54, 57; harm component and
seriousness and, 64, 65, 66–71,
75; imprisonment and theories of,
24–26; moral aspects of, 171, 174;
offender's career and, 80–81;
present act's seriousness and previous record and, 78–80; prior behavior and, 81–85; proportionality and, 30; reinforcing role of,

33–34; reprobation derived from
prevention and, 48–51; reprobation as justifying aim and, 51–53;
retributive justification for,
57–60; rulemakers and seriousness and, 74–76; salient features
of, 52; severe, 140; study analysis
and, 17; treating persons as ends
and, 54–57; underserved, 128,
129. *See also* Desert (deserved
punishment)
Punishment and Desert (Kleinig), 10
Purposeful behavior, 71

Quarantine, 55, 60, 172

RAND Corporation, selective inca-
pacitation studies and, 107–112,
114, 121n, 133, 135–136
Rank-ordering, 40, 163; categorial
incapacitation and, 155, 156, 158;
Morris's argument and, 145
Rawls, John, 9
Reagan administration, 15
Recidivism, 64n, 91, 127; categorial
incapacitation and, 95, 151, 156;
parole and, 105; prediction and,
104, 106, 107, 134n; punishment
and, 132
Reckless behavior, 71, 74
Records, 112, 113, 135, 174. *See also*
Criminal record (previous
convictions)
Rehabilitation, 173; German Penal
Code and, 27n; penal treatment
ethic debate and, 3–6; previous
standards of behavior and, 84
Reiss, Albert, 121
Reprobation: condemnatory aspect
of punishment and, 59; as deriva-
tive from prevention, 48–51; as
independent justifying aim,
51–53
Rescher, Nicholas, 9, 67
Retribution: Morris's view of predic-
tion and, 141; punishment
justification and, 57–60
Retributivism, 38–39, 132, 197n.2
Richards, David, 56
Risk, 63; assessing individual, 134;

criminal acts and, 64; future criminality and, 125; nonadjudicative indicia of, 146; selective incapacitation and conviction, 120; sentencing and, 77; synthesis strategies and, 163, 165

Robbers, 194n.13; categorial incapacitation and, 155, 156, 157–159; high-risk, 144n; long-term risk, 145; Minnesota's sentencing guidelines and, 125; record and, 137; selective incapacitation and, 14, 129; who are the false-positives, 152

Robbery, 56–57, 64, 66, 194n.13; prediction strategies and, 113; RAND study self-reports and, 108, 109n, 110n, 111; selective incapacitation and rates of, 117–120, 126, 129

Rosen, Albert, 6n

Rothman, David, 173

Roxin, Claus, 33

Scheid, Don E., 44n, 57n

Schoeman, Ferdinand D., 55n

School of Criminal Justice (Rutgers), 41

School grades, 35n, 49, 67

Sechrest, Lee B., 4n

Security interests, 69

Selective incapacitation, 164, 171, 178; applied to sentencing, 115; consensus on propriety of predictive sentences ("sunlight" argument"), 130–131; crime control and, 148; decline of deterrence model and, 13; development of strategy of, 104; ethical problems (overview of), 128–129; impact on crime and, 115–123; literature on, 13–15; moral problems of, 129–130; "no-conflict" argument and, 131–138; prison overcrowding and, 123–127; RAND studies and, 107–112, 114, 121n; robbery rate data and, 117–120, 126, 129; sentencing conflict and, 16, 19, 168–169; Shinnar formula and, 116, 117; study analysis and,

17–18; technique improvement and, 112-114. *See also* Incapacitation; Prediction

Self defense, 73n

Self-reported offenses, 135; selective incapacitation study and, 108–109, 111–112, 120

Sellin, Thorsten, 65

Sentencing: accumulative interests and, 70; cardinal proportionality and, 45; categorial incapacitation and, 157–159; consensus on priority of predictive ("sunlight" argument), 130–131; crime prevention and, 171–174; current crime and, 81; desert and, 10, 11, 12, 19, 31, 62, 168–169; desert and sentencing grid model and, 85–90; desert and standards of, 177; determinate, 91n, 123–124, 167; deterrence and, 8–9, 12, 13, 32; distribution of punishment and, 49; "failure" model and, 173; guidelines and, 19, 26–28; guidelines and seriousness of crimes and, 63–64; imprisonment as most severe sanction and, 24–26; ordinal proportionality and, 40; past or future crimes as basis of, 2, 168; penal resources and, 95–100; predictive, 104, 107, 176; problems with reform of, 123; selective incapacitation and, 15–16, 17, 115, 123–127; sentencing commissions and, 20–21, 45, 46, 63–64, 65, 74, 75, 93, 96, 141, 157–159, 160, 161; synthesis strategies and, 160–166

Sentencing grid, 28, 45; cardinal proportionality constraints and, 93–94, 100, 101; categorial incapacitation and, 157–159; crime control and, 95; imprisonment and theories of punishment and, 24–26; the "in-out" line and, 22–24, 85–88, 94, 95, 96, 97, 98, 99, 100, 101, 142, 143, 161, 164, 179, 180; prediction and desert and, 141–144; prior convictions and, 85–88; prison capacity and,

Sentencing grid (*cont.*)
96–100; selective incapacitation and "in-out" line and, 133, 134. *See also* Sentencing
Seriousness (of crime), 63–76, 164, 189n.2; anchoring points and, 92; culpability as component of, 64, 69, 71–74; desert and crime control and, 161; desert and current crime and, 138; desert and prediction and, 145, 146; harm as component of, 64, 65, 66–71, 75; ordinal magnitudes of punishment and, 40–41; parity and, 45; penalty scale anchoring and, 43; previous record and present acts, 78–80; rank ordering and, 40; rulemaking bodies and, 74–76; sentencing grid offense score and, 22.
Sherman, Michael, 96n, 128
Shinnar, Reuel, 116, 117
Shoplifting, 65
Shover, Neal, 109n
Singer, Richard, 77, 88, 133
Social benefits. *See* Benefits-and-burdens theory
Sparks, Richard, 65–66, 162n, 186n.6, 190n.11, 190n.13
Statutory gradations (classification), 75, 76n
Strawson, P. F., 51n
Struggle for Justice (Friends Service Committee), 10
"Sunlight" argument (consensus on predictive sentencing), 130–131
Swedish Criminal Code, 27–28, 187n.26

Technology, 163
Texas, 194n.13; RAND study and, 108
Theft, 70, 74, 92
Thurber, James, 88
Tolerance, 84–85
Tonry, Michael, 72
Treatability, 63

Treating persons as ends, 54–57
Treatment, penal ethic and, 3–7

Underwood, Barbara, 138n
United States Parole Commission, 22
Utilitarianism, 31, 33, 38, 45, 145; punishment justification and, 54–55

Validation, 139–140, 145–146
van den Haag, Ernest, 7, 15, 32
Victimizing acts, 47, 48; condemnation and, 56; moral attitudes and, 50; prevention and, 59; response to, 51–52, 53; seriousness of crimes and, 63; studies of, 66
Visher, Christy, 112n, 121n
von Hirsch, Andrew, 16, 45; desert analysis and, 169–171; sentencing guidelines and, 185n.36, 185n.38. See also *Doing Justice: The Choice of Punishments* (von Hirsch)

Warner, S. B., 105
Washington (state), 11, 167; political pressure and, 125, 126; sentencing commission in, 21, 22, 63–64, 74, 75
Washington, D.C., 151, 153
Wasik, Martin, 79n
Wasserstrom, Richard, 35, 73n
Welfare interests, 67–69, 190n.17
White-collar crimes, 65
White, Susan O., 4n
Wilkins, Leslie, 21n, 132
Williams, Bernard, 9, 49n
Wilson, James Q., 7, 8–9, 13, 15, 16, 115, 116, 131, 142, 171
Wolfgang, Marvin, 65
Wrongfulness: condemnation and, 82; criminal career and, 83–84; as criminal law core conduct, 53; judging degree of, 63; punishment linked with, 55–56; reprobation for, 59; sense of, 50; tolerance and, 84n